ONCE UPON...
A Time for Young People and Their Books:
an annotated resource guide

compiled by
RITA KOHN

The Scarecrow Press, Inc.
Metuchen, N.J., & London
1986

Other Books by Rita Kohn:

Jesse Fell: Planter of Cities. Normal, IL: The Normalite Press, 1968.

You Can Do It: A PR Skills Manual for Librarians (with Krysta Tepper). Metuchen, NJ: Scarecrow Press, 1981.

Have You Got What They Want? A Workbook of Public Relations Strategies for School Librarians/Media Specialists (with Krysta Tepper). Metuchen, NJ: Scarecrow Press, 1982.

Experiencing Displays. Metuchen, NJ: Scarecrow Press, 1982.

Mythology for Young People: A Reference Guide. New York: Garland Publishing, Inc., 1985.

Library of Congress Cataloging-in-Publication Data
Kohn, Rita T.
    Once upon-- a time for young people and their books.

    Includes indexes.
    1. Bibliography--Bibliography--Children's
literature.   2. Children's literature--Bibliography.
3. Bibliography--Bibliography--Young adult literature.
4. Young adult literature--Bibliography.   I. Title.
Z1037.K643 1986   [PN1009.A1]   011'.62   86-14628
ISBN 0-8108-1922-8

For Martin

because I never wrote the one about horses

CONTENTS

v

Few children learn to love books
by themselves. Someone has to
lure them into the wonderful world
of the written word; someone has
to show them the way.

Orville Prescott

The aim of this volume is to provide a resource to materials on print and nonprint children's literature. As a resource guide, it is neither comprehensive nor critical in regard to purchase suggestions. Rather, it lists available aids that could be of value, while at the same time showing where resources currently are lacking.

Some 832 titles are cross-referenced under about 220 subject headings. Current journal articles that are applicable to the scope of this volume are appended to the subject listings but are not included in the main Resource Guide. Neither are the article titles listed in the title index.

Inclusions are based on searches at public, school, and university libraries, as well as on conversations with classroom teachers, parents, researchers in literature for young readers, and librarians. While every effort was made to list in-print titles, it becomes impossible to adhere to such a standard at a time when publishers are forced to remainder so much of their stock because of rulings by the Internal Revenue Service.

Some older titles that are standard works are included in the hope that these can be reprinted and in the understanding that they continue to be used by people who bring children and books together. Some that were omitted, however, deserve to be remembered--like works by Hannah Logasa, who set the pace for other bibliographers, and lists compiled by the early Committee on Recreational Reading of the NCTE, pioneer for the link between teacher-librarian-parent and child.

Some new titles were omitted because they weren't available for perusal prior to the cut-off date for completion of the manuscript. An example is the folklore series from Garland Publishing, Inc., including Street Literature in Great Britain and America by Rainer Wehse, of significance because of the connection between street literature and many of the best-known folktales current in today's literature for young readers. Another example of a seeming omission is in regard to the historical children's literature collection housed in the Lilly Library on the campus of Indiana State University in Bloomington, Indiana.

Comments and suggestions of titles for a revised edition will be welcome and should be sent to the author in care of the publisher. Due acknowledgment will be given.

The term "Young People" here includes infants to young adults; "Their Books" encompasses all genres of trade books for a predominantly English-speaking population. Space limitations necessitate exclusion of collections and anthologies, except for facsimile editions. On the whole, textbooks are not discussed.

The main Resource Guide is alphabetical by author (or title, if there is no author) and provides citations for each title. There is a Subject Index with entry numbers of each appropriate title and a listing of significant recent articles in journals. Subject topics are an amalgamation of standard topics and those suggested as "asked for" during conversations with people who serve young readers.

The Title Index gives entry numbers to the main Resource Guide. Resource Centers, Review Sources, and Publishers with Addresses are included as appendices.

Intensive research was carried out between 1982 and early 1986, but the seed for this work was planted during the years of serving as an Instructor in Literature for Children. I hereby acknowledge the continued friendship and colleagueship of students who have gone on to bring distinction to librarianship, teaching, writing, editing, and parenthood.

A collective note of appreciation goes to the librarians and staffs of Normal Public Library, Zimmerman Library of the Thomas Metcalf Laboratory School, Milner Library of Illinois State University (all in Normal, Illinois); Main Branch of the Chicago Public Library; Fifth Avenue Branch of the New York Public Library; Stratford (Ontario) Public Library; Ball State University Library (Muncie, Indiana); Wabash College Library (Crawfordsville, Indiana); Marian College Library (Indianapolis, Indiana); Indiana University Library (Bloomington, Indiana). A special thank you is due to the librarians and staff of the Riley Room for Children at the Central Branch of the Indianapolis-Marion County Public Library--particularly to Catherine Hanley Lutholtz and Orvella Fields--and to Stephen Bridge of the Broad Ripple Branch.

Mention also must be made of the assistance from Rex Business Machines in Indianapolis, publishers who sent data and who exhibited at the American Library Association annual conferences in San Francisco, Philadelphia, and Chicago, and professionals who reviewed my initial listing and offered suggestions.

However, there are always those who give special encouragement and caring throughout seemingly impossible tasks. Thus, to my family, and to Irene Mitchell, James W. Brown, Mary Ellen Hill, Steven Tuchman, Charles Caron, and William R. Eshelman go my most sincere appreciation.

Rita Kohn
Indianapolis, Indiana, and
Normal, Illinois
March 1986

1. AB BOOKMAN'S WEEKLY Special Children's Book Issue.
   This special issue includes articles on bookselling, publishing, and books for young readers along with adult resources on
   literature for children, ads on special collections for sale, out-
   of-print titles available, and rare titles available. An excellent
   source on dealers and publishers of children's books.
   ANNUAL

2. ADELL, Judith, and Hilary Dole Klein [compilers]. A Guide to
   Non-Sexist Children's Books. Waltrud Schacher, ed.; Introduction by Alan Alda. Chicago: Academy Chicago Limited, 1976.
   Illus. 149p.
   Selective list of about 425 fiction and nonfiction titles in
   three broad readership categories: Preschool-grade 3; grade 3-
   7; grade 7-12; all ages. Full annotations; author and title indexes. ISBN 0-915864-01-0; 0-915864-02-9 paper.
   NONSEXIST

   ALDERSON, Brian. Looking at Picture Books. See DARTON,
   F. J.

3. ALGARIN, Joanne P. Japanese Folk Literature: A Core Collection and Reference Guide. New York: Bowker, 1982. 216p.
   A critical guide to English translations of Japanese anthologies, folk literature, legends, tales. Bibliographies, glossary,
   index. ISBN 0-8352-1516-4.
   JAPAN

4. ALTSHULER, Anne. Books That Help Deal with a Hospital Experience. Rockville, MD: U.S. Department of HEW, 1974. paper. 22p. Reviewed 1978 by the Bureau of Community Health
   Services. [Available through Supt. of Documents, U.S. Government Printing Office, Washington, DC 20402]
   Comprehensive and critical guide to literature for children,
   preschool-elementary grades, about hospitals, illness, and the
   medical procedures children might encounter. Index. ISBN
   0-017-031-00020-1.
   HOSPITAL EXPERIENCE; ILLNESS

5. AMERICAN ASSOCIATION for the Advancement of Science. Science Books and Films. Washington, DC: AAAS, quarterly journal. First published in 1965 under the title: Science Books.

Reviews trade books, textbooks, reference books, and
16mm films in the pure and applied sciences for primary grade
students to adults. ISSN 0036-8253.
SCIENCE

6. AMERICAN BOOKSELLERS ASSOCIATION--Children's Book Coun-
cil Joint Committee. Catalog of the Exhibition of Children's
Books. Briarcliff Manor, NY: The Combined Book Exhibit,
Inc., annual.
In cooperation with the Combined Book Exhibit, "a catalog
of the select children's book display at the ABA convention,
which takes place in late Spring each year," and at other sites,
including at annual conferences of state library associations.
Available from ABA or CBC.
ANNUAL; BEST BOOKS; EXHIBITION

7. AMERICAN LIBRARY ASSOCIATION.* Active Heroines in Folk-
tales for Children. Compiled by the Children's Services Division.
Chicago: American Library Association, 1976. Paper. 6p.
ISBN 0-8389-5498-7.
FOLKTALES; HEROINES

8. _____. Africa: An Annotated List of Printed Materials Suitable for Children. Compiled with the African-American Institute.
New York: UNICEF, Information Center on Children's Cultures,
1968. Paper. 76p.
Arranged by region in Africa; includes addresses of publishers and dealers. Author-title-subject index.
AFRICA

9. _____. Alternatives in Print: An International Catalog of
Books, Pamphlets, Periodicals and Audiovisual Materials. Sixth
edition. Compiled by the Alternatives in Print Task Force of
the Social Responsibilities Round Table of the American Library
Association. New York: Neal-Schuman Publishers, 1980. 668p.
Catalog of publishers; four major indexes per title. ISBN
0-918212-20-0.
ALTERNATIVE TITLES

10. _____. Best Books for Young Adults. Compiled by Young
Adult Services Division. Chicago: American Library Associa-
tion, annual list. Paper.
Annual list of significant books for young adults.
ANNUAL; BEST BOOKS; YOUNG ADULT

11. _____. The Best of the Best Books 1970-1983. Compiled by
Young Adult Services Division. Chicago: American Library
Association, 1984. Paper. ISBN 0-8389-5658-0.
BEST BOOKS; YOUNG ADULT

---

*Also available from ALA, special lists from Booklist.

12. _____. A Bibliography of Non-Sexist Booklists. Compiled
by the ALSC Discussion Group on Sexism in Library Materials
for Children. Chicago: American Library Association, 1977.
Paper. 2p. ISBN 0-8389-6390-0.
         NONSEXIST

13. _____. BOOKLIST Reference and Subscription Books Reviews.
Chicago: American Library Association, annual.
         Reprinted from issues of Booklist. From 1961 to 1969,
published under the title: "Subscription Books Bulletin Reviews."
Biennial until 1974-75, when it changed to annual. Describes
and evaluates encyclopedias, dictionaries, biographical reference
works, atlases and gazetteers, directories, yearbooks, annuals
and statistical compendia, bibliographical reference sources, and
periodical indexes.
         Vols. for 1956-1968 o.p.
         1968-1970   ISBN 0-8389-0092-5
         1970-1972   ISBN 0-8389-0143-3
         1072-1074   ISBN 0-8389-0194-8
         1974-1975   ISBN 0-8389-0229-4
         1975-1976   ISBN 0-8389-0231-6
         1976-1977   ISBN 0-8389-3207-X
         1977-1978   ISBN 0-8389-3221-5
         1978-1979   ISBN 0-8389-3237-1
         1979-1980   ISBN 0-8389-3256-8
         1980-1981   ISBN 0-8389-3269-X
         1981-1982   ISBN 0-8389-0380-0
         1982-1983   ISBN 0-8389-3291-6
         ANNUAL; REFERENCE

14. _____. Books for Children, 1960-1971. Selected and reviewed
by Booklist and Subscription Books Bulletin. Chicago: American
Library Association, annually 1966 until 1970-71.
         Sept. 1960-Aug. 1965   ISBN 0-8389-0016-X
         1965-1966   ISBN 0-8389-0017-8
         1966-1967   ISBN 0-8389-0018-6
         1967-1968   ISBN 0-8389-0019-4
         1968-1969   ISBN 0-8389-0082-8
         1969-1970   ISBN 0-8389-0099-2
         1970-1971   ISBN 0-8389-0119-0
         Selective, critical reviews arranged by a modified Dewey
Decimal classification. Recommendations for purchase. Author,
subject and title index.
         BEST BOOKS

15. _____. Books for Everychild. Chicago: American Library
Association, 1985. Paper booklet.
         Annotated bibliography of 50 titles includes picture books
and fiction. Based on recommended-for-purchase titles from
Booklist. A companion to Junior High Contemporary Classics.
         PRESCHOOL

16. _____. Books for the Youngest Child. Chicago: American
Library Association, 1985. Paper booklet.
      Annotated bibliography of 50 titles includes picture books
and fiction. Based on Booklist recommendations.
      PRESCHOOL

17. _____. Caldecott Medal Books. Chicago: American Library
Association, annual. Paper.
      Annual annotated brochure of award-winning picture
books.
      ANNUAL; AWARD

18. _____. Children's Books of International Interest. Third
Edition. Barbara Elleman, ed.; ALSC. Chicago: American
Library Association, 1984. Paper. 96p.
      Criteria for inclusion is universal appeal within distinctly
American settings. 215 of the 350 annotated entries are new to
this edition. Covers picture books, first reading, folklore, fiction, biography, the arts, history, people, places, science,
nature; directory of publishers. First published in 1972; second edition in 1978. The first list was published in 1955 with
100 titles that appeared from 1930 to 1954. Succeeding annual
lists contained 20 to 60 books each, until the format changed
with the 1972 edition. ISBN 0-8389-3314-9, 1984 edition; ISBN
0-8389-0258-8, 1978 edition [Virginia Haviland, ed.].
      INTERNATIONAL

19. _____. Dictionaries for Children and Young Adults. Helen
Wright, ed.; Reference Books Bulletin Editorial Board. Chicago: American Library Association, 1983. Paper. 38p.
      Critical reviews. ISBN 0-8389-5655-6.
      DICTIONARIES

20. _____. Especially for Children: Outstanding Audiovisual
Materials Selected by the Association for Library Service to
Children. Chicago: American Library Association, 1983. Pa-
per brochure.
      ISBN 0-8389-5641-6.
      AUDIOVISUAL

21. _____. High Interest/Low Reading Level Booklists. Chicago:
American Library Association, annual. Paper.
      1982 ISBN 0-8389-5631-9
      1983 ISBN 0-8389-5657-2
      1984 ISBN 0-8389-5657-2
      Critical reviews of titles with a maximum of 5th-grade
reading level and capability for independent use by teenage
reluctant and poor readers. [Also available: High Interest/
Low Reading Level Information Packet. Chicago: American
Library Association, 1978. Paper. 25p. ISBN 0-8389-6391-9.]
      ANNUAL; HIGH INTEREST/LOW VOCABULARY

22. _____ . I Read, You Read, We Read; I See, You See, We
See; I Hear, You Hear, We Hear; I Learn, You Learn, We
Learn. Compiled by Library Service to the Disadvantaged
Child Committee. Chicago: American Library Association,
1971. Paper. 112p.
     Outgrowth of 1966 list, We Read; divided into four broad
age-level categories: preschool, ages 5-8, 8-11, 12-14; alphabetically by author with listings of books, films and recordings, and program aids and suggested resources for adults
working with disadvantaged children. ISBN 0-8389-3124-3.
     DISADVANTAGED

23. _____ . Junior High Contemporary Classics. Chicago:
American Library Association, 1985. Paper booklet.
     Reprint from December 15, 1984, issue of Booklist; 50
fiction titles. Companion to Books for Everychild.
     JUNIOR HIGH SCHOOL; CONTEMPORARY CLASSICS

24. _____ . Let's Read Together: Books for Family Enjoyment.
Fourth edition. Compiled by Association for Library Service
to Children. Chicago: American Library Association, 1981.
Paper. 111p. [First, second and third editions compiled by
the Special Committee of National Congress of Parents and
Teachers and the Children's Services Division of ALA.]
     577 annotated titles include traditional favorites and new
books "on their way to becoming classics." ISBN 0-8389-
3253-3.
     BEST BOOKS

25. _____ . Libros a Tu Gusto. Compiled by Young Adult Serv-
ices Division. Chicago: American Library Association, 1982.
Paper. 6p.
     Spanish and English annotations of 32 books in Spanish.
ISBN 0-8389-5622-X.
     SPANISH

26. _____ . Media and the Young Adult: A Selected Bibliography 1973-1977. Compiled by Young Adult Services Division.
Chicago: American Library Association, 1981. Paper. 344p.
[1950-1972 edition ©1977, 154p. paper.] 344p.
     ISBN 0-8389-3264-9 [1981]; ISBN 0-8389-3188-X [1977].
     YOUNG ADULT

27. _____ . Newbery Medal Books. Chicago: American Library
Association, annual. Paper.
     Annual pamphlet listing Newbery winners.
     ANNUAL; AWARD

28. _____ . Notable Children's Books 1971-1975. Compiled by
Association for Library Service to Children. Chicago: American
Library Association, 1981. Paper. 36 p. [Companion to

1940-1970 list; Chicago: American Library Association, 1977;
paper; 94p.; ISBN 0-8389-3182-0; which replaced Notable
Children's Books 1940-1959; Chicago: American Library Association, 1966.]

    An Age-Level Guide with Title Index and Illustrator In-
dex; ISBN 0-8389-3252-5. Annual brochures.

1979	©1980 ISBN 0-8389-5572-X
1980	©1981 ISBN 0-8389-5590-8
1981	©1982 ISBN 0-8389-5614-9
1982	©1983 ISBN 0-8389-5633-5
1983	©1984 ISBN 0-8389-5662-9

Notable Children's Books 1976-80, 1986. Paper. 70 p. ISBN
0-8389-3333-5.
    ANNUAL; NOTABLE

29.   . On Death and Dying: A Booklist from the Young
Adult Services Division. Chicago: American Library Association, 1983. Paper. 4p.
    DEATH

30.   . Opening Doors for Preschool Children and Their
Parents. Second edition. Compiled by Preschool Services
and Parent Education Committee, Association for Library Service to Children. Chicago: American Library Association, 1981.
Paper. 90p.
    First edition published 1977. Second edition revised and
expanded with out-of-print titles listed if they are available in
libraries. Three main sections: Books and Nonprint Materials
for Parents and Adults Working with Preschool Children; Books
for Preschool Children; Nonprint Materials for Preschool Children. ISBN 0-8389-3260-6.
    PRESCHOOL

31.   . Openers: America's Library Newspaper. Chicago:
American Library Association, quarterly.
    Seasonal, standard, and newly published titles for chil-
dren and adults in news and feature format. ISSN 0734-6794.
    BOOK REVIEWS

32.   . Outstanding Biographies for the College Bound.
Compiled by the Young Adult Services Division. Chicago:
American Library Association, 1982. Paper. 6p.
    ISBN 0-8389-5607-6.
    BIOGRAPHY; COLLEGE BOUND

33.   . Outstanding Books on the Performing Arts for the
College Bound. Compiled by the Young Adult Services Division. Chicago: American Library Association, 1982. Paper.
6p.
    ISBN 0-8389-5605-X.
    PERFORMING ARTS; COLLEGE BOUND

34. _____. Outstanding Fiction for the College Bound. Compiled by the Young Adult Services Division. Chicago: American Library Association, 1982. Paper. 6p.
    ISBN 0-8389-5606-8.
    FICTION; COLLEGE BOUND.

35. _____. Oustanding Non-fiction for the College Bound.
Compiled by the Young Adult Services Division. Chicago:
American Library Association, 1982. Paper. 6p.
    ISBN 0-8389-5623-8.
    NONFICTION; COLLEGE BOUND

36. _____. Positive Aspects of the Contemporary American
Family: A List of Books and Films. Selected by the Media
and Usage Committee, Young Adult Services Division. Chicago:
American Library Association, 1984. Paper. 6p.
    ISBN not available
    FAMILY

37. _____. Reading Aloud to Children. Compiled by Association for Library Service to Children, Preschool Services and
Parent Education Committee. Chicago: American Library Association, 1980. Paper. 3p.
    ISBN 0-8389-5580-0.
    READING ALOUD

38. _____. Resources for Underachievers in Reading. Compiled by Association for Library Service to Children. Chicago:
American Library Association, 1977. Paper. 5p.
    ISBN not available
    RELUCTANT READERS

39. _____. Role Free Booklist. Compiled by the Young Adult
Services Division, Sexism in Adolescent Materials Committee.
Chicago: American Library Association, 1979. Paper. 4p.
    Annotated list of 31 titles with sex role free contents
and positive sex role images. ISBN not available
    NONSEXIST

40. _____. Selecting Materials for Children and Young Adults:
A Bibliography of Bibliographies and Review Sources. Revised
edition. Compiled by Association for Library Service to Children and the Young Adult Services Division. Chicago: American Library Association, 1980. Paper. 80p.
    Replaces first edition, ©1967 under the title Selecting
Materials for Children and Young Adults. Includes Lists, Review Sources, Reference, Literature, Science and Math, Social
Studies, Special Needs, and Other. Directory of publishers,
title index. ISBN 0-8389-3241-X.
    BIBLIOGRAPHY OF BIBLIOGRAPHIES

41. _____ . Selecting Materials for Children with Special Needs. Compiled by Association for Library Service to Children, Library Service to Children with Special Needs Committee.   Chicago: American Library Association, 1980.   Paper.
ISBN not available
SPECIAL NEEDS, CHILDREN WITH

42. _____ . Sex Education for Adolescents: A Bibliography of Low-Cost Material. Compiled by the Young Adult Services Division, American Academy of Pediatrics and Planned Parenthood Federation of America.   Chicago: American Library Association, 1980.   Paper.   32p.
Critiques over 80 sex-related publications of interest to adolescents.   ISBN 0-8389-3248-7.
SEX EDUCATION

43. _____ . Sources for Young Adult Book Reviews.   Compiled by the Young Adult Services Division.   Chicago: American Library Association, 1974.   Paper.   3p.
ISBN not available
YOUNG ADULT

44. _____ . Still Alive: The Best of the Best, 1960-1974. Compiled by the Young Adult Services Division.   Chicago: American Library Association, 1976.   Paper.   8p.
72 titles published between 1960 and 1974 that were still read by YA's in 1975.   ISBN 0-8389-5477-4.
YOUNG ADULT; BEST BOOKS

45. _____ . Storytelling: Readings, Bibliographies, Resources. Compiled by Association for Library Service to Children, Margaret Bush, Ed.   Chicago: American Library Association, 1978.   Paper.   16p.
Lists sources of stories and materials on storytelling. Replaces 1968 list, For Storytellers and Storytelling.   ISBN 0-8389-3216-9.
STORYTELLING

46. _____ . Subject and Title Index to Short Stories for Children.   Compiled by ALA Editorial Committee, Julia F. Carter, Chair.   Chicago: American Library Association, 1955.   333p.
372 books indexed alphabetically by author within grade ranges.   Includes Subject and Title indexes.   LC 55-10208.
SHORT STORY

47. _____ . Subject Index to Children's Plays.   Compiled by a subcommittee of the ALA Board on Library Service to Children and Young People, Elizabeth D. Briggs, Chair, with Lesley Newton and Margaret McFate.   Chicago: American Library Association, 1940.   277p.
Suitable for presentation by pupils in grades 1-8; by

subject, cross-referenced under types. 202 books indexed.
DRAMATIC LITERATURE/PLAYS

48. _____. Subject Index to Poetry for Children and Young
People. Violet Sell, compiler. Great Neck, NY: Core Collection Books, Inc. 1982. 582p.
   157 poetry collections indexed for K-High School. Full
citations with subject headings and form headings. ISBN 0-
8486-0013-4.
POETRY

49. _____. Subject Index to Poetry for Children and Young
People, 1957-1975. Dorothy B. Frizzell-Smith and Eva L.
Andrews, editors. Chicago: American Library Association,
1977. 1035p.
   Supplement to 1957 edition [see above]; does not super-
sede. Includes 263 new anthologies with subject headings
drawn mainly from Sears List of Subject Headings: 10th edition
and others of contemporary significance added. ISBN 0-8389-
0242-1. [See SELL, Violet for 1982 edition.]
POETRY

50. AMERICAN SOCIETY for Aerospace Education. The Directory
of Aviation and Space Education. Third Edition. Washington,
DC: American Society for Aerospace Education, 1981. Paper.
70p.
   Basic sources of information, including books and resource organizations.
AEROSPACE

51. ANCHORAGE PRESS. Plays for Young People: 50th Anniver-
sary Catalog. New Orleans, LA: Anchorage Press, 1985.
Paper. 75p.
   Anchorage Press was founded in 1935 as the Children's
Theatre Press. This catalog is a descriptive listing of available plays, by title. Indexes of playwrights and plays in
categories. Also includes texts and guides on children's theatre.
DRAMATIC LITERATURE/PLAYS

52. ANDERSON, William Davis, and Patrick Groff. A New Look at
Children's Literature. Bibliography compiled by Ruth Robinson. Belmont, CA: Wadsworth Publishing Co., 1972. Illus.
362p.
      ISBN 0-534-00177-7.
   CHILDREN'S LITERATURE, TEXTBOOKS ON

53. ANDREWS, Siri [editor]. The Hewins Lectures, 1947-1962.
Introduction by Frederic G. Melcher. Boston: Hornbook,
1963. 375p.
   Presentation on books for children by New England

residents. LC 63-21644.
CHILDREN'S LITERATURE, HISTORY & CRITICISM

54. ANNO, Mitsumasa. The Unique World of Mitsumasa Anno:
Selected Works (1968-1977). Translated and adapted by Samuel
Crowell Morse. New York: Philomel Books, 1980. Illus. 48p.
[International edition ©Kodansha, Ltd., Tokyo, 1980; Original
Japanese edition ©Mitsumasa Anno, 1977.]
Retrospective of his work. ISBN 0-399-20743-0.
ILLUSTRATORS

55. AQUINO, John. Fantasy in Literature. West Haven, CT:
National Education Association, 1977. 64p.
ISBN 0-8106-1817-6.
FANTASY

56. ARBUTHNOT, May Hill; Dorothy M. Broderick, Shelton L. Root
Jr., Mark Taylor, and Evelyn L. Wenzel. The Arbuthnot
Anthology of Children's Literature. Fourth edition. Revised
by Zena Sutherland. Glenview, IL: Scott, Foresman, 1976.
Illus. 1089p. First edition ©1961.
A collection of poetry, folklore, short stories, biogra-
phies and other nonfiction. Includes a history and discussion
of children's literature. Bibliographies; subject and general in-
dexes. ISBN 0-673-15000-1.
CHILDREN'S LITERATURE, TEXTBOOKS ON

57. THE ARBUTHNOT LECTURES, 1970-1979. With a biographical
sketch of May Hill Arbuthnot by Zena Sutherland. Chicago:
American Library Association, 1980. 214p.
Lectures on literature for children. ISBN 0-8389-3240-1.
CHILDREN'S LITERATURE, HISTORY & CRITICISM
ARBUTHNOT, May Hill. See SUTHERLAND, Zena.

58. _____. Children's Books Too Good to Miss. Revised,
seventh edition. Cleveland: Press of Case Western Reserve
University, 1980. Illus. Paper. 125p.
First published 1948, periodically revised. Highly selective and critical appraisal of over 200 books for children K-
grade 8. ISBN 0-8295-0287-4.
BEST BOOKS

59. ARCHER, Marion Fuller [editor]. Reading for Young People:
The Upper Midwest. Chicago: American Library Association,
1981. Paper. 135p.
Part of a series; an annotated bibliography of 278 fiction
and nonfiction titles for the states of Michigan, Minnesota, and
Wisconsin. Directory of regional publishers; Author-Title-
Subject Index. ISBN 0-8389-0339-8.
U.S. REGIONAL LITERATURE

60. ARNOLD, Arnold. Pictures and Stories from Forgotten Children's Books. New York: Dover Publications, 1970. Paper. Facsimile edition of materials for children in grades K-6. ISBN 0-486-22041-9.
    FACSIMILE EDITION

61. ASIAN AMERICAN MATERIALS. San Mateo, CA: Japanese American Curriculum Project, 1984. Paper. 22p.
    Catalogue of materials for elementary and secondary levels, in English and other languages and including stories, folktales, poetry, nonfiction, fiction, journals, periodicals, and reference works. Covers Chinese, Filipino, Japanese, Korean, Samoan, and Vietnamese heritages. Available from the Project.
    ASIAN; ANNUAL

62. ASSOCIATION FOR CHILDHOOD Education International. Bibliography of Books for Children. Washington, DC: ACEI, 1984. Paper. 112p. Triennial; first published 1937.
    Selected listing grouped by subject or form for suggested age levels. Index of titles and authors; directory of publishers; major awards. Also now includes "Magazines and Newspapers for Children and Young Adolescents." ISBN 0-8713-095-2, 1980 edition; ISBN 0-8713-105-3, 1983 edition.
    BEST BOOKS

63. _____. Guide to Children's Magazines, Newspapers, Reference Books. Washington, DC: ACEI, biennial. Paper. 12p.
    Comprehensive coverage of available magazines and newspapers and selective listing of reference titles recently published. ISBN 0-87173-078-2 [1972].
    MAGAZINES; NEWSPAPERS; REFERENCE BOOKS

64. _____. Literature with Children. Washington, DC: ACEI, 1972. 64p.
    Tips on selection, reading, storytelling. ISBN 0-87173-031-6.
    ACTIVE READERS, DEVELOPING

65. AUBREY, Irene [compiler]. Mystery and Adventure in Canadian Books for Children and Young People. Ottawa: National Library of Canada, 1984. Paper. 18p.
    ISBN 0-6625-24845.
    CANADA

66. AUSTIN, Mary, and Esther Jenkins. Promoting World Understanding Through Literature, K-8. Littleton, CO: Libraries Unlimited, 1983. 300p.
    Annotated list, historical highlights, and introduction to the culture of ethnic groups in the U.S., including Blacks, Native Americans and Asian Americans. ISBN 0-87287-356-0.
    MULTIETHNIC

67. AVERY, Gillian Elise. Childhood's Pattern: A Study of the
     Heroes and Heroines of Children's Fiction, 1770-1950. London:
     Hodder & Stoughton Ltd., 1975.
          HEROES/HEROINES; FICTION

68. AZARNOFF, Pat. Best Books on Health for Children. New
     York: Bowker, 1982. 600p.
          Descriptions of 4000 nonfiction books under 700 subject
     areas. Title and author indexes. ISBN 0-8352-1518-0.
          HEALTH

69. _____ . Health, Illness and Disability: A Guide to Books
     for Children and Young Adults. New York: Bowker, 1983.
     432p.
          Annotations for over 1000 titles on physical, psychologi-
     cal and social aspects of specific health problems. ISBN 0-
     8352-1518-0.
          HEALTH; ILLNESS; DISABILITIES

70. BADER, Barbara. American Picture Books from Noah's Ark to
     the Beast Within. New York: Macmillan, 1976. Illus. 624p.
          Arranged topically and chronologically; history and
     criticism; biographies with critical analysis. ISBN 0-02-
     708080-3.
          PICTURE BOOKS

71. BAGSHAW, Marguerite [editor]. Assisted by Doris Scott.
     Books for Boys and Girls: A Standard Work of Reference for
     Librarians. Fourth edition. Toronto: Toronto Public Li-
     brary, 1966.
          First edition published 1927; supplement 1932; 2nd edition
     1940; 3rd edition 1954; supplement 1960. ISBN 0-919486-60-6.
          CANADA

72. Baker, Augusta. Books About Negro Life for Children. New
     York: New York Public Library, 1957. Paper. 24p.
          Now recognized as a basic list.
          BLACKS

73. _____ , and Ellin Greene. Storytelling: Art and Technique.
     New York: Bowker, 1977. 142p.
          History of storytelling in the United States; biographies
     of early known storytellers; storytelling literature, principles
     of selection, techniques, special settings for groups with spe-
     cial needs and handicaps. Appendix lists stories by age group
     and special needs. ISBN 0-8352-0840-0.
          STORYTELLING

74. BALDWIN, Ruth M. [collector and editor]. 100 Nineteenth-
     Century Rhyming Alphabets in English. Carbondale, IL:

Southern Illinois University Press, 1972. Illus. 296p.
ISBN 0-8093-0509-7
ALPHABET BOOKS

75. BALDWIN LIBRARY of Childrens Literature. Index to Children's Literature in English Before 1900: Catalog of the Baldwin Library of the University of Florida at Gainesville. Boston: G. K. Hall, 1981. ISBN 0-686-69555-0
SPECIAL COLLECTIONS

76. BARING-GOULD, William S., and Ceil Baring-Gould [editors]. The Annotated Mother Goose. New York: Bramhall House, 1962. Illus. 350p.
844 entries grouped by topic and kind. Bibliography: "A Chronological Listing of Some Important Books of Nursery Rhymes (and Books About Them) (1719-1960)." Index of first lines. LC 62-21606.
MOTHER GOOSE

77. BARRON, Neil [editor]. Anatomy of Wonder: A Critical Guide to Science Fiction. Second Edition. New York: Bowker, 1981. 724p.
ISBN 0-8352-1404-4.
SCIENCE FICTION

78. BARRON, Pamela Petrick, and Jennifer Q. Burley. Jump Over the Moon: Selected Professional Readings. New York: Holt, Rinehart and Winston, 1984. Paper. 512p.
Outgrowth of the telecourse, "Jump Over the Moon: Sharing Literature with Young Children," which was created to introduce viewers to the world of picture books for children from birth to age nine. Co-producers of the telecourse are the University of South Carolina and the South Carolina Educational Television Network. This collection contains 60 essays on twelve types of picture books. ISBN 0-03-063383-4.
PICTURE BOOKS

79. BARRY, Florence V. A Century of Children's Books. Detroit: Singing Tree Press, 1968. Illus. 257p. Reissue of 1922 edition published by Methuen & Co. Ltd., London.
Retrospective from chap-books to a garden of verses-- 1700-1823. ISBN 0-87968-828-9.
CHILDREN'S LITERATURE, HISTORY & CRITICISM

80. BARTH, Edna. A Christmas Feast: Poems, Sayings, Greetings and Wishes. Line drawings by Ursula Arndt. Boston: Houghton Mifflin/Clarion Books, 1979. 176p.
Collection encompasses five centuries of traditions and customs for middle elementary grade students. ISBN 0-395-28965-3.
CHRISTMAS

81.   A BASIC COLLECTION for Elementary Grades. First to
      seventh editions. Chicago: American Library Association,
      1922-1951.
            A standard during the thirty years of publication, it was
      published under the title: Graded List of Books for Children
      from 1922 to 1936. Compilers included A. S. Cutter [1922];
      N. Beust [1930-36]; G. Westervelt [1943]; M. S. Mathes [1951].
      BASIC COLLECTION

82.   A BASIC COLLECTION for Junior High Schools. First to third
      editions. Chicago: American Library Association, 1950-1960.
            E. R. Berner was editor for the first [1950] and second
      [1956] editions; M. V. Spengler edited the third edition [1960].
      The title served as an authoritative buying list for first pur-
      chases in small and medium-size junior high school libraries,
      and as a checklist to evaluate established collections.
      BASIC COLLECTION

83.   BASKIN, Barbara H., and Karen H. Harris. Books for the
      Gifted Child. New York: Bowker, 1980. 263p. Part of the
      Serving Special Populations Series.
            Evaluates 150 challenging books for the pre-reader to
      age 12. Directory of United Kingdom Publishers/Distributors.
      Indexes. ISBN 0-8352-1428-1 paper; ISBN 0-8352-1161-4.
      GIFTED CHILD, BOOKS FOR THE

84.   _____. More Notes from a Different Drummer: A Guide to
      Juvenile Fiction Portraying the Disabled. Second edition. New
      York: Bowker, 1984. Illus. 495p. Part of the Serving Spe-
      cial Populations Series. First edition: Notes from a Different
      Drummer [New York: Bowker, 1977, Illus. 375p, ISBN 0-
      8352-0978-4.]
            348 titles published 1976-1981; includes picture books,
      novels, foreign titles available in the U.S. Coded for reading
      levels. Indexes. ISBN 0-8352-1871-6.
      DISABILITIES

85.   BATOR, Robert [editor]. Signposts to Criticism of Children's
      Literature. Chicago: American Library Association, 1983.
      346p.
            Critical essays examining and identifying the special as-
      pects of literature for children. ISBN 0-8389-0372-X.
      CHILDREN'S LITERATURE, HISTORY & CRITICISM

86.   BAUER, Caroline Feller. Celebrations: Read-Aloud Holiday
      and Theme Book Programs. Illustrated by Lynn Gates Brede-
      son. New York: H. W. Wilson, 1985. 301p.
            16 programs that include prose and poetry selections,
      activities, and selective book lists. ISBN 0-8242-0708-4.
      HOLIDAYS

87. _____. Handbook for Storytellers. Chicago: American Library Association, 1977. 381p.
     Includes sources and techniques for using a variety of
media, including films, music, crafts, puppetry, and magic in
storytelling. Also available: Creative Storytelling Techniques:
Mixing the Media with Dr. Caroline Bauer. 30 minute videocassette. Rental from ALA. Purchase from The Public Television Library, 425 L'Enfant Plaza SW, Washington, DC 20024.
ISBN 0-8389-0225-1; ISBN 0-8389-0293-6 paper.
     STORYTELLING

88. _____. This Way to Books. Drawings by Lynn Gates. New
York: H. W. Wilson, 1983. 363p.
     In the author's words, "a collection of ideas, programs,
techniques and activities to involve children in books...."
Book lists; directory of publishers; index. ISBN 0-8242-
0678-9.
     STORYTELLING; GAMES; POETRY; BOOKTALKING;
     ACTIVE READERS, DEVELOPING

89. BAY AREA Young Adult Librarians. Book Waves. Modesta,
CA: BAYA, annual. Paper booklet.
     First issue in 1979; a compilation of reviews of books for
teenagers on fiction, science fiction/fantasy, mystery, nonfiction, hi/lo. Title and author indexes.
     ANNUAL; YOUNG ADULT

90. BEDARD, Roger L. [editor]. Dramatic Literature for Children:
A Century in Review. New Orleans: Anchorage Press, 1984.
705p.
     Retrospective; plays; listings of anthologies; selected
bibliography. ISBN 0-87602-045-7.
     DRAMATIC LITERATURE

90a. BENARDETE, Jane, and Phyllis Moe [editors]. Companions
of Our Youth: Stories by Women for Young Peoples Magazines, 1865-1900. New York: Frederick Ungar Publishing
Co., 1980. 216p.
          Contains 19 stories. ISBN 0-8044-2043-2; ISBN 0-8044-
6047-7 paper.
     STORIES

91. BENNET, Jill. Learning to Read with Picture Books. Revised
and enlarged second edition. Stroud, Glos, England: Thimble
Press, 1982. Illus. 48p.
     120 main entry and 150 supplementary titles from which
children learn to read. ISBN 0-903355-08-6.
     PICTURE BOOKS

92. _____. Reaching Out: Stories for Readers of 6 to 8.
Stroud, Glos, England: Thimble Press, 1980. 36p.

100 books annotated and 50 titles listed that children particularly enjoy just after they have learned to read. ISBN 0-903355-06-X.
PRIMARY GRADES

93-   BENNET, Rowena. Creative Plays and Programs for Holidays:
94.   Royalty-free Plays, Playlets, Group Readings, and Poems for Holiday and Seasonal Programs for Boys and Girls. Boston: Plays, Inc., 1976 ©1966. 448p. ISBN 0-8238-0005-9.
HOLIDAYS

95.   BERNSTEIN, Joanne E. [compiler]. Books to Help Children Cope with Separation and Loss. Second edition. New York: Bowker, 1983. 439p. First edition published 1977.
420 recommended books for ages 3 to 16. Indexes for Author, Title, Subject, Interest Level, Reading Level. ISBN 0-8352-1484-2.
BIBLIOTHERAPY

96.   BETTELHEIM, Bruno. The Uses of Enchantment: The Meaning and Importance of Fairy Tales. New York: Knopf, 1976. 328p. New York: Random House, 1977. Paper. 328p.
Discusses children's needs for fairy tales to gain emotional maturity. ISBN 0-394-4971-6 [Knopf]; ISBN 0-394-72265-5 [Random House].
FAIRY TALES

97.   BIENSTOCK, June Klein, and Ruth Bienstock Anolik. Careers in Fact and Fiction. Chicago: American Library Association, 1985. 178p.
160 fields cross-referenced with 1,000 autobiographies, biographies, nonfiction books, novels. Author and title indexes. Replaces Vocations in Fact and Fiction [ALA, 1953 and 1962]. ISBN 0-8389-0424-6.
CAREERS

98.   BILLINGTON, Elizabeth T. [editor]. The Randolph Caldecott Treasury. An Appreciation by Maurice Sendak. New York: Frederick Warne, 1978. Illus. 288p.
Essays about and selections from the work of Caldecott. Index. ISBN 0-7232-6139-3
ILLUSTRATORS

99.   BINGHAM, Jane, and Grayce Scholt [editors]. Fifteen Centuries of Children's Literature: An Annotated Chronology of British and American Works in Historical Context. Westport, CT: Greenwood Press, 1980. Illus. 540p.
Lists significant or representative books from the sixth century to 1945. Appendices include chronological listing of

periodicals and facsimiles and reprints. Bibliography of secondary sources. Index by titles and index with authors, illustrators, translators, and publishers. ISBN 0-313-22164-2.
CHILDREN'S LITERATURE, HISTORY & CRITICISM; BRITISH

100. BISSHOPP, Patricia [compiler]. Books About Handicaps for Children and Young Adults: The Meeting Street School Annotated Bibliography. East Providence, RI: The Meeting Street School, 1978. 64p.
Selected list of over 200 fiction and nonfiction titles on topics including: deafness and hearing impairment, blindness and visual impairment, learning disabilities, speech and emotional dysfunction, orthopedic handicaps, mental retardation, and brain damage. Update forthcoming.
DISABILITIES

101. BLACK AMERICA: A Selected List for Young Adults. New York: New York Public Library, annual. Paper.
BLACKS; YOUNG ADULT

102. BLICKLE, Calvin, and Frances Corcoran. Sports: A Multimedia Guide for Children and Young Adults. New York: Neal-Schuman Publishers, 1980. 245p. Selection Guide Series No. 6.
Almost 600 print and nonprint titles on various sports, critically reviewed for grade levels. Indexes by author, title, series, subject, high interest/low vocabulary; also biography/ autobiography index, periodical index, multimedia index, and women/girls sports index. ISBN 0-87436-283-0.
SPORTS

103. BLOSTEIN, Fay. Invitations, Celebrations: A Handbook of Ideas and Techniques for Promoting Reading in Junior and Senior High Schools. Toronto: Ontario Library Association, 1980. Illus. 223p.
Bibliography by title; index; addresses of Canadian publishers. ISBN 0-88969-013-8 paper.
CANADA; YOUNG ADULT

104. _____. New Paperbacks for Young Adults: A Thematic Guide. 2 vols. Toronto: Ontario Library Association, 1979-1981. 127p.; 148p.
ISBN 0-88969-022-7 [Vol. 1]; ISBN 0-88969-024-3 [Vol. 2].
PAPERBOUND; YOUNG ADULT

105. BLOUNT, Margaret. Animal Land: The Creatures of Children's Fiction. New York: William Morrow, 1975. 336p.
FICTION

106. BODART, Joni. Booktalk! Booktalking and School Visiting
for Young Adult Audiences. Second edition. New York:
H. W. Wilson, 1985. 246p. First edition, 1980, 249p.
Bibliography; index. ISBN 0-8242-0650-9, 1980; ISBN
0-8242-0716-5, 1985.
BOOKTALKING; YOUNG ADULT

107. BOGART, Gary, and Richard H. Isaacson [editors]. Children's Catalog. Fourteenth edition. New York: H. W. Wilson, 1981. 1296p. With four annual supplements, 1982-1985.
First edition published in 1909. Part of Standard Catalog
Series.
5,901 fiction and nonfiction titles for preschoolers to
grade six, selected by an advisory committee. Suggestions
for a basic core collection based on critical reviews. ISBN
0-8242-0662-2.
CORE COLLECTION; ANNUAL

108. _____. Junior High School Library Catalog. Fourth edition. New York: H. W. Wilson, 1980. 939p. First published
in 1965, edited by Rachel Shor and Estelle Fidell, with 3310
titles. Part of Standard Catalog Series.
Fourth edition catalogs 3,775 books and includes 9,061
subject and author and title analytical entries. Kept up-to-
date with annual supplements. ISBN 0-8342-0652-5.
CORE COLLECTION; ANNUAL; JUNIOR HIGH SCHOOL

109. _____. Senior High School Library Catalog. Twelfth edition. New York: H. W. Wilson, 1982. 1300p. With four
annual supplements, 1983-1986. First published 1918. Part
of Standard Catalog Series.
ISBN 0-8242-0677-0.
CORE COLLECTION; ANNUAL; SENIOR HIGH SCHOOL

110. BOOKS FOR ALL TIME: A Guide to Current Editions of Classics for Young People. Compiled by the North West Branch,
Youth Libraries Group of the Library Association. Birmingham: Combridge Jackson Ltd., 1973. Illus. 123p.
Compilers state that they "attempt[ed] to find the
most important and interesting works of fiction which have
endured for more than 50 years ... and to point out good
editions within various categories of price." Listed by author
and title. ISBN 0-85197-0478; 0-85197-0486 [paper].
CLASSICS

111. BOOKS FOR [ELEMENTARY] School Libraries (Grades K-8).
Williamsport, PA: Bro-Dart, annual.
A jobber's catalog that includes more than 34,000 titles,
with a fully annotated selection guide of over 8,500 titles, arranged by subject.

BUYING GUIDE; ANNUAL

112. BOOKS FOR FRIENDSHIP: A List of Books Recommended for
      Children. Fourth edition. Published simultaneously by
      Philadelphia: American Friends Service Committee; New York:
      Anti-Defamation League of B'nai B'rith, 1968. Paper. 46p.
      First published in 1953 under title: Books Are Bridges.
      Some 300 titles in five broad categories: Neighbors at
      home; Neighbors abroad; Races and Nations; Beliefs into ac-
      tion; Holidays and holy days. Title index; author-illustrator
      index.
      MULTICULTURAL

113. BOOKS ON DIVORCE. Woodbridge, CT: Children's Divorce
      Center Press, 1984. Paper. 31p.
      Includes fiction and nonfiction titles for children.
      DIVORCE

114. BOOKS TO SHARE. Compiled by Children's Librarians of
      Westchester County, NY. Elmsford, NY: Westchester Library
      System, 1984. Paper. 10p.
      60 titles selected from over 2000 published in 1983.
      Under four headings: Picture books; For young readers; For
      older readers; For parents and other professionals.
      BEST BOOKS

115. R. R. BOWKER COMPANY. Bilingual Educational Publications
      in Print. New York: Bowker, 1983. 600p.
           Covers all grade levels and subject areas with materials
      in a range of languages including Chinese, French, German,
      Hebrew, Russian, Spanish, and Vietnamese. Indexed by lan-
      guage, subject, author, title, and series. ISBN 0-8352-1605-5.
      BILINGUAL

116. _____. Books for Secondary School Libraries. Sixth Edi-
      tion. Compiled by the Ad Hoc Library Committee of the Na-
      tional Association of Independent Schools. New York: Bow-
      ker, 1981. 844p.
           Lists over 9000 nonfiction and series titles. ISBN 0-
      8352-1111-8.
      SECONDARY SCHOOL

117. _____. Books in Print. New York: Bowker, annual.
           Separate volumes by author, by title, by subject.
      Books in Print Supplement gives price changes, titles which
      have gone out-of-print and new books published or announced
      in the six months following publication of Books in Print.
      ANNUAL

118. _____. Children's Books in Print. New York: Bowker,

annual.
        First edition in 1969 was an expansion from and replace-
ment for Children's Books for Schools and Libraries. Separate volumes by author, by title, by subject. Comprehensive
listing of publishers and distributors appended to the title
index.
        ANNUAL

119.   _____. Children's Fiction 1876-1984. 2 vols. New York:
        Bowker, 1984. 2000p.
            ISBN 0-8352-1831-7.
            FICTION

120.   _____. El-Hi Textbooks in Print. New York: Bowker,
        annual.
            Includes texts, atlases, dictionaries, encyclopedias,
        maps, professional books, teaching aids, supplementary AV
        materials for K-12. Indexed by author, title, subject, series;
        publishers index.
            REFERENCE; ANNUAL

121.   _____. Forthcoming Books. New York: Bowker, bi-
        monthly.
            Listing of all books due to appear in the coming five-
        month period to supplement the annual Books in Print.
        Subject Guide to Books in Print companion publication.
            FORTHCOMING BOOKS; ANNUAL

122.   _____. Growing Up with Books. New York: Bowker,
        annual. Paper booklet.
            Annual list of approximately 250 of the best children's
        books in print, including old and new, classic and contempo-
        rary. BEST BOOKS; ANNUAL

123.   _____. Growing Up with Paperbacks. New York: Bow-
        ker, annual. Paper booklet.
            Guide to approximately 200 of the best paperbacks in
        print for children, including classics and newer titles.
            PAPERBOUND; ANNUAL

124.   _____. Growing Up with Science Books. New York:
        Bowker, annual. Paper booklet.
            Listing of approximately 250 of the best books in Sci-
        ence for children.
            SCIENCE; ANNUAL

125.   _____. Large Type Books in Print. New York: Bowker,
        annual.
            Lists books in oversize type for visually handicapped.
        Main index arranged by subject under "general reading" and

"textbooks." Grade levels. Author, title, and publisher/
service association indexes.
LARGE TYPE; ANNUAL

126. _____. Literary and Library Prizes. Tenth edition.
New York: Bowker, 1980. 650p.
Comprehensive data on 450 literary prizes, library
awards, fellowships and grants in the United States, Canada,
and Great Britain. ISBN 0-8352-1249-1.
PRIZES

127. _____. LMP 1985: Literary Market Place: The Directory
of American Book Publishing. New York: R. R. Bowker
Co., 1984. Paper. 945p.
Comprehensive coverage on publishing with additional
data on juvenile book clubs and a compilation of readily avail-
able juvenile book lists and catalogs. ISBN 0-8352-1919-4;
ISSN 0075-9899.
PUBLISHING; ANNUAL

128. _____. Paperbound Book Guide for Elementary Schools.
New York: Bowker, annual.
Subject guide to reprints and originals.
PAPERBOUND; ANNUAL

129. _____. Paperbound Books for Young People: From Kindergarten Through Grade 12. Second edition. New York:
Bowker, 1980. Paper. 325p. First edition, ©1979.
15,000 titles [includes trade books for young readers
and professional titles for teachers and librarians] annotated
in subject, author, title, and illustrator indexes. Index to
publishers and distributors. ISBN 0-8352-1280-7.
PAPERBOUND; ANNUAL

130. _____. The Publishers' Trade List Annual: A Buying and
Reference Guide to Books and Related Products. Ruth Traub,
editor. New York: R. R. Bowker, multivolume, annual.
The American Catalog, begun in 1873, grew into the
PTLA. Publishers choose to be included. Coverage of pub-
lishers of children's books is fairly comprehensive, providing
a good listing from any particular house.
PUBLISHING; ANNUAL

131. BRACKEN, Jeanne, and Sharon Wigutoff [editors]. Books for
Today's Child: An Annotated Bibliography of Non-Stereotyped
Picture Books. Old Westbury, NY: The Feminist Press, 1979.
Paper. 42p.
Annotated listing of approximately 200 picture books, in
categories that include single parents, working mothers, handi-
caps, multiracial, and sensitive boys and adventurous girls.
Indexes. ISBN 0-912670-53-3.
NONSTEREOTYPED; PICTURE BOOKS

132.   _____, with Ilene Baker. Books for Today's Young Read-
        ers: An Annotated Bibliography of Recommended Fiction for
        Ages 10-14. Old Westbury, NY: The Feminist Press, 1981.
        Paper. 64p.
            200 titles in seven thematic sections: gender and self-
        awareness; peer friendships; ethnicity; acculturation and
        racism; children with special needs; families in transition;
        foster care and adoption; and intergenerational relationships
        between young and old. Author, title, subject indexes.
        ISBN 0-935-312-03-X.
            FICTION; INTERRELATIONSHIPS

133.   BRAILLE INSTITUTE OF AMERICA. Expectations: The An-
        nual Braille Anthology of Current Children's Literature. Los
        Angeles: Braille Institute Press, annual.
            Available free to any blind child in the United States.
        Lists recent materials transcribed into Braille for children
        ages 8 to 12.
            BRAILLE BOOKS; ANNUAL

134.   BRANSON, Margaret; Margaret Bush; Lazer Goldberg; Beverly
        Kobrin; Phylis and Philip Morrison; Barbara Ann Porte; and
        Judith S. Wooster. Everychild Informational Books: Appre-
        ciating the Elements of Effective Factual Books for Young
        People. New York: Children's Book Council, 1983.
            Introduced at "Everychild: The American Conference"
        in New York City, August 29-September 1, 1983.
            INFORMATIONAL

135.   BREWTON, John E., and Sara W. Brewton [compilers]. Index
        to Children's Poetry: A Title, Subject, Author and First
        Line Index to Poetry in Collections for Children and Youth.
        New York: H. W. Wilson, ©1942, 966p; First Supplement
        ©1954, 405p; Second Supplement ©1965, 453p.
            A dictionary index with title, subject, author, and first
        line entries. First volume indexes some 15,000 poems from
        130 collections; first supplement indexes some 7,000 poems
        from 66 collections, published 1938 to 1951; second supplement
        indexes approximately 8,000 poems from 85 collections pub-
        lished 1949 to 1963. These three and the following three vol-
        umes are part of the Index to Poetry for Children and Young
        People Series. ISBN 0-8242-0021-7, 1942; 0-8242-0022-5, 1954;
        0-8242-0023-3, 1965.
            POETRY

136.   _____, and G. Meredith Blackburn III [compilers]. Index
        to Poetry for Children and Young People: 1964-1969. New
        York: H. W. Wilson, 1972.
            Indexes approximately 11,000 poems from 117 collections.
        ISBN 0-8242-0435-2.
            POETRY

137. BREWTON, John E.; G. Meredith Blackburn III; and Lorraine
      A. Blackburn [compilers]. Index to Poetry for Children
      and Young People: 1970-1975. New York: H. W. Wilson,
      1978. 471p.
            Indexes approximately 10,000 poems from 109 collections.
      ISBN 0-8242-0621-5.
            POETRY

138. _____. Index to Poetry for Children and Young People:
      1976-1981. New York: H. W. Wilson, 1983. 320p.
            Indexes approximately 7,000 poems from 110 collections.
      ISBN 0-8242-0681-9.
            POETRY

139. BRIGGS, Katharine Mary. An Encyclopedia of Fairies: Hob-
      goblins, Brownies, Bogies and Other Supernatural Creatures.
      New York: Pantheon, 1978. Paper. Illus. 448p. ISBN
      0-394-73467-X.
            FAIRIES

140. _____. Fairies in Tradition and Literature. Boston, MA:
      Routlege & Kegan Paul, Ltd., 1977. Paper.
            ISBN 0-7100-8687-3.
            FAIRIES

141. _____. Personnel of Fairyland: A Short Account of the
      Fairy People of Great Britain for Those Who Tell Stories to
      Children. Detroit: Gale Research Co., 1971. Illus. Re-
      production of 1953 edition.
            ISBN 0-8103-3374-4.
            FAIRIES

142. BRIGGS, Nancy E., and Joseph A. Wagner. Children's Lit-
      erature Through Storytelling and Drama. Second edition.
      Dubuque, IA: Wm. C. Brown, 1979. 201p.
            First edition ©1970 by J. A. Wagner under title Chil-
      dren's Literature Through Storytelling.
            Includes bibliography and indexes. ISBN 0-697-06212-0.
            STORYTELLING; DRAMATIC LITERATURE/PLAYS

143. BRITISH BOOKS IN PRINT; British Children's Books in Print.
      Published annually in November by J. Whitaker and Sons
      Ltd.; distributed in the United States by R. R. Bowker Com-
      pany.
            ANNUAL; BRITISH

144. BRODERICK, Dorothy M. Image of the Black in Children's
      Fiction. New York: Bowker, 1973. Illus. 219p.
            Over 100 children's books published between 1909 and
      1968 analyzed to determine the image of Blacks. ISBN 0-
      8352-0550-9.
            BLACKS; FICTION

145. BROWN, Lucy Gregor, and Betty McDavid. <u>Core Media Col-</u>
      <u>lection for Elementary Schools</u>. Second edition. New York:
      Bowker, 1978. 224p.
           First edition published in 1971. 3,000 nonprint titles
      recommended for grades K-8 that were produced since the first
      edition and a list of "classic" titles from the first edition.
      Title and media indexes; directory of producers and distrib-
      utors. ISBN 0-8352-1096-0.
           CORE COLLECTIONS

146. _____ . <u>Core Media Collection for Secondary Schools</u>.
      Second edition. New York: Bowker, 1979. 263p.
           Supplement to the first edition; mainly titles produced
      after 1973. Qualitative selection guide to nonprint media for
      students in grades 7 to 12. Title and subject indexes.
      Producer/distributor directory. ISBN 0-8352-1162-2.
           SECONDARY SCHOOLS; CORE COLLECTIONS

147. THE BUCKLEY-LITTLE CATALOGUE of Books Available from
      Authors, 1984. New York: The Buckley-Little Book Cata-
      logue Co., Inc., 1984. Paper. 151p.
           First annual listing contains over 750 titles by 450 au-
      thors in the U.S. and Canada whose books were published
      by reputable houses but have been remaindered and would
      be out-of-print but for the willingness to store and sell on
      their own. Along with adult titles, an extensive listing un-
      der "Children's Literature." Indexes by author, title and
      subject. ISBN 0-916667-01-4.
           ANNUAL

148. BUTLER, Dorothy. <u>Babies Need Books</u>. Drawings by Shirley
      Hughes. New York: Atheneum, 1980. First published Lon-
      don: The Bodley Head, 1980.
           Discussion and booklists. ISBN 0-689-11112-6.
           PRESCHOOL; ACTIVE READERS, DEVELOPING

149. _____ . <u>Cushla and Her Books</u>. Boston: Horn Book, 1980.
      Illus. 128p.
           Biographical account of a handicapped child's experi-
      ences with books, from birth to age four. ISBN 0-87675-279-
      2 cloth; 0-87675-283-0 paper.
           BIBLIOTHERAPY

150. _____ , and Marie Clay. <u>Reading Begins at Home</u>. Exeter,
      NH: Heinemann Educational Books, ©1979; first U.S. edition,
      1982. Paper. 43p.
           How to select and use books; selected bibliography.
      ISBN 0-435-08201-9.
           ACTIVE READERS, DEVELOPING

151. BUTLER, Francelia, and Compton Rees. <u>Children's Litera-</u>
      <u>ture, Volume 12: Annual of the Modern Language Association</u>

Division on Children's Literature and the Children's Literature Association. New Haven: Yale University Press, 1984.
226p. Volumes 1-6, 1972-1979, published by Temple University Press; since 1980 published by Yale University Press.
Each volume includes far-ranging interpretative articles
by critics and reviewers.
ANNUAL

152. BUTLER, Francelia, and Richard W. Rotert [editors]. Reflections on Literature for Children: Selected from the Annual, Children's Literature. Hamden, CT: Library Professional Publications, 1984. Paper. 352p.
Foreword by Leland B. Jacobs; 26 articles by leading
professionals in children's literature. Index. ISBN 0-208-
02054-3.
CHILDREN'S LITERATURE, HISTORY & CRITICISM

153. BUTLER, Marian [editor]. Canadian Books in Print 1985:
Author and Title Index; Canadian Books in Print 1985: Sub-
ject Index. Toronto: University of Toronto Press, 1985.
ISBN 0-8020-4621-5 [Author and Title Index]; ISBN 0-
8020-4622-3 [Subject Index].
ANNUAL, CANADA

154. BUTTLAR, Lois, and Lubomyr R. Wynar. Building Ethnic
Collections: An Annotated Guide for School Media Centers
and Public Libraries. Littleton, CO.: Libraries Unlimited,
1977. 434p.
Selective listing. Author, title, and audiovisual indexes. ISBN 0-87287-130-4. LC 73-82110.
MULTIETHNIC

155. BYLER, Mary Gloyne [compiler]. American Indian Authors
for Young Readers: A Selected Bibliography. New York:
Association on American Indian Affairs, 1973. Paper. 26p.
Includes publishers directory.
AMERICAN INDIAN

156. CALIFORNIA LIBRARY ASSOCIATION. Annual Booklist.
Compiled by the Young Adult Reviewers of Southern Califor-
nia. Sacramento, CA: California Library Association, annual.
Paper.
Begun in 1965, this annual list includes fiction and non-
fiction titles that appeal to young adults.
ANNUAL; YOUNG ADULTS

157. CALIFORNIA STATE COLLEGE. Chicano Children's Literature:
Annotated Bibliography. Compiled by the Mexican-American
Children's Literature 490 class. Sonoma, CA: California

State College, Chicano Studies Department, 1973. Paper.
39p.
    Selection made on a five-point rating system.
    CHICANO

158. CAMERON, Eleanor. The Green and Burning Tree: On the
Writing and Enjoyment of Children's Books. Boston: Little,
Brown and Co., ©1962, 1969. Paper. 377p.
    Essays. ISBN 0-316-12522-9 paper [published by the
Atlantic Monthly Press]; LC 69-11780 cloth.
    CHILDREN'S LITERATURE, HISTORY & CRITICISM

159. CAMPBELL, Harriet. Children's Literature. Cincinnati, OH:
Mosaic Press, 1981. Paper. 48p.
    Emphasis is on readers at the high school level. ISBN
0-88014-032-1.
    CHILDREN'S LITERATURE, HISTORY & CRITICISM

160. CAMPBELL, Patty. Sex Education Books for Young Adults,
1892-1979. New York: Bowker, 1979. 282p.
    Examines aspects of societal influence on adolescent sex-
uality in books with a core collection of recommended titles.
ISBN 0-8352-1157-6.
    SEX EDUCATION

CANADIAN BOOKS in Print see BUTTLER, Marian

161. CARLSEN, G. Robert. Books and the Teenage Reader: A
Guide for Teachers, Librarians and Parents. Second Revised
Edition. New York: Bantam Books, Inc., 1980. Paper.
New York: Harper and Row, 1980. Cloth. 290p.
    First published in 1967; revised and updated in 1971.
Includes discussions and bibliographies in diverse categories:
The teenager's world; subliterature; the adolescent novel;
the popular adult novel; significant modern literature; the
classics; poetry; biography; drama; nonfiction; literature by
and about women; science fiction and fantasy. ISBN 0-553-
13332-2 paper; ISBN 0-06-010626-3 cloth.
    TEENAGE

162. CARLSON, Ruth Kearney. Emerging Humanity: Multi-ethnic
Literature for Children and Adolescents. Dubuque, IA.:
Wm. C. Brown Co., 1972.
    MULTIETHNIC

163. _____. Literature for Children: Enrichment Ideas; Spark-
ling Fireflies. Pose Lamb, consulting editor. Dubuque, IA:
Wm. C. Brown Co., 1970. Illus. Paper. 109p. Part of
Literature for Children Series.
    Emphasis is on the uses of literature; this volume covers
enjoyment of language, Oriental poetry, and the theme of

loneliness. Each section has a selected list for children and
for professionals/adults. ISBN 0-697-06200-7.
POETRY

164. CARPENTER, Humphrey. Secret Gardens: A Study of the
Golden Age of Children's Literature, from Alice in Wonder-
land to Winnie-the-Pooh. Boston: Houghton Mifflin, 1985.
235p.
Biographical sketches and literary criticism of writers
of children's literature from 1860 to 1930. ISBN 0-395-
35293-2.
AUTHORS; CHILDREN'S LITERATURE, HISTORY &
CRITICISM

165. _____, and Mari Prichard. The Oxford Companion to Children's Literature. New York: Oxford University Press,
1984. 587p.
Over 2,000 entries, including 900 biographical sketches
of authors, illustrators, printers, and publishers. The other
entries cover titles, characters, genres, and publication ter-
minology. ISBN 0-19-211582-0.
CHILDREN'S LITERATURE, REFERENCES FOR

166. CARR, Jo [compiler]. Beyond Fact: Nonfiction for Children
and Young People. Chicago: American Library Association,
1982. Paper. 224p.
Twenty-nine essays cover science, history, biography,
and controversial issues. Includes a list of awards for nonfiction books. Gives professional titles, journals, and notable
lists. ISBN 0-8389-0348-7.
NONFICTION

167. CARROLL, Frances Laverne, and Mary Meacham [editors].
Exciting, Funny, Scary, Short, Different, and Sad Books
Kids Like About Animals, Science, Sports, Families, Songs,
and Other Things. Chicago: American Library Association,
1984. Paper. 180p.
Combines comments by children with critiques by li-
brarians. ISBN 0-8389-0423-8.
BEST BOOKS

168. CASS, Joan E. [selecter]. Books for Under Five. London:
National Book League, 1973. Paper. 15p.
PRESCHOOL

169. CATHON, Laura E.; Marion McC. Haushalter; Virginia A.
Russell; and Margaret Hodges, Consultant. Stories to Tell
Children: A Selected List. Eighth edition. Pittsburgh:
University of Pittsburgh Press for Carnegie Library of Pitts-
burgh Children's Services, 1974. Illus. 168p. 1st edition,
1916 compiled by Edna Whiteman; 2nd, 3rd, 4th editions, 1918,

1921, 1926, revised by Margaret Carnegie and Elizabeth Nesbitt; 5th edition, 1932, compiled and revised by Esther Fleming (Elva S. Smith); 6th edition, 1950, revised and edited by Laura E. Cathon, Kathryn Kohberger, and Virginia A. Russell; 7th edition, 1960, compiled by Laura E. Cathon, Margaret Hodges, and Virginia A. Russell.

Stories under a variety of topics, including Africa and Southeast Asia. Classified list; aids for the storyteller. Includes stories of special interest to preschool children; aged 6 to 10 and older boys and girls. ISBN 0-8229-3280-6; 0-8229-5246-7 paper.

STORYTELLING

170. CATTERSON, Jane H. [editor]. Children and Literature. Newark, DE: International Reading Association, 1970. 104p.

Twelve essays on three topics: Point of View, Choosing the Books, and Using the Books. Includes book lists. LC 75-119755.

CHILDREN'S LITERATURE, HISTORY & CRITICISM

171. CECH, John [editor]. American Writers for Children, 1900-1960. Detroit, MI: Gale Research Co., 1983. Illus. 412p. Dictionary of Literary Biography Series: Vol 22.

43 authors are examined in critical essays containing biographical and bibliographical data. ISBN 0-8103-1146-1.

AUTHORS

172. CENTER FOR INTERNATIONAL COOPERATION. Peace Issues Bibliography Service. Evanston, IL: Center for International Cooperation, National College of Education, annual. Paper.

Computerized, selective bibliographies by grade levels on peace-related topics.

ANNUAL; PEACE

173. CHAMBERS, Aidan. Introducing Books to Children. Second Edition Completely Revised and Expanded. Boston: The Horn Book, 1983. 224p. First published 1973.

Bibliography, index, and discussion on bringing books and children together. ISBN 0-87675-284-9 cloth; 0-87675-285-7 paper.

ACTIVE READERS, DEVELOPING

174. _____. Plays for Young People to Read and Perform. Stroud, Glos., England: The Thimble Press, 1983. Paper. 84p.

Over 80 plays for 8 to 18 year olds, discussed in relation to literature and performance. Descriptive and critical bibliography. ISBN 0-903355-10-8.

DRAMATIC LITERATURE/PLAYS

175. _____. The Reluctant Reader. Elmsford, NY: Pergamon Press, 1969.
     RELUCTANT READERS

176. CHAMBERS, Dewey W. Children's Literature in the Curriculum. Chicago: Rand McNally, 1971. Illus. 227p. Rand McNally Education Series.
     Multiple bibliographies.
     CHILDREN'S LITERATURE, STUDY & TEACHING

177. _____. Literature for Children: Storytelling and Creative Drama. Pose Lamb, consulting editor. Dubuque, IA: Wm. C. Brown Co., 1970. Illus. 92p. Part of series.
     Covers techniques and provides selected titles. Index.
     ISBN 0-697-0620-5.
     STORYTELLING; CREATIVE DRAMA

178. CHAMBERS, Joanna [compiler]. Hey, Miss! You Got a Book for Me?: A Model Multicultural Resource Collection. Second edition. Austin, TX: Austin Bilingual Language Editions, 1981. 91p.
     Offers a model resource collection of approximately 350 book and audiovisual titles. Includes Chinese, French, Greek, and Vietnamese dual-language items, with an emphasis on Spanish. Author, Subject, and Publisher/Distributor indexes.
     ISBN 0-940048-01-9.
     MULTICULTURAL

179. CHAMBERS, Nancy [editor]. The Signal Approach to Children's Books: A Collection. Metuchen, NJ: Scarecrow Press, 1981. Illus. 352p. First published Harmondsworth, Middlesex, England: Kestrell Books, 1980.
     A collection of articles drawn from the first ten years of Signal: Approaches to Children's Books, published by Aidan and Nancy Chambers. ISBN 0-8108-1447-1.
     CHILDREN'S LITERATURE, HISTORY & CRITICISM

180. _____. The Signal Review of Children's Books 1: A Selective Guide to Picture Books, Fiction, Plays, Poetry, Information Books Published During 1982. Stroud, Glos., England: The Thimble Press, 1983. Illus. Paper. 80p.
     400 hardback and paperback books for preschool to mid-teen readers. Index. ISBN 0-903355-12-4.
     SELECTION GUIDES

181. CHAMPLIN, Connie. Puppetry and Creative Dramatics in Storytelling. Illus. by Nancy Renfro. Ann W. Schwalb, editor. Austin, TX: Nancy Renfro Studios, 1980. Paper. 132p.
     Includes an extensive listing of titles. ISBN 0-931044-03-0.
     STORYTELLING

182.   _____, and Nancy Renfro. Storytelling with Puppets.
        Chicago: American Library Association, 1984. 308p.
            Comprehensive coverage of techniques, activities, and
        sources for puppets, stages, and titles. Also by Champlin,
        but not available for review, are Books in Bloom: Developing
        Creativity Through Children's Literature and Storytelling with
        the Computer. Renfro has her own puppetry and storytelling
        company. ISBN 0-8389-0421-1.
                STORYTELLING

183.   CHARLES, Sharon Ashenbrenner, and Sari Feldman [com-
        pilers]. Drugs: A Multimedia Sourcebook for Young Adults.
        New York: Neal-Schuman Publishers, 1980. Selection Guide
        Series 4.
            Print materials include general nonfiction, personal nar-
        rative, and fiction. Nonprint materials and other sources are
        included. Directory of Publishers and Distributors; author,
        title, subject index. ISBN 0-87436-281-4.
                DRUGS

184.   CHELTON, Mary K. Booktalking: You Can Do It. Chicago:
        American Library Association, 1976. Paper. 5p. Reprint
        from School Library Journal, April 1976.
                ISBN 0-8389-5485-5.
                BOOKTALKING

185.   CHICOREL, Marietta [editor]. Chicorel Theatre Index to
        Plays for Young People. Vol. 9. New York: American Li-
        brary Publishing Co., 1974. 500p.
                ISBN 0-934598-34-7.
                DRAMATIC LITERATURE/PLAYS

186.   THE CHILD IMMIGRANT: Establishing Roots in a New Coun-
        try. Compiled by a Committee of the Association of Children's
        Librarians of Northern California, 1983. 64p. Available from
        Sherrill Kumler, 245 Ocean View Avenue #B, Santa Cruz, CA
        95062.
            Selective bibliography under headings of fiction, non-
        fiction, series by title, origin and period of immigration. In-
        dexes.
                IMMIGRANTS

187.   CHILD STUDY ASSOCIATION of America. Children's Books
        of the Year. Compiled by the Child Study Children's Book
        Committee. New York: Bank Street College of Education,
        annual. Originally published by The Child Study Press.
            Describes approximately 500 titles selected from the ap-
        proximately 3,000 new books published the previous year.
        Grouped by age, 3 to 13, and by interest, and includes pa-
        perbacks, reprints, and new editions of old favorites.
                1968; ©1969 paper ISBN 0-87183-170-8

```
1969; ©1970 paper  ISBN 0-87183-171-6
1970; ©1971 paper  ISBN 0-87183-172-4
1971; ©1972 paper  ISBN 0-87183-173-2
1972; ©1973 paper  ISBN 0-685-41668-2
1973; ©1974 paper  ISBN 0-685-41669-0
1975; ©1976 paper  ISBN 0-87183-177-5
1976; ©1977 paper  ISBN 0-87183-178-3
ANNUAL; BEST BOOKS
```

188. _____. Reading with Your Child Through Age 5. Revised
     edition. Prepared by the Children's Book Committee. New
     York: Child Study Association of America-Wel-Met, Inc.,
     1976. Paper. 40p. First edition, ©1972.
        Includes books on: Children and Families; Animals;
     City Stories; Real Things and Machine; ABC & Counting
     Books; Fantasy, Humor & Folk Tales; Collections of Verse,
     of Songs, and of Mother Goose; Inexpensive Books. Index.
     ISBN 0-685-23774-5 [1972 ISBN 0-87183-211-9].
        PRESCHOOL

189. _____. Sex Education: Recommended Reading. New York:
     Child Study Association of America, 1969. Paper.
        ISBN 0-87183-243-7.
        SEX EDUCATION

190. CHILD STUDY Children's Book Committee. Paperback Books
     for Children: A Selected List Through Age Twelve. New
     York: Bank Street College, 1984. Paper. 49p.
        PAPERBOUND

191. _____. Reading Aloud with Children Through Age 8. New
     York: Bank Street College, 1985. Paper.
        400 titles selected from the best current books and the
     classics.
        BEST BOOKS; READING ALOUD

192. CHILDREN'S BOOK COUNCIL, Inc. CBC FEATURES. New
     York: The Children's Book Council, Inc., quarterly.
        Newsletter, formerly titled "The Calendar." Lists free
     and inexpensive promotional materials available from publish-
     ers; news about Children's Book Week, publishing, authors,
     and CBC activities.
        PUBLISHING; PROMOTIONAL MATERIALS

193. _____. Children's Books: Awards & Prizes. New York:
     The Children's Book Council, Inc., biennial revisions. First
     published 1969 under CBC sponsorship. Editions from 1960
     to 1968 were by the Westchester [NY] Library System.
        Non-evaluative, fairly comprehensive compilation of hon-
     ors awarded in U.S., British Commonwealth, and internation-
     ally, giving description of the award, recipients, brief

history, and address of headquarters. Each successive edition lists discontinued awards and awards not included in that edition. ISBN 0-844-0267-2, 1981; ISSN 0069-3472.
AWARDS

194. _____. The Children's Book Showcase. New York: The Children's Book Council, Inc., annual.
The catalog of books on display at The Bank Street College of Education, 610 West 112th Street in New York City. Selections are made for the best illustrated and/or designed children's books published in the U.S. during the calendar year preceding the Showcase.
BEST BOOKS; EXHIBITION; ANNUAL

195. _____. Choosing a Child's Book. New York: The Children's Book Council, Inc., annual. Paper. 4p.
Suggestions on how to select books for children, from infancy onwards. Lists book selection resources.
SELECTION GUIDES; ANNUAL

196. _____. PRELUDE: Mini-Seminars on Using Books Creatively. New York: The Children's Book Council, Inc.
On cassettes, the presentations, as of 1985, are in seven series, each covering a range of topics that are presented by authorities in the field. Printed supplements with each album.
ACTIVE READERS, DEVELOPING

197. _____. Sports and Books and Books and Sports: An Annotated Bibliography for Grades 4-8. New York: The Children's Book Council, Inc., 1979.
Covers 50 books, in conjunction with Sports Kit.
SPORTS

198. CHILDREN'S BOOKS in the Rare Book Division of the Library of Congress. Totowa, NJ: Rowman and Littlefield, 1975. Vol. I, 900 p.; Vol. II, 493p.
Reproduces cards of the holdings. For Volume I: Author, the cards are reproduced in their entirety. For Volume II: Chronological, the cards are overlapped. ISBN 0-87471-579-2, I; ISBN 0-87471-579-2, II.
RARE BOOKS

CHILDREN'S CATALOG see ISAACSON, Richard H.

CHILDREN'S CHOICES see INTERNATIONAL READING ASSOCIATION/Children's Book Council

199. CHILDREN'S CHOICES of Canadian Books. Compiled by Citizens' Committee on Children; Margaret Caughey, editor. Ottawa: Citizens' Committee on Children, biennial. Paper. Vol. I, 880.; Vol. II, 118p.

Rates books by reader enjoyment.   Covers approximately
200 fiction titles per volume.   ISBN 0-9690205-0-3, I: ISBN
0-9690205-1-1, II.
BEST BOOKS; CANADA

200. CHILDREN'S INDEX.   Edited by Bibliotheca Press Research
Staff.   Fresh Meadows, NY: Biblio Press, 1982.   Paper.
200p.
ISBN 0-939476-44-4.
BIBLIOGRAPHY OF BIBLIOGRAPHIES

201. CHILDREN'S LITERATURE: Annual of the Modern Language
Association and the Children's Literature Association.   New
Haven: Yale University Press, annual.   Paper.
Since 1973, a compilation of articles, reviews, and varia.
No. 11, ©1983, edited by Francelia Butler and Compton Rees,
Jr., 224p.   ISBN 0-300-02991-8; ISBN 0-300-02992-6 paper.
ANNUAL; CHILDREN'S LITERATURE, HISTORY &
CRITICISM

202. CHILDREN'S LITERATURE in Education.   London: Ward Lock
Educational, published three times a year.
CHILDREN'S LITERATURE, STUDY & TEACHING

203. CHILDREN'S LITERATURE Review: Excerpts from Reviews,
Criticism, and Commentary on Books for Children and Young
People.   Ann Block and Carolyn Riley, editors for Volume 1;
Carolyn Riley, editor for Volume 2; Gerard J. Senick, editor
for volumes 3-8.   Detroit: Gale Research Co., 1976-1985 and
ongoing.
Excerpts of recent reviews of fiction and nonfiction ar-
ranged alphabetically by author, with reviews of each of the
author's books following.   Cumulative index to authors,
critics, titles, and nationalities.
Vol. 1, ©1976 ISBN 0-8103-0077-X 201p
Vol. 2, ©1976 ISBN 0-8103-0078-8 239p.
Vol. 3, ©1978 ISBN 0-8103-0079-6 254p.
Vol. 4, ©1982 ISBN 0-8103-0080-X 310p.
Vol. 5, ©1983 ISBN 0-8103-0330-2 298p.
Vol. 6, ©1984 ISBN 0-8103-0331-0 294p.
Vol. 7, ©1984 ISBN 0-8103-0332-9 350p.
Vol. 8, ©1985 ISBN 0-8103-0333-7 277p.
BOOK REVIEWS

204. CHILDREN'S MAGAZINE GUIDE.   Madison, WI: Children's
Magazine Guide, 1985-86:   Volume 38.
Subject Index to 49 magazines for students in elementary
and junior high schools.   Also indexes magazines for media
specialists and teachers.   Published nine times a year with
six-month cumulations.   ISSN 0743-9873.
MAGAZINES

CHILDREN'S MEDIA MARKET PLACE   see   EMMENS, Carol A.

205. CHILDREN'S RIGHTS WORKSHOP. Children's Books in Multi-
      racial Britain. New York: Writers & Readers. Paper. 75p.
      Essays. ISBN 0-904613-39-9.
      BRITAIN

206. _____. Little Miss Muffet Fights Back. New York: Writ-
      ers & Readers, 1974. Paper. 75p. First edition, 1971.
      Nonsexist children's books for all ages. Also includes
      titles from alternative publishers and children's books from
      The People's Republic of China. ISBN 0-904613-38-0.
      NONSEXIST; PEOPLE'S REPUBLIC OF CHINA

207. _____. Racist and Sexist Images in Children's Books.
      New York: Writers & Readers. Paper. 45p.
      Well-known children's books examined for their images
      of Blacks. Sexist attitudes discussed. A look at children's
      books from The People's Republic of China. ISBN 0-904613-
      09-7.
      RACISM; SEXISM; PEOPLE'S REPUBLIC OF CHINA

208. _____. Sexism in Children's Books: Facts, Figures and
      Guidelines: Papers on Children's Literature. New York:
      Writers and Readers, 1981. Illus. 60p.
      Articles analyze sexism in children's books and use the
      McGraw-Hill Guidelines to show how to recognize and overcome
      sexism in literature. ISBN 0-904613-22-4.
      SEXISM

209. CHILDREN'S SCIENCE Book Review Committee. Appraisal:
      Children's Science Books. Book Review Service. triennial.
      First published in 1967.
      50-75 books are analyzed and rated in each issue. Sup-
      ported by the Harvard Graduate School of Education and New
      England Libraries. A subject expert examines each title and a
      librarian verifies how each fits into a collection. ISBN 0003-7052.
      SCIENCE

210. CHILDREN'S THEATRE REVIEW. Washington, D.C.: Chil-
      dren's Theatre Association, quarterly.
      Describes plays that are available and discusses produc-
      tion.
      DRAMATIC LITERATURE

      CIANCIOLO, Patricia [editor]. Adventuring with Books.
      See ROOT, Shelton; WHITE, Mary Lou.

211. _____. Illustrations in Children's Books. Second edition.
      Dubuque, IA: William C. Brown, 1976. Illus. Paper. 210p.
      First edition ©1970.

Discusses style of art, artist's media and techniques and uses of illustrations. Extensive bibliography. Index. ISBN 0-697-06208-2.
ILLUSTRATION IN BOOKS

212. _____. Picture Books for Children. Second Edition, Revised and Enlarged. Edited with The Picture Book Committee of NCTE. Chicago: American Library Association, 1981. Illus. Paper. 237p. First edition ©1973.
Most of the 375 titles in the second edition are new entries. The preschool to teen selections are hardbound editions; however, many are available in paperback. Books chosen are those with illustration and story in concert for aesthetic and educational value. Four categories include: Me and My Family; Other People; The World I Live In; The Imaginative World. Includes a title index. ISBN 0-8389-0315-0; [ISBN 0-8389-0157-3, ©1973].
PICTURE BOOKS

213. CIANI, Alfred J. [editor]. Motivating Reluctant Readers. Newark, DE: International Reading Association, 1981. Paper. 104p.
Articles describing techniques to bring readers and books together. ISBN 0-87207-530-3.
RELUCTANT READERS

214. CLARK, Catherine H., and Florence Widutis [editors]. Books for New Age Children & Youth. College Park, MD: Beautiful Day Books, 1977.
Preschool to grade nine listing. ISBN 0-930296-00-1.
CONTEMPORARY TITLES

215. CLEMENTS, Andrew. "A Note to Grownups: The Picture Book Studio Journal 1" Designed by Michael Neugebauer. Natick, MA: Picture Book Studio USA, 1984. Paper.
First in a projected series, available from Picture Book Studio USA, 60 North Main Street, Natick, MA 01760.
PICTURE BOOKS

216. CLENDENING, Corinne P., and Ruth Ann Davies. Creating Programs for the Gifted: A Guide for Teachers, Librarians and Students. New York: Bowker, 1980. 574p. A volume in Serving Special Populations Series.
Appendix with basic reference titles for gifted students. ISBN 0-8352-1265-3.
GIFTED

217. CLEVELAND PUBLIC LIBRARY. Children's Books for Holiday Giving and Year 'Round Reading. Cleveland, OH: Children's Dept., Cleveland Public Library, annual. Paper. 20p.
Selected list with age levels.
ANNUAL; GIFT BOOKS

218. CLINE, Ruth K. J., and William G. McBride. A Guide to
Literature for Young Adults: Background, Selection and
Use. Glenview, IL: Scott, Foresman and Company, 1983.
Paper. 200p.
        ISBN 0-673-16030-0.
        YOUNG ADULT

COHEN, David see MULTI-ETHNIC MEDIA

219. COHEN, Monroe D. Excellent Paperbacks for Children.
Washington, DC: Association for Childhood Education, 1979.
        ISBN 0-87173-001-4.
        PAPERBOUND

220. COLWELL, Eileen. Storytelling. Topsfield, MA: Bodley
Head, distributed by Merrimack Publishing Circle, 1983.
Paper. 96p.
        Commentary on storytelling in England. ISBN 0-370-
30228-1.
        STORYTELLING; BRITAIN

221. COMMIRE, Anne [editor]. Something About the Author:
Facts and Pictures About Authors and Illustrators of Books
for Young People. Detroit: Gale Research Company, ongoing
series. Volume 1, ©1971; volume 39, ©1985. Illus. Approx.
300p.
        According to the description, "many of the biographical
sketches in this [series] have appeared in Contemporary Authors. There are new listings and updates of previous listings in succeeding volumes." Obituaries begin with volume 20.
        AUTHORS; ILLUSTRATORS

222. _____ . Yesterday's Authors of Books for Children: Facts
and Pictures About Authors and Illustrators of Books for
Young People. 2 vols. Detroit: Gale Research Company.
Vol. 1, ©1977, 275p.; Vol. 2, ©1978, 335p. Illus., Photos.
Part of series.
        Provides extensive biobibliographical information on chil-
dren's authors and illustrators who died before 1961. ISBN
0-8103-0073-3.
        AUTHORS; ILLUSTRATORS

223. A COMMUNITY OF PEOPLE: A Multi-ethnic Bibliography for
Grades K-8. Portland, OR: Portland Public Schools, 1983.
Paper. 139p.
        Indexes by geocultural groups, and by curriculum sub-
ject headings, for print and nonprint materials.
        MULTIETHNIC

224. CONTEMPORARY LITERARY CRITICISM; Volume 12: Young
Adult Literature. Edited by Sharon R. Gunton. Detroit:

Gale Research Company, 1979. 737p. Part of the Contempo-
rary Literary Criticism series.
  ISBN 0-8103-0122-9.
  YOUNG ADULT

225. CONWELL, Mary K., and Pura Belpre. Libros en Español:
An Annotated List of Children's Books in Spanish. Sponsored
by the South Bronx Project. New York: The New York Public Library, 1971. Paper. 52p.
       Comprehensive listing in nine categories: picture books,
young readers, books for the middle age, books for older boys
and girls, folklore, myths, & legends, songs & games, bilingual
books, books for learning Spanish, anthologies. Includes a
list of sources and an author/title index.
       SPANISH LANGUAGE BOOKS

226. COOK, Elizabeth. The Ordinary and the Fabulous: An Introduction to Myths, Legends and Fairy Tales. Second edition. New York: Cambridge University Press, 1978. 204p.
First published in 1962 and reprinted with an addendum in
1978.
       Source also for "modern hybrids" and lists titles from
the Third World and Eastern Europe. Includes professional
literature (up to 1977) on myths, legends, and tales. ISBN
0-521-09961-7 paper; ISBN 0-521-20825-4 cloth.
       MYTHS; LEGENDS; FAIRY TALES

227. CORRIGAN, John T., CFY [editor]. What Today's Youth Is
Reading and Why. Haverford, PA: Catholic Library Associa
tion, 1981. Paper. 32p.
       Three papers focusing on selection of materials for chil-
dren, elementary to high school, in light of the "role of the
librarian in promoting traditional Catholic values through media selection." ISBN 0-87507-022-1.
       CATHOLIC

228. COTT, Jonathan [editor]. Beyond the Looking Glass; Extra-
ordinary Works of Fairy Tales and Fantasy. Introductions by
Jonathan Cott and Leslie Fiedler. New York: R. R. Bowker,
1974. Illus. 519p.
       ISBN 0-8352-0794-3.
       FAIRY TALES; FANTASY

229. _____. Masterworks of Children's Literature, Fifteen Fifty
to Nineteen Hundred. 8 vols. New York: Chelsea House,
1985. Illus. Vols. 1 and 2: The Early Years, 1550-1739,
ed. Francella Butler, 1983, ISBN 0-87754-375-5; ISBN 0-
87754-376-3; Vols. 3 and 4: The Middle Period, 1740-1836,
ed. Robert Bator, 1984, ISBN 0-87754-377-1; ISBN 0-87754-
378-X; Vol. 5: The Victorian Age, 1837-1900, ed. Robert L.
Wolff, 1984, ISBN 0-87754-379-8, Part 1; ISBN 0-87754-380-1,

Part 2; Vol. 6: The Victorian Era, 1837-1900, ed. Robert L.
Wolff, 1984, ISBN 0-87754-449-2; Vol. 7: Victorian Color
Picture Books, ed. Jonathan Cott, 1984, ISBN 0-87754-381-X;
Vol. 8: Supplemental Volume, 1900-Present, 1985, ISBN 0-
317-04769-8; 8-vol. set: ISBN 0-87754-089-6.
CHILDREN'S LITERATURE, HISTORY & CRITICISM

230.   . Pipers at the Gates of Dawn: The Wisdom of Chil-
dren's Literature. New York: Random House, 1983. Illus.
327p. New York: McGraw-Hill, 1985. Illus. Paper. 327p.
        Critical and informative essays on writers, including
Dr. Seuss, Maurice Sendak, William Steig, Astrid Lindgren,
Chinua Achebe, P. L. Travers, and Iona and Peter Opie.
ISBN 0-394-50464-X [Random House]; ISBN 0-07-013220-8
[McGraw-Hill].
AUTHORS

231. COUGHLAN, Margaret N. [compiler]. Books for Children.
Washington, DC: Library of Congress, 1985. Paper.
        New format succeeds Children's Books, which was pub-
lished from 1964 to 1984. Old lists still available. New list
is a selection of 100 titles published January-November 1984,
arranged by age group (preschool to junior high) and cate-
gory (picture books, fiction, nonfiction).
BEST BOOKS

232.   . Creating Independence, 1763-1789; Background
Reading for Young People; A Selected Annotated Bibliography.
Washington, DC: Library of Congress, 1972. Illus. 62p.
        ISBN 0-8444-0029-7.
AMERICAN HISTORY

233.   . Folklore from Africa to the United States: An
Annotated Bibliography. Washington, DC: Library of Congress, 1976. Illus. 161p.
        Selective bibliography of 190 items available in the col-
lections of the Library of Congress, with single-tale picture
books excluded. Descriptions include story contents, information about the story's derivation, an analysis of the reteller's
methods and data on related stories. ISBN 0-8444-0175-7.
BLACKS; FOLKLORE

234. COUNCIL ON INTERRACIAL BOOKS for Children. Guidelines
for Selecting Bias Free Textbooks and Story Books. New
York: Council on Interracial Books for Children, Inc. N.d.
Paper. 104p.
        Terminology and definitions, survey and analysis of bias
in children's storybooks, textbooks, U.S. history textbooks,
with criteria and checklists to analyze for racism, sexism, and
bias against disabled people and older people. Lists of

materials available from CIBC and other resources. ISBN 0-
930040-33-3.
     BIAS-FREE

235. _____. Human and Anti-human Values in Children's Books:
A Content Rating Instrument for Educators and Concerned
Parents; Guidelines for the Future. Compiled by the Racism
and Sexism Resources Center for Educators. New York:
Council on Interracial Books for Children, 1976. 280p.
     BIAS-FREE; HUMAN VALUES

236. CRAGO, Maureen, and Hugh Crago. Prelude to Literacy: A
Preschool Child's Encounter with Picture and Story. Carbondale, IL: Southern Illinois University Press, 1983. 320p.
     ISBN 0-8093-1077-5.
     PRESCHOOL

237. CRIDLAND, Nancy C. Books in American History: A Book
List for High Schools and Junior Colleges. Second edition.
Bloomington, IN: Indiana University Press, 1981. First edition, ©1964, by John E. Wiltz.
     Arranged chronologically, colonial period to recent times,
in four segments, and including biography, historical fiction,
and fiction for each. ISBN 0-253-15255-0; ISBN 0-253-20266-3
[paper].
     AMERICAN HISTORY

238. CRISCUOLO, Nicholas. You Can Use Television to Stimulate
Your Child's Reading Habits. Newark, DE: International
Reading Association, 1980. Paper.
     TELEVISION AND BOOKS

239. CROUCH, Marcus. The Nesbit Tradition: Children's Novels
1945-1970. Totowa, NJ: Rowman and Littlefield, 1972. 239p.
     ISBN 0-87471-146-0.
     FICTION

240. _____, and Alec Ellis [editors]. Chosen for Children.
Third edition. Phoenix: Oryx Press, 1977. Illus. 180p.
First edition ©1957. All editions published by the Library
Association, London.
     Reviews Carnegie Medal winners, 1936-1975. ISBN 0-
85365-349-6.
     AWARDS; BRITAIN

241. CULLINAN, Bernice E., and M. Jerry Weiss [editors]. Books
I Read When I Was Young: The Favorite Books of Famous
People. New York: Avon Books, 1980. Paper. Illus. 192p.
     "A project of the Commission on Literature of the Na-
tional Council of Teachers of English." In a national poll,
students were invited to name their "heroes" from among living

personalities. Those individuals most often named were in
turn invited to describe three books or three authors who had
influenced her or his life. ISBN 0-380-76638-8.
    FAVORITE BOOKS

242. CULLINAN, Bernice E., and Carolyn W. Carmichael [editors].
      Literature and Young Children. Champaign, IL: National
      Council of Teachers of English, 1977. Paper. 180p.
          100 best books and authors for young children. In-
      dexes. ISBN 0-8141-2972-2.
          BEST BOOKS

243. CULLINAN, Bernice E., et al. Literature and the Child.
      New York: Harcourt Brace Jovanovich, 1981. 594p. ISBN
      0-15-551110-6.
          CHILDREN'S LITERATURE, TEXTBOOKS ON

244. CUTT, Margaret Nancy. Ministering Angels: A Study of
      Nineteenth-Century Evangelical Writing for Children. Brox-
      bourne, Herts, England: Five Owls Press Ltd., 1979. 226p.
          Discussion of the tract tales published by Christian So-
      cieties, for the Dominions, that provided the bulk of reading
      materials directed to the theologically illiterate population, in-
      cluding children and newly literate adults. ISBN 0-903838-
      01X.
          RELIGION; CANADA

245. CUYAHOGA COUNTY (OH) Public Library. Computer Books
      for Children: A Basic List. Cleveland, OH: Children's
      Services Dept., Cuyahoga County Public Library, 1985.
          50 basic computer books, by grade levels, with full
      annotations.
          COMPUTERS

246. DALE, Doris Cruger. Bilingual Books in Spanish and English
      for Children. Littleton, CO: Libraries Unlimited, 1985.
      163p.
          Critical analysis of 254 bilingual books for preschool to
      elementary age children. ISBN 0-87287-477-X.
          SPANISH, BOOKS IN; BILINGUAL

247. DALPHIN, Marcia. Light the Candles! A List for Christmas
      Reading. Boston: The Horn Book, Inc., 1953. Paper. 24p.
      First published 1944.
          Sections include: Stories and poems to set the mood for
      the season; Legends of Christmas; Christmas carols; Animals
      at Christmas; Stories to tell; Christmas in the family in the
      United States and world wide; Christmas parties and games;
      Christmas handicrafts.
          CHRISTMAS

248. DANIEL, Elouise [compiler]. A Treasury of Books for Family
     Enjoyment: Books for Children from Infancy to Grade 2.
     Pontiac, MI: Blue Engine Express, 1983. Illus. 122p.
         ISBN 0-9611370-0-2.
         PRESCHOOL; PRIMARY

249. DARLING, Richard L. The Rise of Children's Book Reviewing
     in America, 1865-1881. New York: R. R. Bowker, 1968.
     Illus. 452p.
         Includes bibliographies.
         BOOK REVIEWING

250. DARRELL, Margery [editor]. Once Upon a Time: The Fairy
     Tale World of Arthur Rackham. New York: [A Studio Book]
     The Viking Press, 1972. Illus. 296p.
         A compendium of illustrations, including those for Rip
     Van Winkle, seven of the Grimms' tales, Alice's Adventures
     in Wonderland, three tales from Shakespeare (by Charles and
     Mary Lamb); A Christmas Carol; Aesop fables; and Peter Pan
     in Kensington Gardens. ISBN 0-670-52574-X.
         ILLUSTRATORS

251. DARTON, F. J. Harvey. Children's Books in England: Five
     Centuries of Social Life. Third edition. Revised by Brian
     Alderson. Cambridge: Cambridge University Press, 1982.
     Illus. 398p. First edition ©1932; second edition ©1958, re-
     vised by Kathleen Lines, with a reprint ©1960.
         Contains general booklists. It remains a standard in
     the treatment of publishing decisions. As a book about chil-
     dren's books it is considered a benchmark contribution. Each
     chapter ends with a brief booklist. ISBN 0-521-24020-4.
         BRITAIN; CHILDREN'S LITERATURE, HISTORY &
         CRITICISM

252. DAVIS, Enid. A Comprehensive Guide to Children's Literature
     with a Jewish Theme. New York: Schocken Books, 1981.
     190p.
         ISBN 0-8052-3760-7.
         JEWISH THEME, BOOKS ON

253. _____. The Liberty Cap; A Catalogue of Non-Sexist Mate-
     rials for Children. Chicago: Academy Press, 1978. Paper.
     236p.
         ISBN 0-915864-15-0.
         NONSEXIST

254. DAVIS, Lenwood G., and Belinda S. Daniels. Black Athletes
     in the United States: A Bibliography of Books, Articles,
     Autobiographies, and Biographies on Black Professional Ath-
     letes in the United States, 1800-1981. Westport, CN: Green-
     wood Press, 1981. 265p.
         Of special interest to junior and senior high school

readers are part 5 (Books by Black Athletes) and part 6
(Books about Black Athletes). ISBN 0-313-22976-7.
BLACKS; ATHLETES

255. DEASON, Hilary J. [compiler]. AAAS Science Books List for
      Children. Third edition. Washington, DC: American Asso-
      ciation for the Advancement of Science Publications, 1972.
      268p.
           Comes from critical reviews originally published in Sci-
      ence Books and Films, an AAAS journal. ISBN 0-87168-202-8.
      SCIENCE

256. DELAMAR, Gloria T. Children's Counting-Out Rhymes, Fin-
      gerplays, Jump-Rope and Bounce-Ball Chants and Other
      Rhymes. Jefferson, NC: McFarland, 1983. 224p.
           Broad in scope and inclusive in content. Indexes of
      Author, Subject, Title, and First Line. ISBN 0-89950-064-1.
      RHYMES

257. DEMERS, Patricia, and Gordon Moyles [editors]. From In-
      struction to Delight: An Anthology of Children's Literature
      to 1850. Toronto: Oxford University Press, 1982. Illus.
      Paper. 310p.
           Historical materials in eight sections: Books of Courtesy
      and Early Lessons; "Hell Fire" Tales of the Puritans; The Ly-
      rical Instruction of Isaac Watts; Chapbooks and Penny His-
      tories; John Newbery, "Instruction with Delight"; Rational
      Moralists; Sunday School Moralists; Harbingers of the Golden
      Age. Extensive bibliography; index. ISBN 0-19-540384-3.
      CHILDREN'S LITERATURE, HISTORY & CRITICISM

258. DeMONTREVILLE, Doris, and Elizabeth D. Crawford [editors].
      Fourth Book of Junior Authors and Illustrators. New York:
      H. W. Wilson, 1978. 370p. Part of the Junior Authors and
      Illustrators series.
           242 autobiographical or biographical sketches of authors
      and illustrators who have come to prominence since the third
      book, with some older authors of continuing or renewed popu-
      larity. Entries in alphabetical order by name appearing most
      frequently on the title page; cross-referenced with pseudonym.
      Index includes all authors and illustrators in the series. ISBN
      0-8242-0568-5. [See also HOLTZE, Sally Holmes; Fifth Book
      of Junior Authors and Illustrators.]
      AUTHORS; ILLUSTRATORS

259. DeMONTREVILLE, Doris, and Donna Hill [editors]. Third
      Book of Junior Authors. New York: H. W. Wilson Co.,
      1972. 370p.
           Continues work of The Junior Book of Authors and
      More Junior authors. 255 sketches of authors and illustrators
      who came to prominence since 1963 or who are older but were
      not in volumes one or two in the series. Indexes.

ISBN 0-8242-0408-5.
AUTHORS; ILLUSTRATORS

260. DEQUIN, Henry C. Librarians Serving Disabled Children and
      Young People. Littleton, CO: Libraries Unlimited, 1983.
      306p.
          Comprehensive overview on serving the disabled, with
      guidelines for locating, evaluating, selecting materials and
      equipment. Selective listing of sources of information. ISBN
      0-87287-364-1.
      DISABILITIES

261. deWIT, Dorothy. Children's Faces Looking Up: Program
      Building for the Storyteller. Chicago: American Library As-
      sociation, 1979. 156p.
          Bibliography of folklore and fairy tale anthologies; ba-
      sic sources; and professional sources. Index. ISBN 0-8389-
      0272-3.
      STORYTELLING

262. DIRECTORY of Specialized American Bookdealers. Prepared
      by the staff of American Book Collector. New York: The
      Moretus Press, Inc., 1984. Annual.
          Dealers of children's books are listed along with dealers
      of other books. ISBN 0-89679-012-6.
      BOOK DEALERS

263. DIXON, Bob. Catching Them Young: Sex, Race and Class
      in Children's Fiction. Vol. 1. New York: Pluto Press,
      1980. 160p.
          ISBN 0-904383-51-2; ISBN 0-904383-50-4 paper.
      FICTION; SEXISM; CONTEMPORARY ISSUES

264. _____. Catching Them Young: Political Ideas in Children's
      Fiction. Vol. 2. New York: Pluto Press, 1980. 192p.
          ISBN 0-904383-59-8; ISBN 0-904383-58-X paper.
      FICTION; POLITICAL IDEAS

265. DIZER, John T., Jr. Tom Swift & Company: "Boys' Books"
      by Stratemeyer and Others. Jefferson, NC: McFarland and
      Co., 1982. Illus. 192p.
          Comprehensive look at the publishing history of pulps
      and a bibliography of Tom Swift and other series books. In-
      dex. ISBN 0-89950-024-2.
      BOYS' BOOKS IN SERIES; PULPS; SERIES, BOOKS IN

266. DOBLER, Lavinia, and Muriel Fuller [compilers and editors].
      Dobler World Directory of Youth Periodicals. Third enlarged
      edition. New York: Citation Press, 1970. Paper. 108p.
          Periodicals published in the United States and outside
      the U.S., in English and non-English languages. Subject

listing and title index.   LC 75-125919.
                    PERIODICALS

267.   DODDS, Barbara.   Negro Literature for High School Students.
       Champaign, IL: National Council of Teachers of English, 1968.
       157p.
            Discussion of contents, quality of writing and reading
       level for books in four categories: Historical Survey of Negro
       Writers; Words about Negroes; The Junior Novel; and Biogra-
       phy.   Index.
                    BLACKS

       DONELSON, Kenneth.   Books for You: A Booklist for Senior
       High School.   See NATIONAL COUNCIL of Teachers of Eng-
       lish, 1976.

268.   _____, and Alleen Pace Nilsen.   Literature for Today's
       Young Adults.   Glenview, IL: Scott Foresman, 1980.   484p.
       [See NILSEN for second edition.]
            Covers realistic problem novels, romances, excitement
       and suspense stories, science fiction, fantasy, informational
       books and biographies.   ISBN 0-673-15165-4.
                    YOUNG ADULT

269.   DOOLEY, Patricia [compiler and editor].   The First Steps:
       Articles and Columns from the ChLA Newsletter/Quarterly,
       Volume I-VI.   West Lafayette, IN: ChLA Publications, 1984.
       148p.
            Articles cover range of subjects, including award books.
       ISBN 0-318-17736-6.
                    CHILDREN'S LITERATURE, HISTORY AND CRITICISM

270.   DORSETT, Cora Matheny.   Reading for Young People: The
       Mississippi Delta.   Chicago: American Library Association,
       1984.   157p.   Part of the series.
            Listing of books on the Mississippi Delta.   ISBN 0-
       8389-0395-9.
                    UNITED STATES, REGIONAL LITERATURE

271.   DOYLE, Brian [editor].   The Who's Who of Children's Litera-
       ture.   New York: Schocken, 1971.   Illus.   380p.   First
       published 1968.
            Biographies, bibliographies and discussion of over 400
       major authors and illustrators of children's titles from 1800 to
       1970s.   Principal annual awards in Britain and the U.S. for
       children's books.   ISBN 0-8052-3290-7; ISBN 0-8052-0307-9
       paper.
                    AUTHORS; ILLUSTRATORS

272.   THE DRAMATIC PUBLISHING COMPANY.   Centennial Catalog
       of Plays and Musicals.   Chicago, IL: The Dramatic Publishing
       Co., 1985.   Illus.   Paper.

Includes extensive listing of plays for children and young adults. Author index, classified index.
DRAMATIC LITERATURE/PLAYS

273. DREYER, Sharon Spredemann. The Bookfinder: A Guide to Children's Literature About the Needs and Problems of Youth Aged 2-15. Circle Pines, MN: American Guidance Service, Vol. 1 [1977, 1031p]; Vol. 2 [1981, 520p]; Vol. 3 [1985, 522p].
Each discusses books on behavioral, developmental, and psychological themes on problems children and young adults face in their daily lives. ISBN 0-913476-48-X; ISBN 0-913476-49-8 [paper], Vol. 3; ISBN 0-913476-44-7, Vol. 2; ISBN 0-913476-45-5, Vol. 1.
BIBLIOTHERAPY

274. DUFF, Annis. "Bequest of Wings": A Family's Pleasures with Books. New York: Viking Press, 1944. 207p.
Remains a warm and charming sharing for all new parents.
FAMILY

275. _____. "Longer Flight": A Family Grows Up with Books. New York: Viking Press, 1955. 269p.
Sequel to "Bequest of Wings...."
FAMILY

276. DUKE, Judith S. Children's Books and Magazines: A Market Study. White Plains, NY: Knowledge Industry Publications, 1979. 236p. Part of Communications Library.
Includes a study of trade and mass-market juvenile books, children's book clubs, magazines, and audiovisual products that are based on juvenile books. Textbooks are excluded. Features profiles of leading juvenile publishers. Selected bibliography on juvenile publishing and marketing. ISBN 0-914236-17-2.
PUBLISHING

277. DUNDES, Alan. Cinderella: A Casebook. New York: Garland Publishing, 1982. 350p.
Diverse essays on the folktale, with a selected bibliography of scholarship. ISBN 0-8240-9295.
FOLKTALES

278. DUNNING, Stephen, and Alan B. Howes. Literature for Adolescents. Glenview, IL: Scott Foresman, 1975. 491p.
Also, in the series, Teaching Literature to Adolescents: Poetry and Short Stories. ISBN 0-673-05841-7.
YOUNG ADULTS

279. DURAN, Daniel Flores. Latino Materials: A Multimedia Guide

for Children and Young Adults. New York: Neal Schuman,
1979. 249p. Part of Selection Guide Series.
Comprehensive coverage of resources and titles. Subject index and author/title index. ISBN 0-87436-262-8.
LATINO

280. EAGLEN, Audrey [editor]. Reflections on Fantasy and Science Fiction. Chicago: American Library Association, 1982.
Paper. 60p. Reprint from Top of the News, Fall 1982 issue.
Overview and analysis, with an emphasis on women authors and women characters in science fiction. Bibliography
includes periodicals and nonfiction books as well as fiction.
FANTASY, SCIENCE FICTION

281. EAKIN, Mary K. [compiler]. Good Books for Children: A
Selection of Outstanding Children's Books Published 1950-65.
Third edition. Chicago: University of Chicago Press, 1966.
407p.
Revised and enlarged edition of outstanding children's
books published between 1948 and 1961. [Chicago: University of Chicago Press, 1962, 362p.] The 1,391 titles recommended in the third edition encompass data from previous
editions. ISBN 0-226-17916-8. [See also SUTHERLAND,
Zena, The Best in Children's Books.]
BEST BOOKS

282. _____. Subject Index to Books for Intermediate Grades.
Third edition. Chicago: American Library Association, 1963.
308p. First edition ©1940; second edition ©1950; compiled by
Eloise Rue.
1,800 trade books listed by author, with full citation
and no content description. Subject index with cross-
references. LC 63-12951.
INTERMEDIATE GRADES

283. _____. Subject Index to Books for Primary Grades. Third
edition. Chicago: American Library Association, 1967. 113p.
First edition ©1943 compiled by Eloise Rue as a revision and
expansion of Subject Index to Readers; Second edition ©1961,
compiled by Mary Eakin and Eleanor Merritt.
Covers approximately 1,000 trade and text books published between 1903 and 1965 but with an emphasis on 1950-
1965 publications. List by author with a subject index cross-
reference. Full citation, no content description. LC 66-30062.
PRIMARY GRADES

284. EASTMAN, Mary Huse. Index to Fairy Tales, Myths and
Legends. Boston: The F. W. Faxon Co., second edition,
1926, 610p.; supplement, 1937, 566p.; second supplement,
1952, 370p. Part of index series.

Main list by title, cross-reference by variant titles and under subject with author and title of book in which tale, myth or legend is to be found. Includes geographical and racial list and country and continent list. ISBN 0-87305-061-4 [1937 Supplement]. [See also IRELAND, Norma Olin.]
FAIRY TALES; MYTHS; LEGENDS

285. EBSCO SUBSCRIPTION SERVICE. Periodicals for Elementary and Secondary School Libraries. Birmingham, AL: Ebsco Subscription Service, annual. Paper.
Promotional, comprehensive listing of available periodicals.
PERIODICALS

286. ECKENSTEIN, Lina. Comparative Studies in Nursery Rhymes. Detroit: Singing Tree Press, 1968. 231p. First published London: Duckworth & Co., 1906.
Covers all types of rhymes. Alphabetical index of first lines. List of foreign collections of rhymes. LC 68 23469.
RHYMES

287. EGOFF, Shiela A. [editor]. Children's Periodicals of the Nineteenth Century: A Survey and Bibliography. London: Library Association, 1951. 55p. Library Association Pamphlet No. 8.
PERIODICALS

288. _____. One Ocean Touching: Papers from the First Pacific Rim Conference on Children's Literature. Metuchen, NJ: Scarecrow Press, 1979. 260p.
Papers by "writers, illustrators, retellers of folklore, educators, librarians, publishers, editors [which show] children's books ... as important in themselves and not merely as tools for social training or adjuncts to formal education."
ISBN 0-8108-1199-5.
CHILDREN'S LITERATURE, HISTORY & CRITICISM

289. _____. The Republic of Childhood; A Critical Guide to Canadian Children's Literature in English. Second edition. Toronto: Oxford University Press, 1975. Paper. 335p. First published 1967.
Important books published to 1974, in all genres.
ISBN 0-19-540231-6; ISBN 0-19-540232-2.
CANADA; CHILDREN'S LITERATURE, TEXTBOOKS ON

290. _____. Thursday's Child: Trends and Patterns in Contemporary Children's Literature. Chicago: American Library Association, 1981. 340p.
Discusses children's literature since 1957, with an overview for a variety of genres, including realistic fiction, the problem novel, new fantasy, science fiction, historical fiction,

folklore, myth and legend, poetry, picture books, and the
European novel in translation. ISBN 0-8389-0327-4.
CONTEMPORARY LITERATURE

291. _____ ; G. T. Stubbs; and L. F. Ashley [editors]. Only
Connect; Readings on Children's Literature. Second edition.
New York: Oxford University Press, 1980. Illus. Paper.
457p. First published 1969.
38 essays, most published originally in periodicals in
the 1960s to 1970s. ISBN 0-19-540309-6.
CHILDREN'S LITERATURE, HISTORY & CRITICISM

292. THE ELEMENTARY SCHOOL Library Collection: A Guide to
Books and Other Media, Phases 1-2-3. Fourteenth edition.
Newark, NJ: The Bro-Dart Foundation, 1984. 1070p. First
published 1965.
Classified catalog divided into reference, nonfiction,
fiction, easy, periodicals, and professional collection. Author,
title, subject indexes. Appendices include media for preschool children, books for independent reading, and directory
of publishers and producers. Recommends materials of high
quality. ISBN 0-87272-090-X.
SELECTION AIDS/GUIDES; ELEMENTARY SCHOOL

293. ELLEMAN, Barbara [editor]. Popular Reading for Children:
A Collection of Booklist Columns. Chicago: American Library
Association, 1981. 60p.
Compilation of ten retrospective lists of books in high
demand by readers in grades 2 to 9. Published in Booklist
since 1976. ISBN 0-8389-0322-3.
BEST BOOKS

_____ . See also AMERICAN LIBRARY ASSOCIATION, Children's Books of International Interest

294. _____ , and Betsy Hearne [compilers]. Books for Every-
child: Contemporary Titles That Families Should Know. New
York: Children's Book Council, 1983. Paper.
Introduced at "Everychild; The American Conference,"
August 29-September 1, 1983.
CONTEMPORARY

295. ELLIS, Alec. A History of Children's Reading and Literature.
Elmsford, NY: Pergamon Press, 1968.
ISBN 0-08-01258-7.
CHILDREN'S LITERATURE, TEXTBOOKS ON

296. _____ . How to Find Out About Children's Literature.
Third edition. Elmsford, NY: Pergamon Press, 1973.
ISBN 0-08-016970-8; ISBN 0-08-018230-5 paper.
CHILDREN'S LITERATURE, TEXTBOOKS ON

297. ELLIS, Anne W. The Family Story in the 1960's. Hamden,
      CT: Archon Books, 1970. 105p.
      ISBN 0-208-00881-0.
      FAMILY; FICTION

298. ELLIS, John M. One Fairy Story Too Many: The Brothers
      Grimm and Their Tales. Chicago: University of Chicago
      Press, 1985. 219p.
      ISBN 0-226-20546-0.
      FAIRY TALES; CHILDREN'S LITERATURE, HISTORY &
      CRITICISM

299. EMMENS, Carol A. [editor]. Children's Media Market Place.
      Second edition. New York: Neal-Schuman Publishers, 1982.
      Paper. 353p.
          Comprehensive guide to sources for print and nonprint
      materials for children, parents, and teachers. ISBN 0-918212-
      33-2.
          SELECTION GUIDE; PERIODICALS; PICTURE BOOKS;
          AWARDS; GRANTS; PUBLISHERS

300. EMPORIA STATE UNIVERSITY. The May Massee Collection:
      Creative Publishing for Children, 1923-1963, A Checklist.
      Edited by George V. Hodowancec. Annotations by Jeanne
      Frederickson. Emporia, KS: Emporia State University, 1979.
      Illus. 316p.
          Catalogs material on May Massee as editor of children's
      books and includes books edited, correspondence with authors,
      articles, and other materials. ISBN 0-934068-00-3.
          PUBLISHING

301. ENGLE, Rosalind; Ruth Jones; and Dorothy Pinsky. Books
      for Young Children: How to Choose. Ames, IA: Cooperative
      Extension Service at Iowa State University, 1978. Paper.
          SELECTION GUIDE

302. ESTES, Glenn E. [editor]. American Writers for Children
      Before 1900. Detroit, MI: Gale Research, 1985. 350p.
      Dictionary of Literary Biography, v. 42.
      ISBN 0-8103-1720-6
      AUTHORS

303. ETTLINGER, John R. T.; and Diana Spirt. Choosing Books
      for Young People: A Guide to Criticism and Bibliography,
      1945-1975. Chicago: American Library Association, 1982.
      220p.
          A key to the comment and criticism published since
      World War II. Arrangement by author or main entry. Sub-
      ject Index. ISBN 0-8389-0366-5.
          CHILDREN'S LITERATURE, HISTORY & CRITICISM

304. EYRE, Frank. British Children's Books in the Twentieth
      Century. Revised and enlarged edition. New York: E. P.
      Dutton, 1973. 208p. Originally published as 20th Century
      Children's Books; London: for the British Council by Long-
      mans, Green and Co., 1952.
            Discusses publishing developments in fiction for chil-
      dren. Appendices cover Regional Writing, Award Winners,
      and a select bibliography of books about children's books.
      Index. ISBN 0-525-27230-5.
            BRITISH; CHILDREN'S LITERATURE, HISTORY &
      CRITICISM

305. FADER, Daniel. The New Hooked on Books. Revised edition.
      New York: Berkley, 1977. First published 1966.
            Reading list of approximately 1,000 authors arranged
      topically for readers up to twelfth grade. ISBN 0-399-
      11954-X; ISBN 0-425-03426-7 paper (Berkley Medalion Books,
      10th edition).
            TEENAGE

306. FASSLER, Joan. Helping Children Cope. Illus. by William B.
      Hogan. New York: The Free Press, 1978. 162p.
            Especially for children four to eight years old, books
      that deal with stress areas including death, separation, hos-
      pitalization and illness, lifestyle changes, family changes,
      emergency situations, financial changes, moving, adoption,
      and poverty. ISBN 0-02693500-7.
            BIBLIOTHERAPY

307. FAVAT, F. Andre. Child and Tale: The Origins of Interest.
      Urbana, IL: National Council of Teachers of English, 1977.
      102p. Research Report No. 19 of NCTE.
            CHILDREN'S LITERATURE, HISTORY & CRITICISM;
      ACTIVE READERS, DEVELOPING

308. FEAVER, William. When We Were Young: Two Centuries of
      Children's Book Illustration. New York: Holt, Rinehart and
      Winston, 1977. Illus. 96p.
            Overview of popular styles of art and techniques with
      123 illustrations in black and white and 44 in full color. ISBN
      0-03-020306-6; ISBN 0-03-020301-1 [paper].
            ILLUSTRATION

      FIDELL, Estelle A. see PLAY INDEX.

309. FIELD, Carolyn W. [editor]. With consultants Margaret N.
      Coughlan and Sharyl G. Smith for the National Planning for
      Special Collections Committee, Association for Library Service
      to Children, American Library Association. Special Collections

in Children's Literature. Chicago: American Library Association, 1982. Illus. 257p.
Includes collections in Canada and the United States. Index. ISBN 0-8389-0345-2.
SPECIAL COLLECTIONS

310. _____. With Consultants Virginia Haviland and Elizabeth Nesbitt for the National Planning for Special Collections Committee, Association for Library Service to Children, American Library Association. Subject Collections in Children's Literature. New York: R. R. Bowker, 1969. Illus. 142p.
SUBJECT COLLECTIONS

311. FIELD, Elinor Whitney [editor]. Horn Book Reflections: On Children's Books and Reading: Selected from Eighteen Years of the Horn Book Magazine, 1949-1966. Boston: The Horn Book, 1969. 367p.
Articles within seven broad categories: Inspiration--How it Comes; Goals and Guidelines for Writers and Illustrators; Recreating Other Times; The Matter of Poetry; Fantasy, Yesterday and Today; People and Places; Family Reading and Storytelling. ISBN 0-87675-033-1.
CHILDREN'S LITERATURE, HISTORY & CRITICISM

312. FIELD, Louise Frances Story. The Child and His Book. Second edition. Detroit: Singing Tree Press, 1968. Originally published London: Gardner & Darton, 1892.
Reproduction of the history and progress of children's literature in England up to 1890. ISBN 0-8103-3480-1.
BRITAIN; CHILDREN'S LITERATURE, HISTORY & CRITICISM

313. FINNEY, James E. The Long Road to Now: A Bibliography of Material Relating to the American Black Man. Farmingdale, NY: Charles W. Clark Co., Inc., 1969. Illus. Paper. 54p.
Selective listing of titles "that reflect the Negro ... in the context of American history." Covers materials in history, reference, fiction, music, biography. LC 75-84466.
BLACKS

314. FISHER, Margery Turner. Intent Upon Reading: A Critical Appraisal of Modern Fiction for Children. Second edition, revised and enlarged. New York: Franklin Watts, Inc., 1965. First published Leicester, England: Brockhampton Press Ltd., 1961; second edition, 1964; Franklin Watts, 1962.
Discusses fiction 1930 to 1960. LC 62-10374.
FICTION

315. _____. Matters of Fact: Aspects of Non-Fiction for Children. New York: Thomas Y. Crowell, 1972. 488p.

Covers single subject and multiple subject titles.
ISBN 0-690-52537-0.
NONFICTION

316. _____. Who's Who in Children's Books: A Treasury of the
Familiar Characters of Childhood. London: Weidenfeld and
Nicolson, 1975. New York: Holt, Rinehart & Winston, 1975.
Illus. 399p.
Alphabetical listing of characters central to fiction titles.
Gives description of the character and full bibliographic data
on the book. Index of authors and of titles. ISBN 0-297-
77037-3.
FICTION

317. FITZGERALD, Bonnie. Bibliography of Literature and Cross-
culture Values. Urbana, IL: National Council of Teachers of
English, 1973? Paper. 16p.
Description of each title, with reading levels. Includes
Black fiction, biography, poetry and informational titles;
American folktales; American Indian fiction, poetry, legends
and informational titles; Chinese folktales; Oriental poetry and
fiction; Spanish folktales; Chicano music, fiction and informa-
tional titles.
MULTICULTURAL

318. FITZGERALD, Randall. The Complete Book of Extraterrestrial
Encounters. New York: Collier, 1979. Paper. 200p.
Approximately 100 detailed summaries of popular works
dealing with UFOs. Most are adult books suitable for young
adults. ISBN 0-02-095500-6.
EXTRATERRESTRIAL

319. FLEMING, Margaret, and Jo McGinnis [editors]. Portraits:
Biography and Autobiography in the Secondary School. Ur-
bana, IL: National Council of Teachers of English, 1985.
Paper. 104p.
ISBN 0-8141-3648-6.
BIOGRAPHY; AUTOBIOGRAPHY; SECONDARY SCHOOL

320. FLEMMING, Carolyn Sherwood, and Donna Schatt. Choices:
A Core Collection for Young Reluctant Readers. Evanston,
IL: John Gordon Burke Pub. Inc., 1983. 554p.
First in a series for reluctant readers. Includes popu-
lar titles in trade editions in addition to designated hi/lo titles
for children in grades one to six. ISBN 0-934272-10-7.
RELUCTANT READERS

321. FOOD AND NUTRITION Quarterly Resource Guide. Phoenix:
Oryx Press, quarterly beginning in 1984. Paper. Supersedes
Food and Nutrition Bibliography, pubished up to its 11th
edition.

Indexing system is by main entry, subject, title, author, media, intellectual level and sponsoring agency. Includes print and nonprint materials in food, human nutrition
and food service management. Fairly comprehensive coverage
for young readers. ISSN 0732-1171.
NUTRITION

322. FORDYCE, Rachel. Children's Theatre and Creative Dramatics: An Annotated Bibliography. Boston: G. K. Hall,
1975. 275p. Part of G. K. Hall Reference Series.
Includes children's plays and titles for drama in education. ISBN 0-8161-1161-8.
DRAMATIC LITERATURE/PLAYS

323. FORINASH, Melissa R. [compiler]. Reader Development Bibliography. Syracuse, NY: New Readers Press, 1977, 109p.;
supplement 1978, 24p.
Designed for adults and young adults who are reading
on or below eighth grade level. Includes books for leisure
reading and on community and family life, jobs, and the world
and its people. Over 90 percent of the titles are in paperback. The bibliography is part of the Reader Development
Program of the Free Library of Philadelphia.
RELUCTANT READERS; HIGH INTEREST/LOW VOCAB-
ULARY

324. FOX, Geoff; Graham Hammond; Terry Jones; Frederick Smith;
and Kenneth Sterck [editors]. Writers, Critics and Children:
Articles from Children's Literature in Education. New York:
Agathon Press, 1976. 245p.
23 critical essays in three sections: Writers, Critics,
and Children. Children's Literature in Education was first
published in Great Britain and since 1972 has been published
four times a year by APS Publications Inc. ISBN 0-87586-
054-0.
CHILDREN'S LITERATURE, HISTORY & CRITICISM

325. FRANK, Josette. Your Child's Reading Today. Fourth edition, new and revised. Garden City, NY: Doubleday &
Company, Inc., 1969. 368p. First edition 1953; second edition 1954; third edition 1960.
Selected lists for various ages and interests. Frank
also wrote What Books for Children? LC 68-11816.
SELECTION GUIDE

326. FRASER, James H. [compiler]. Children's Authors and Illus-
trators: A Guide to Manuscript Collections in United States
Research Libraries. New York: K. G. Sauer, 1980. 119p.
Phaedrus Bibliographic Series No. 1.
Lists collections by title with location and description
of the collection. ISBN 0-89664-950-4.
AUTHORS; ILLUSTRATORS; SPECIAL COLLECTIONS

327. _____. Society and Children's Literature. Chicago:
American Library Association, in association with David R.
Godine, 1978. Paper. 218p.
Includes papers on regionalism, foreign language pub-
lishing, 18th-century influences, American comics and film.
Index. ISBN 0-8389-3213-4.
CHILDREN'S LITERATURE, HISTORY & CRITICISM

328. FREEMAN, Judy. Books Kids Will Sit Still For: A Guide to
Using Children's Literature for Librarians, Teachers and
Parents. Hagerstown, MD: Upstart Press, 1984. Illus.
Paper. 210p.
Over 1,200 selected titles for reading aloud for children
K-6. Indexes. ISBN 0-913853-02-X.
ACTIVE READERS, DEVELOPING

329. FREEMAN, Ruth Sunderlin. Children's Picture Books: Yes-
terday and Today, An Analysis. Watkins Glen, NY: Century
House, 1967. Illus. 200p.
Extensive bibliography.
PICTURE BOOKS

330. FRIEDBERG, Joan Brest; June B. Mullins; and Adelaire Weir
Sukiennik. Accept Me As I Am: Best Books of Juvenile Non-
fiction on Impairments and Disabilities. New York: R. R.
Bowker, 1985. Illus. 378p. Part of Serving Special Needs
Series.
Biographies, autobiographies, and informational books
within four categories of disability: Physical; Sensory; Cog-
nitive and Behavioral; and Multiple/Severe. Subject, author
and title indexes. ISBN 0-8352-1974-7.
DISABILITIES

331. FRIEDMAN, Leslie. Sex Role Stereotyping in the Mass Media:
An Annotated Bibliography. New York: Garland, 1977.
342p.
Covers over 1,000 pieces of scholarship on the media,
including literature for children. ISBN 0-8420-9865-X.
SEXISM

332. FRITZ, Jean. Tracking the Past. Chicago: American Li-
brary Association, 1983. Paper.
ISBN 0-8389-5640-8.
HISTORICAL FICTION

FRYATT, Norma R. see HORN BOOK, A Horn Book Sampler

333. FULLER, Muriel. More Junior Authors. New York: H. W.
Wilson Co., 1963. Illus. 235p. Companion volume to The
Junior Book of Authors. Second edition revised.
Covers 268 authors and illustrators, the majority of

whom have become prominent since 1951. Subsequent printings list date of death. ISBN 0-8242-0036-5.
AUTHORS

334. FULTON, Len, and Ellen Ferber [editors]. Small Press Record
of Books in Print. Thirteenth edition. Paradise, CA: Dustbooks, 1984. First edition, 1966-1968; became annual publication with third edition in 1974.
Subject heading: Children and Youth; also indexes by
author, title, and publisher. Dustbooks also publishes a
monthly, Small Press Review. ISBN 0-913219-56-1.
ANNUAL

335. GAER, Joseph. California in Juvenile Fiction. New York:
Burt Franklin Publishing, 1972. Illus. 62p. California Lit-
erary Research Monographs: No. 12.
Reproduction of 1935 edition. ISBN 0-8337-1255-1
FICTION; U.S., REGIONAL LITERATURE

336. GALLAGHER, Kathleen, and Alice Peery [compilers]. Bib-
liography of Materials on Sexism in Children's Books. Chapel
Hill, NC: Lollipop Power, Inc., annual. Paper.
A pamphlet listing articles on sexism in books for young
readers.
ANNUAL; SEXISM

337. GALLIVAN, Marion F. [compiler]. Fun for Kids: An Index
to Children's Craft Books. Metuchen, NJ: Scarecrow Press,
1981. 340p.
Listed by author or main title entry; cross-reference
by crafts and by types of materials. ISBN 0-8108-1439-0.
CRAFTS

338. GARDNER, Frank M., and Lisa-Christina Persson. Sequels:
Volume 2, Junior Books. London: Library Association, 1976.
112p. Previous editions, which combined adult and junior
books, 1922, 1928, 1947, 1955, 1967.
Includes 7,000 titles that feature the same character or
group of characters, that have a connected narrative or developing theme, or that have an interior connection, either
topographical or historical. ISBN 0-900092-27-0.
SEQUELS; FICTION

339. GEORGE, Jean Craighead. Exploring the Out-of-Doors. Chi-
cago: American Library Association, 1983. Paper.
Titles set in nature. ISBN 0-8389-5621-1.
NATURE

340. GEORGIOU, Constantine. Children and Their Literature.

Englewood Cliffs, NJ: Prentice Hall, 1969. Part of education series.
ISBN 0-13-132167-6.
CHILDREN'S LITERATURE, TEXTBOOKS ON

341. GERSONI-STAVN, Diane [compiler]. Sexism and Youth. New York: R. R. Bowker, 1974. 464p.
Part III is a review of children's literature and textbooks. ISBN 0-8352-0710-2.
SEXISM

342. GERSONI-EDELMEN, Diane. Work-Wise: Learning About the World of Work from Books--A Critical Guide to Book Selection and Usage. New York: Neal Schuman Publishers, 1980. 258p.
493 books, by grade, on career planning, job hunting, and careers. Includes standard reference works, general nonfiction, and fiction. Directory of career publishers. Indexes by author, title, series, and occupation. ISBN 0-87-436-264-4.
CAREERS; ECONOMICS

343. GIAMBRA, Carolyn [compiler]. The Lois Lenski Children's Collection in the Edward H. Butler Library. Buffalo, NY: State University College at Buffalo, 1972. Paper. Unpp.
Comprehensive coverage of books written and illustrated, plays, recordings, magazine articles, unpublished material by Lois Lenski and material about Lois Lenski.
SPECIAL COLLECTIONS

344. GILLESPIE, John T. [editor]. More Junior Plots: A Guide for Teachers and Librarians. New York: R. R. Bowker, 1977. 253p.
Plots of, and material related to, 88 books organized by basic behavior themes for young people ages 11 to 15. ISBN 0-8352-1002-2.
FICTION; BOOKTALKING

345. _____ [compiler]. Paperback Books for Young People: An Annotated Guide to Publishers and Distributors. Second edition. Chicago: American Library Association, 1977. Paper. 232p. New York: Dell Publishing Co.
Comprehensive listing for the United States and Canada. Gives available series, special services, ordering procedures. ISBN 0-8389-0248-0 [ALA]. Paper teacher's edition, ISBN 0-317-06456-8 [Dell].
PAPERBOUND; CANADA

346. _____, and Christine B. Gilbert [editors]. Best Books for Children: Pre-School Through the Middle Grades. Third edition. New York: R. R. Bowker, 1985. 635p. Originally published 1959, paper, with 5000 titles. First edition in new

format, ©1978. Second edition in new format, ©1981.
13,000 books in 500 subject areas with grade range.
ISBN 0-8352-2131-8.
BEST BOOKS

347. GILLESPIE, John T., and Diana L. Lembo. Introducing
Books: A Guide for the Middle Grades. New York: R. R.
Bowker, 1970. 318p.
    Companion to Junior Plots and More Junior Plots. Plot
summaries of 88 books, for students grades 4 to 6; organized
around "life goal" themes. ISBN 0-8352-0215-1.
    FICTION; MIDDLE GRADES; BOOKTALKING

348. _____. Juniorplots: A Book Talk Manual for Teachers
and Librarians. New York: R. R. Bowker, 1967. 222p.
    Plot summaries of 88 books for sixth to tenth-grade
students. Arranged in basic behavioral themes with supplementary discussion materials and other related titles. ISBN
0-8352-0063-9.
    FICTION; BOOKTALKING; YOUNG ADULTS

349. GILLESPIE, John T., and Diana L. Spirt. The Young Phe-
nomenon: Paperbacks in Our Schools. Chicago: American
Library Association, 1972. Paper. 140p. ALA Studies in
Librarianship #3.
    1967 and 1970 surveys reported and analyzed. De-
scribes master programs utilizing paperbacks. ISBN 0-8389-
0133-6.
    PAPERBOUND

350. GILLESPIE, Margaret C. Literature for Children: History
and Trends. Pose Lamb, consulting editor. Dubuque, IA:
Wm. C. Brown, 1970. Illus. Paper. 128p. Part of Literature for Children series.
    Covers librarianship and early publishing, fantasy,
poetry, and realism. Index. ISBN 0-697-06205-8.
    CHILDREN'S LITERATURE, HISTORY & CRITICISM

351. _____, and John W. Conner. Creative Growth Through
Literature for Children and Adolescents. Columbus, OH:
Charles E. Merrill Publishing Co., 1975. Illus. 405p.
    "Illustrates the relationship between developmental
stages and the literature that young people find relevant at
various stages of their growth." Listing by age range.
Subject, author, illustrator, title indexes. ISBN 0-675-8751-1.
    CHILDREN'S LITERATURE, TEXTBOOKS ON

352. GILLILAND, Hap. Indian Children's Books. Billings, MT:
Council for Indian Education, 1980. Paper. 230p.
    List of 1,650 books evaluated by selection criteria.
ISBN 0-89992-503-0.
    AMERICAN INDIAN

353.   GILLIS, Ruth J. [compiler; with technical assistance by Lou-
       ise S. Spear]. Children's Books for Times of Stress: An
       Annotated Bibliography. Bloomington, IN: Indiana Univer-
       sity Press, 1978. 322p.
           261 books selected according to specific criteria for
       seven broad categories: Emotions, Behavior, Family, Difficult
       Situation, New Situation, Self Concept, Friendship. Cross-
       references also with subheadings. Indexes for title, author,
       illustrator. ISBN 0-253-31348-1.
           BIBLIOTHERAPY

354.   GLAZER, Joan I., and Gurney Williams III. Introduction to
       Children's Literature. New York: McGraw-Hill Book Co.,
       1979. Illus. 737p.
           Central thesis is that the basis for selection is in re-
       gard to concepts of child growth and development. Index.
       Extensive bibliography. ISBN 0-07-023380-2.
           CHILDREN'S LITERATURE, TEXTBOOKS ON

355.   GOODMAN, Cynthia. Native Americans. North Canton, OH:
       Stark County District Library, 1984. 24p.
           Fiction and nonfiction titles.
           AMERICAN INDIAN

356.   GORDON, Sol, and Susan Untener Snyder. Parents as Sex
       Educators: An Annotated Print and Audiovisual Bibliography.
       Phoenix: Oryx Press, 1984. 144p.
           Description of "materials that parents can use to pro-
       vide accurate and up-to-date information on sexuality for
       their children." ISBN 0-89774-087-4.
           SEX EDUCATION

357.   GOTTLIEB, Gerald. Early Children's Books and Their Illus-
       tration. Photographs by Charles V. Passela. Boston: David
       R. Godine, 1975. Illus.
           Based on the collection at the Pierpont Morgan Library.
       225 examples to provide "a sense of the evolution of the vari-
       ous types of children's literature." Extensive bibliography.
       Index. ISBN 0-87598-051-1; ISBN 0-87923-158-0.
           SPECIAL COLLECTIONS

358.   GOTTLIEB, Robin. Publishing Children's Books in America,
       1919-1976: An Annotated Bibliography. New York: Chil-
       dren's Book Council, 1978. Paper. 224p.
           707 entries arranged chronologically, in general cate-
       gories with brief descriptions.
           PUBLISHING; CHILDREN'S LITERATURE, HISTORY &
           CRITICISM

359.   GRANGER'S INDEX TO POETRY. Seventh Edition, Indexing
       Anthologies Published from 1970-1981. Edited by William James

Smith and William F. Bernhardt. New York: Columbia University Press, 1982. 1329p. First published, Chicago: A. C. McClurg & Co., 1904; edited by Edith Granger. Other editions 1918, 1929 and 1940. Columbia University Press 1945, 1953, 1957, 1962, 1973, 1978.

Title and first line index; author index; subject index. Includes adult and children's poetry. The sixth edition is the most comprehensive survey of poetry anthologies up to 1970. ISBN 0-231-05002-X.

POETRY

360. GRAUSTEIN, Jean McCarthy, and Carol L. Jaglinski [editors]. An Annotated Bibliography of Young People's Fiction on American Indians. Curriculum Bulletin #11 and #12. Albuquerque: Bureau of Indian Affairs, Language Arts Branch, 1972.

AMERICAN INDIAN; FICTION

361. GREEN, Roger Lancelyn. Tellers of Tales: British Authors of Children's Books From 1800-1964. Revised edition. New York: Franklin Watts, Inc., 1965. 320p. First published, London: Edmund Ward Ltd., 1946.

Includes a chronological table of famous children's books to 1965, together with lists of titles by each author. LC 65-12428.

BRITISH, AUTHORS

362. GREENE, Ellin, and Mary Alice Hunt [compilers and editors]. A Multimedia Approach to Children's Literature. Third edition. Chicago: American Library Association, 1983. Paper. 182p. First published 1972; second edition 1977.

Includes media adaptations, films, filmstrips and recordings based on children's books. Indexes to subjects and each of the media, to authors and illustrators, and to books. Directory of distributors. ISBN 0-8389-3289-4.

MULTIMEDIA

363. GROBANI, Anton [editor]. Guide to Football Literature. Detroit: Gale Research Co., 1975. Illus. 319p.

For young adults, includes biographies, anthologies, fiction, humor, drama, verse and ballads. ISBN 0-8103-0964-5.

SPORTS

364. GUILFOILE, Elizabeth. Books for Beginning Readers. Illustrated by Norma Phillips. Champaign, IL: National Council of Teachers of English, 1962. 73p. Reprinted from Elementary English, April 1963.

Approximately 320 titles of specific interest to a new reader. Includes descriptions, discussions, and book lists.

BEGINNING READERS

365. HAAS, Elizabeth [compiler]. Everything You Always Wanted
      to Know About Book Fairs But Didn't Know Who to Ask.
      New York: Association of American Publishers, 1985. Pa-
      per.
           A self-help guide.
      BOOK FAIRS

366. HALSEY, Rosalie Vrylina. Forgotten Books of the American
      Nursery: A History of the Development of the American
      Story Book. Detroit: Reissued by Singing Tree Press,
      1969. Illus. 245p. Originally published Boston: Charles
      E. Goodspeed & Co., 1911.
           Comprehensive coverage of early preschool books. In-
      dex. ISBN 0-8103-3483-6.
      CHILDREN'S LITERATURE, HISTORY & CRITICISM

367. HAMAN, Albert C., and Mary K. Eakin. Assisted by Kath-
      ryn Kessler. Library Books on Environmental Biology for
      the Elementary and Junior High School. Cedar Falls: Exten-
      sion Service, University of Northern Iowa, 1973. Paper.
      89p. Educational Service Publication, No. 35.
           This listing replaces "Library Materials for Elementary
      School" by the same authors. Titles, by biology subject, in-
      clude a content description and reading levels. Title/author
      index.
      ENVIRONMENTAL BIOLOGY

368. HARING-SMITH, Tori. A. A. Milne: A Critical Bibliography.
      New York: Garland Publishing, Inc., 1982. 382p.
           Arranged chronologically, primary entries include data
      on later editions, adaptations, translations, and reviews.
      Cross-referenced with author-title index. ISBN 0-8240-
      9282-1.
      AUTHORS

369. HARMON, Elva A., and Anna L. Milligan. Reading for Young
      People: The Southwest. Chicago: American Library Asso-
      ciation, 1982. 245p. Part of a series.
           Covers material on The Southwest in fiction and nonfic-
      tion. ISBN 0-8389-0362-2.
      U.S., REGIONAL LITERATURE

370. HARRAH, Barbara K. Sports Books for Children: An Anno-
      tated Bibliography. Metuchen, NJ: Scarecrow Press, Inc.,
      1978. 540p.
           3,509 books in print as of January 1977 for preschool
      to twelfth grade, by subject headings according to sport.
      Includes selected periodical guide per sport; author and title
      indexes. ISBN 0-8108-1154-5.
      SPORTS

371. HART, J. A. [editor]. Books for the Retarded Reader.
     Hawthorn, Vic.: Australian Council for Educational Re-
     search. Periodic revisions. First edition ©1959. First to third
     editions edited by J. A. Hart and J. A. Richardson. Fourth
     and fifth editions by J. A. Hart, ©1970; ©1973. See RICH-
     ARDSON, J. A. for sixth edition.
         Includes trade book lists. ISBN 0-8426-0037-X.
         RETARDED READERS

372. HAUSSLEIN, Evelyn B. Children and Divorce: An Anno-
     tated Bibliography and Guide. New York: Garland Publish-
     ing, Inc., 1983. 164p.
         Comprehensive survey of books and of journal and maga-
     zine articles form 1975 to 1980 and selected seminal titles prior
     to 1975. Also includes books and articles for parents; books
     for children; list of resource organizations, newsletters and
     audiovisual materials. ISBN 0-8240-9391-7.
         DIVORCE

373. HAVILAND, Virginia [editor]. The Best of Children's Books,
     1964-1978: With 1979 Addenda. Washington, DC: Library of
     Congress, 1980. 126p.
         Includes top choices for picture and picture-story
     books, stories for the middle group and older boys and girls,
     folklore, poetry, plays, songs, arts, hobbies, biography, his-
     tory, people, places, nature, science, psychology, sociology.
     The preface synthesizes publishing decisions from 1964 to
     1978. ISBN 0-8295-0289-0.
         BEST BOOKS

374. _____. Children and Literature: Views and Reviews.
     Glenview, IL: Scott, Foresman, 1973. 448 p. New York:
     Lothrop, Lee & Shepard Co., 1974.
         Selection of essays, criticisms, and statements of trends
     for the nineteenth and twentieth centuries. ISBN 0-673-
     07676-8 [Scott, Foresman]; ISBN 0-370-01595-9 [Lothrop, Lee
     & Shepard].
         CHILDREN'S LITERATURE, HISTORY & CRITICISM

375. _____. Children's Literature: A Guide to Reference
     Sources. Second Supplement. Washington, DC: Library of
     Congress, 1977. Illus. 413p. First published 1966, 341p.,
     by Haviland, with Elizabeth Wenning Davidson and Barbara
     Quinnam. First supplement, 1972, 315p., by Haviland with
     Margaret N. Coughlin.
         Covers books, articles and pamphlets of value to
     adults. Includes Indexes. LC 66-62734 [1966]; ISBN 0-
     8444-0022-X [1972]; ISBN 0-8444-0215-X [1977].
         CHILDREN'S LITERATURE, REFERENCES FOR

376. _____, and Anne Pellowski. Some Suggestions for Finding

Friends Through Books. Chicago: American Library Asso-
ciation, 1972.   Paper.   4p.   Reprint form "Top of the News,"
January 1972.
ISBN 0-8389-5581-6.
BIBLIOTHERAPY

377. _____, and William Jay Smith.   Children and Poetry: A
Selective, Annotated Bibliography.   Second revised edition.
Washington, DC: Library of Congress, 1979.   Illus.   84p.
First edition 1969.
Includes rhymes, poetry of the past, twentieth-century
poets, anthologies, world poetry.   Omitted are traditional bal-
lads, Mother Goose rhymes, textbooks, and collections in-
tended for classroom use.   ISBN 0-8444-0267-2.
POETRY

378. _____, and Lois Watt.   Children's Books.   Washington, DC:
Library of Congress, annual.   Paper.   First published 1964.
Annotated list for preschool to junior high school age,
in categories, with reading levels.
ANNUAL; BEST BOOKS

379. HAZARD, Paul.   Books, Children and Men.   Fifth edition.
Translated from the French by Marguerite Mitchell.   Introduction by Sheila Egoff.   Boston: Horn Book, 1983.   Paper.
176p.   First published in the United States 1944.
"An analysis of the distinctive national traits and common values in children's books of different countries."   ISBN
0-87675-059-5.
CHILDREN'S LITERATURE, HISTORY & CRITICISM

380. HEALD, Dorothy [regional editor].   Reading for Young People: The Southeast.   Chicago: American Library Association,
1980.   Paper.   174p.
444 titles of fiction, folktales, poetry, drama, biography
and personal accounts, and other informational books on the
states of Alabama, Florida, Georgia, North Carolina, South
Carolina, and Virginia.   Includes a directory of regional publishers and author and subject index.   ISBN 0-8389-0300-2.
U.S., REGIONAL LITERATURE

381. HEARNE, Betsy.   Choosing Books for Children: A Common-
sense Guide.   New York: Delacorte Press, 1981.   228p.
New York: Dell Publishing Co., 1982.   Paper.   176p.
Emphasis on finding books "that will challenge and ex-
cite a child's imagination."   ISBN 0-440-01930-3 [Delacorte];
ISBN 0-440-31576-X [Laurel].
SELECTION GUIDE

382. _____, and Marilyn Kaye [editors].   Celebrating Children's
Books: Essays on Children's Literature in Honor of Zena

Sutherland. New York: Lothrop, Lee and Shepard, 1981.
244p.
    23 critical essays by writers and critics within four
broad categories: creating the books; producing the books;
understanding the books; reaching the readers. ISBN 0-
688-00752-X.
    CHILDREN'S LITERATURE, HISTORY & CRITICISM

383. HEEKS, Peggy. Ways of Knowing: Information Books for 7
to 9 Year Olds. Stroud, Glos, England: Thimble Press,
n.d. Paper. 56p.
    Recommends over 100 titles in all main subject areas.
ISBN 0-903355-11-6.
    INFORMATIONAL BOOKS

384. HEINS, Ethel [compiler]. Contemporary Classics: Thirty
Children's Books for Adults. Boston: Horn Book, annual.
Paper.
    Intended primarily to introduce parents to some of the
best books for young readers.
    ANNUAL; CONTEMPORARY CLASSICS; ADULTS, CHIL-
DREN'S BOOKS FOR

385. HEINS, Paul [editor]. Crosscurrents of Criticism: Horn
Book Essays, 1968-1977. Boston: The Horn Book, 1977.
359p. Follows A Horn Book Sampler and Horn Book Reflections.
    47 critical essays on a range of topics. Index to titles
and authors. ISBN 0-87675-034-X.
    CHILDREN'S LITERATURE, HISTORY & CRITICISM

386. HENDRICKS, Robert H.; George G. Dawson; Andrew T.
Nappi; and Rita Haniff. Learning Economics Through Children's Stories. Fourth edition. New York: Joint Council
on Economic Education, 1982. Paper. 107p. JCEE Checklist
No. 320. First published 1978, edited by Andrew T. Nappi.
    Listed by title, with description of contents, reading
levels. Keyed to economics topics.
    ECONOMICS

387. HERBERT, Cynthia. Child's Play Horizons: An Annotated,
Non-Sexist Bibliography on Books for Children with Special
Problems. Brooklyn, NY: Highly Specialized, 1981. Paper.
18p.
    ISBN 0-686-75166-3.
    BIBLIOTHERAPY

388. HERDEG, Walter [editor]. Graphis: Children's Book Illustration (4). Natick, MA: Alphabet Press, 1984. Illus.
148p. First published, Zurich, Switzerland: The Graphis
Press, Spring 1979.

Features European and U.S. illustrators and their
work.   Indexes to illustrators and publishers.
ILLUSTRATORS

389.   HEWINS, Caroline M. A Mid-Century Child and Her Books.
Detroit: Gale Research Co., 1969. Reproduction of 1926
edition. Edition under title Caroline M. Hewins, Her Book:
Containing A Mid-Century Child and Her Books published,
Boston: Horn Book, 1954.
ISBN 0-8103-3857-2.
CHILDREN'S LITERATURE, HISTORY & CRITICISM

390.   HIGGINS, Judith H. Energy: A Multimedia Guide for Children and Young Adults. Santa Barbara, CA: Neal-Schuman
Publishers, 1979. 195p. Selection Guide Series No. 2.
   433 print and nonprint materials. ISBN 0-87436-266-0.
ENERGY

391.   HILL, Janet [editor]. Books for Children: The Homelands
of Immigrants in Britain: Africa, Cyprus, India and Pakis-
tan, Ireland, Italy, Poland, Turkey, the West Indies. London: Institute of Race Relations, 1971. Paper. 85p. Institute of Race Relations Special Series.
   Description includes a critical recommendation. Includes
trade books only. ISBN 0-85001-012-8.
BRITAIN

392.   HINMAN, Dorothy, and Ruth Zimmerman. Reading for Boys
and Girls: Illinois: A Subject Index and Annotated Bibliography. Chicago: American Library Association, 1970.
128p.
   200 titles with a historical emphasis for eighteenth,
nineteenth, and twentieth centuries. Biography and fiction
predominate. Appendix on books about athletes and sports.
ISBN 0-8389-0075-5.
U.S., REGIONAL LITERATURE

393.   _____. Reading for Young People: The Midwest. Chicago: American Library Association, 1979. Paper. 250p.
Part of a series.
   440 titles of Illinois, Iowa, Missouri, Ohio, and the Midwest in general for students in grades 4 to 10. Emphasis is
on fiction, history, and biography. ISBN 0-8389-0271-9.
U.S., REGIONAL LITERATURE

394.   HIRSCHFELDER, Arlene B. [compiler]. American Indian and
Eskimo Authors: A Comprehensive Bibliography. New York:
Association on American Indian Affairs, 1973. 104p. [Inter-
book Inc.] First compiled 1970.
   400 titles written or narrated by nearly 300 Indian and
Eskimo authors representing more than 100 tribes are cited.

Tribal index. ISBN 0-686-24118-5.
AMERICAN INDIAN; ESKIMO; AUTHORS

395. _____. American Indian Stereotypes in the World of Children: A Reader and Bibliography. Metuchen, NJ: Scarecrow Press, 1982. 312p.
Scrutinizes children's attitudes about Indians and images of Indians in children's stories. Annotated bibliography of approximately 125 titles. ISBN 0-8108-1494-2.
AMERICAN INDIAN

396. A HISTORY OF CHILDREN'S BOOKS and Juvenile Graphic Art: Virtues, Adventures and Delights. London: Visual Publications, 1975.
Film strip of six rolls; color; 35mm; with six guides compiled and annotated by Laurence Scarfe.
CHILDREN'S LITERATURE, HISTORY & CRITICISM

397. HODGES, Elizabeth D. [compiler and editor]. Books for Elementary School Libraries: An Initial Collection. Chicago: American Library Association, 1969. Paper. 321p.
Designed as a buying guide to a quality collection for initial library service for pupils in grades K-8. Includes fiction and nonfiction by subject and with reading levels. ISBN 0-8389-0069-0.
CORE COLLECTION

398. HOFFMAN, Miriam, and Eva Samuels. Authors and Illustrators of Children's Books: Writings on Their Lives and Works. New York: R. R. Bowker, 1972. Illus. 471p.
Selective choice of 50 individuals on whom articles are reprinted from periodicals, newspapers, and journals published between 1950 and 1971. ISBN 0-8352-0523-1.
AUTHORS; ILLUSTRATORS

399. HOLTZE, Sally Holmes [editor]. Fifth Book of Junior Authors and Illustrators. New York: H. W. Wilson, 1983. Illus. 357p. Part of series. First volume published 1934.
239 sketches of authors and illustrators who have come to prominence since the Fourth Book [1979]. Cumulative index for series; cross-reference to pen names. ISBN 0-8242-0694-0.
AUTHORS; ILLUSTRATORS

400. HOPKINS, Lee Bennett. Books Are by People: Interviews with 104 Authors and Illustrators of Books for Young Children. New York: Citation Press, 1969. Photographs. 349p.
Human interest and anecdotal data limited to authors and illustrators of books for children, preschool to grade 3. LC 70-96312.
AUTHORS; ILLUSTRATORS

401.   . More Books by More People: Interviews with
Sixty-five Authors of Books for Children.   New York: Cita-
tion Press, 1974.   Photographs.   410p.
        Especially notes how the book came to be written.
ISBN 0-590-07357-5; ISBN 0-590-09401-7 paper.
        AUTHORS

402.   THE HORN BOOK, INC.   A Horn Book Sampler on Children's
Books and Reading.   Selected From Twenty-five Years of the
Horn Book Magazine.   1924-1948.   Edited by Norma R. Fryatt.
Introduction by Bertha Mahony Miller.   Boston: Horn Book,
1959.   261p.
        Articles on authors and artists and reviews and criti-
cisms on books.   LC 59-15028.
        CHILDREN'S LITERATURE, HISTORY & CRITICISM

403.   . "Why Children's Books?"   Boston: Horn Book,
quarterly.
        A newsletter for parents that features articles and sug-
gestions for choosing, using, and enjoying books with children.
        SELECTION GUIDE

404.   HORNER, Catherine Townsend.   The Aging Adult in Children's Books and Nonprint Media: An Annotated Bibliography.   Metuchen, NJ: Scarecrow Press, 1982.   266p.
        400 books by reading levels, preschool to high school,
in which aging adults are portrayed.   ISBN 0-8108-1475-7.
        AGING ADULT

405.   . The Single Parent Family in Children's Books:
An Analysis and Annotated Bibliography with an Appendix
on Audiovisual Material.   Metuchen, NJ: Scarecrow Press,
1978.   180p.
        ISBN 0-8108-1157-X.
        SINGLE-PARENT FAMILY

406.   HOTCHKISS, Jeanette [compiler].   African Asian Reading
Guide for Children and Young Adults.   Metuchen, NJ:
Scarecrow Press, 1976.   269p.
        Includes multiple indexes.   ISBN 0-8108-0886-2.
        AFRICA; ASIA

407.   . American Historical Fiction and Biography for
Children and Young People.   Metuchen, NJ: Scarecrow
Press, 1973.   318p.
        1,600 novels and biographies on both Americas, ar-
ranged chronologically in the first section and topically in
the second section.   ISBN 0-8108-0650-9.
        HISTORICAL FICTION; BIOGRAPHY

408. _____. European Historical Fiction and Biography for
Children and Young People. Second edition. Metuchen,
NJ: Scarecrow Press, 1972. 272p. First published 1967
with title: European Historical Fiction for Children and
Young People.
        Lists 1,341 selected titles set in the British Isles and
continental Europe, grouped under geographical regions by
historical period. Author, title and biographical indexes.
ISBN 0-8108-0515-4.
        HISTORICAL FICTION; BIOGRAPHY; EUROPE

409. HOYLE, Karen Nelson [compiler]. Danish Children's Literature in English: A Bibliography Excluding H. C. Andersen.
Minneapolis: University of Minnesota, 1982.
        DENMARK

410. HUCK, Charlotte S. Children's Literature in the Elementary
School. Fourth revised edition. New York: Holt, Rinehart
and Winston, 1979. 804p. First published 1961 by Charlotte
Huck and Doris Young Kuhn.
        Discusses all genres and aspects of literature for chil-
dren; extensive lists for each genre and age. ISBN 0-03-
046086-7.
        CHILDREN'S LITERATURE, TEXTBOOKS ON

411. HUNT, Abby Campbell. The World of Books for Children:
A Parent's Guide. New York: Sovereign Books, 1979.
Illus. 242p.
        Grouped by age and subject for children, preschool to
grade four. Author, title indexes. ISBN 0-671-18383-4;
ISBN 0-671-18350-8 paper.
        SELECTION GUIDE

HUNT, Mary Alice see GREENE, Ellin.

412. HURLIMANN, Bettina. Three Centuries of Children's Books
in Europe. Translated and edited by Brian W. Alderson.
Cleveland: World Publishing Co., 1968. Illus. 297p. First
published Zurich: Atlantis Verlag AG, 1959 and London:
Oxford University Press, 1967.
        Comparative and historical treatment for all genres pub-
lished in the eighteenth, nineteenth, and twentieth centuries.
Index. LC 68-14703.
        EUROPE

413. _____. Picture-Book World: A Critical Survey of Modern
Picture Books for Children. Translated and edited by Brian
W. Alderson. Modern Picture-Books for Children from 24
Countries with a Biographical Supplement by Elisabeth Wald-
mann. Cleveland: World Publishing Co., 1969. Illus.
216p.

Discussion by country and genre.   Index.   LC 69-
13066.
PICTURE BOOKS

414.   INGLIS, Fred.   The Promise of Happiness: Value and Mean-
ing in Children's Fiction.   New York: Cambridge University
Press, 1981.   250p.
ISBN 0-521-23142-6; ISBN 0-521-27070-7 [paper].
FICTION

415.   INTERNATIONAL READING ASSOCIATION and the Children's
Book Council Joint Committee.   Children's Choices....   New
York: Children's Book Council, annual.   Paper.   "Classroom
Choices: Children's Trade Books...."
Yearly selective, descriptive list appears first in the
October issue of The Reading Teacher and is then available
from the CBC.
ANNUAL; BEST BOOKS

416.   IRELAND, Norma Olin [compiler].   Index to America: Life
and Customs--19th Century.   Metuchen, NJ: Scarecrow
Press, 1984, 374p.; --17th Century, Westwood, MA: F. W.
Faxon Co., 1978, 250p.; --18th Century, Westwood, MA:
F. W. Faxon Co., 1976, 186p.
Each volume contains a representative selection of adult
and young adult titles usually found in major public, school,
and academic libraries, with an emphasis on family and home
life, the arts, education, sports and recreation, science,
clothing and furniture, and personalities.   ISBN 0-8108-
1661-X [1984]; ISBN 0-87305-107-6 [1978]; ISBN 0-87305-
108-4 [1976].
AMERICA, LIFE & CUSTOMS

417.   _____.   Index to Fairy Tales, 1949-1972:   Including Folklore, Legends and Myths in Collections.   Third Supplement.
Westwood, MA: F. W. Faxon Co., 1973.   741p.; dist.,
Metuchen, NJ: Scarecrow Press.   Useful Reference Series
No. 101.
406 books published between 1949 and 1972 indexed,
under title and subject.   Stories in collections only are included (no individual story books).   ISBN 0-87305-101-7.
FAIRY TALES; FOLKLORE; LEGENDS; MYTHS

418.   _____.   Index to Fairy Tales, 1973-1977.   Including Folklore, Legends and Myths in Collections.   Fourth Supplement.
Westwood, MA: F. W. Faxon Co., 1979.   259p.; reprint,
Metuchen, NJ: Scarecrow Press, 1985.
130 titles indexed.   Selection is on the basis of avail-
ability and favorable reviews in professional journals.

ISBN 0-8108-1855-5.
FAIRY TALES; FOLKLORE; LEGENDS; MYTHS

419. IRWIN, Leonard Bertram [compiler]. A Guide to Historical
Fiction for the Use of Schools, Libraries, and the General
Reader. Nineteenth edition, new and revised. Brooklawn,
NJ: McKinley Pub. Co., 1971. 255p. McKinley Bibliogra-
phies, v. 1.
    First to ninth editions, 1927-1968, compiled by Hannah
Logasa, under title Historical Fiction. ISBN 0-910942-26-9.
    HISTORICAL FICTION

420. _____. A Guide to Historical Reading: Non-Fiction. For
the Use of Schools, Libraries and the General Reader. Tenth
revised edition. Washington, DC: Heldreff Publications,
1976. 289p. McKinley Bibliographies, v. 2.
    "Formerly a part of the first-sixth editions of Historical
Fiction by Hannah Logasa...." Since 1960 published as Historical Nonfiction. Compilation by Irwin begins with the 1970
edition.
    General interest titles in a selective listing for adults
and senior and junior high school students. Includes the
Ancient World, Europe, Asia, Africa, The Pacific, The United
States, Canada, and Latin America. ISBN 0-916882-02-0.
    HISTORICAL NONFICTION

ISAACSON, Richard H. see BOGART, Gary L.

421. JACOB, Gale Sypher. Independent Reading Grades One-
Three: An Annotated Bibliography with Reading Levels.
Williamsport, PA: Bro Dart Pub. Co., 1975. Paper. 86p.
    By subject headings, describes 849 tradebooks. Read-
ing levels cited. ISBN 0-87272-064-0.
    INDEPENDENT READING

422. JAMES, Philip. Children's Books of Yesterday. C. Geoffrey
Holme, editor. Detroit: Gale Research Co., 1976. Illus.
128p. Reproduction of 1933 edition published by Studio
Productions.
    Catalog of the 1932 exhibit at London's Victoria and
Albert Museum. ISBN 0-8103-4135-2.
    SPECIAL COLLECTIONS

423. JEFFREE, Dorothy, and Margaret Skeffington. Reading Is
for Everyone: A Guide for Parents and Teachers of Exceptional Children. Englewood Cliffs, NJ: Prentice Hall, 1984.
Illus. 168p.
    Discussion and list of selected books. ISBN 0-13-
755224-6; ISBN 0-13-755216-5 paper.
    EXCEPTIONAL CHILDREN

424. JEWETT, Claudia L. Helping Children Cope with Separation and Loss. Cambridge, MA: Harvard Common Press, 1984. Paper. 164p.
     ISBN 0-916782-53-0.
     BIBLIOTHERAPY

425. JOHNSON, Deidre [editor]. Stratemeyer Pseudonyms and Series Books: An Annotated Checklist of Stratemeyer and Syndicate Publications. Westport, CT: Greenwood Press, 1982. 343p.
     ISBN 0-313-22632-6.
     SERIES BOOKS; PSEUDONYMS

426. JOHNSON, Ferne [editor]. Start Early for an Early Start: You and the Young Child. Chicago: American Library Association, 1976. Paper. 181p.
     Extensive reading lists and suggestions for developing readers. ISBN 0-8389-3185-5.
     ACTIVE READERS, DEVELOPING

427. JOHNSON, James P. [compiler]. Africana for Children and Young People: A Current Guide for Teachers and Librarians. Westport, CT: Greenwood Press, 1971. Paper. 172p. Special Bibliographic Series, Vol. 8, No. 1.
     ISBN 0-8371-6261-0.
     AFRICA

428. JONES, Cornelia, and Olivia R. Way. British Children's Authors: Interviews at Home. Chicago: American Library Association, 1976. 192p.
     The philosophies, methods of working, and personalities of twenty British authors and illustrators. ISBN 0-8389-0224-3.
     AUTHORS; ILLUSTRATORS; BRITAIN

429. JONES, Dolores Blythe [editor]. Children's Literature Awards and Winners: A Directory of Prizes, Authors, and Illustrators. Supplement. Detroit: Gale Research Co., 1984. Paper. 136p. First edition, ©1983, current up to 1980; 495p.
     ISBN 0-8103-0171-7.
     AWARDS

430. JORDAN, Alice M. Children's Classics: With Lists of Recommended Editions by Paul Heins. Fifth edition. Boston: Horn Book, 1976. Illus. Paper. 16p. Appeared first as an article in The Horn Book, February 1947, as a booklist prepared by Alice M. Jordan. Revisions in 1952, 1960, and 1967 were by Helen Adams.
     Purpose is to serve as an aid in selecting editions of the classics for purchase by school or public libraries. See

also MANTHORNE, Jane. ISBN 0-87675-136-2.
CLASSICS

431. JORDAN, Lois B. Mexican Americans: Resources to Build
Cultural Understanding. Littleton, CO: Libraries Unlimited,
1973. 265p.
Selective annotated bibliography of print and nonprint
materials for young adults. Approximately 1,028 titles of
biography, fiction, history, and the arts. Author, title,
subject indexes. ISBN 0-87287-059-6.
MEXICAN AMERICAN

JUNIOR AUTHORS AND ILLUSTRATORS SERIES see
HOLTZE, Sally Holmes; DEMONTREVILLE, Doris; FULLER,
Muriel; KUNITZ, Stanley J.

JUNIOR HIGH SCHOOL LIBRARY CATALOG, Fourth edition
see BOGART, Gary L.

432. KAMENETSKY, Christa. Children's Literature in Hitler's
Germany: The Cultural Policy of National Socialism. Athens,
OH: Ohio University Press, 1984. Illus. 359p.
Bibliography along with discussion. Index. ISBN 0-
8214-0688-X.
GERMANY

433. KATZ, Bill, and Ruth Fraley [editors]. Reference Services
for Children and Young Adults. New York: The Haworth
Press, 1983. The Reference Librarian Series: Nos. 7 & 8.
ISBN 0-86656-201-X.
REFERENCE

434. KATZ, Bill, and Linda Sternberg Katz. Self-Help: 1400
Best Books on Personal Growth. New York: R. R. Bowker,
1985. 379p.
Fully annotated listing on books published from 1980 to
1984 on a broad range of self-help topics: including careers,
grooming, well-being. Detailed Table of Contents. ISBN 0-
8352-1939-9.
SELF-HELP

435. _____. How-To: 1400 Best Books on Doing Almost Everything. New York: R. R. Bowker, 1985. 377p.
Fully annotated listing of titles published from 1980 to
1984 on a broad range of how-to activities that young people
enjoy. Detailed table of contents. ISBN 0-8352-1927-5.
HOW TO

436. KEATING, Charlotte Matthews. Building Bridges of Understanding Between Cultures. Tucson, AZ: Palo Verde

Publishing Co., Inc. 1971. 233p. Outgrowth of and companion to Building Bridges of Understanding [1967; LC 67-
27778].
    Approximately 575 books in twelve categories arranged
by three broad school levels. Author and title indexes.
LC 72-147259.
    MULTIETHNIC

437. KELLY, R. Gordon [editor]. Children's Periodicals of the
      United States. Westport, CT: Greenwood Press, 1984.
      688p. Historical Guides to the World's Periodicals and News-
      papers series.
          Bibliography; index. ISBN 0-313-22117-0.
          PERIODICALS

438. _____. Mother Was a Lady: Self and Society in Selected
      American Children's Periodicals, 1865-1890. Westport, CT:
      Greenwood Press, 1974. Illus. 233p.
          Presents a study of social factors that are mirrored by
      writers for children. ISBN 0-8371-6451-6.
          PERIODICALS

439. KENNEDY, Carol J. [editor]. Child Drama: A Selected and
      Annotated Bibliography, 1974-1979. Washington, DC: Chil-
      dren's Theatre Association of America, 1981. Paper.
          ISBN 0-940528-21-5.
          DRAMATIC LITERATURE

440. KERLAN, Irvin. Newbery and Caldecott Awards: A Bibliog-
      raphy of First Editions. Introduction by Frederic G. Melcher.
      Minneapolis: University of Minnesota Press, 1949. 51p.
          A descriptive bibliography covering Newbery Medal
      Award books, 1922-1949, and Caldecott Medal Award books,
      1938-1949.
          AWARDS

441. KIEFER, Monica. American Children Through Their Books,
      1700-1835. Foreword by Dorothy Canfield Fisher. Philadel-
      phia: University of Pennsylvania Press, 1948. Illus. 248p.
          Covers the "book-diet" of "long ago children" by trac-
      ing the "changing status of the American child in the Colonial
      and National Periods."
          CHILDREN'S LITERATURE, HISTORY & CRITICISM

442. KIMBALL, Judith A. Children's Caravan: A Reading Activ-
      ities Idea Book for Use with Children. Phoenix, AZ: Oryx
      Press, 1983. Illus. Paper. 75p. A Fun With Reading Book.
          Includes bibliographies. ISBN 0-89774-043-2.
          ACTIVE READERS, DEVELOPING

443. KIMMEL, Margaret Mary, and Elizabeth Segel. For Read-
      ing Out Loud! A Guide to Sharing Books with Children.

Foreword by Betsy Byars. Illustrated by Trina Schart Hyman. New York: Delacorte Press, 1983. 230p.
Describes approximately 140 favorite titles while explaining the importance of reading aloud. ISBN 0-385-28304-0.
READING ALOUD

444. KINGMAN, Lee; Joanna Foster; and Ruth Giles Lontoft [compilers]. Illustrators of Children's Books, 1957-1966. Boston: The Horn Book, 1968. Illus. 295p. One of a series.
Biographies and critical analysis of work of illustrators active from 1957 to 1966. LC 47-31264.
ILLUSTRATORS

445. _____. The Illustrator's Notebook. Boston: Horn Book, Inc., 1978. Illus. 153p.
Articles about and by illustrators of children's books. Index. Bibliography of each body of work. ISBN 0-87675-013-7.
ILLUSTRATORS

446. _____. Newbery and Caldecott Medal Books: 1956-1965. "Origin of Newbery and Caldecott Medals" by Frederic G. Melcher. "Twenty Medal Books: In Perspective" by Elizabeth H. Gross. Boston: Horn Book, 1965. Illus. 300p.
ISBN 0-87675-002-1.
AWARDS

447. _____. Newbery and Caldecott Medal Books: 1966-1975. Boston: Horn Book, 1975. Illus. 321p. Fourth in the Series [See also MILLER, Bertha].
Format follows for series: a book note, excerpts from the book, the award acceptance by the author/illustrator, and biographical sketch of the award recipient. ISBN 0-87675-003-X.
AWARDS

110. KINGSTON, Carolyn T. The Tragic Mode in Children's Literature. New York: Teachers College Press, 1974. 177p.
New Aims in Children's Literature Series.
Analysis of books along thematic content. LC 73-14665.
CHILDREN'S LITERATURE, HISTORY & CRITICISM

449. KIRCHER, Clara J. [compiler]. Behavior Patterns in Children's Books: A Bibliography. Washington, DC: The Catholic University of America Press, 1966. 132p.
Replacement for "Character Formation Through Books: An Application of Bibliotherapy to the Behavior Problems of Childhood," which discussed 386 titles.
This volume treats 507 titles, preschool to grade nine. LC 66-18693.
BIBLIOTHERAPY

74   Once Upon

450. KIRKPATRICK, Daniel. Twentieth-Century Children's Writ-
      ers. Second edition. New York: St. Martin's Press, 1983.
      1024p. First edition ©1978, 1507p.
         Writers included are "the main 20th-century contribu-
      tors, in English, of fiction, poetry and drama for children
      and young people." Entries include a biography, a fully
      annotated list of books published and a signed critical essay.
      Living writers were invited to make a comment on their work.
      Appendix lists major nineteenth-century writers. ISBN 0-
      312-82413-0.
         AUTHORS

451. KISTER, Kenneth F. Dictionary Buying Guide: A Consumer
      Guide to General English Language Wordbooks in Print. New
      York: R. R. Bowker, 1977. 358p.
         Sections on dictionaries for use in secondary, middle,
      and elementary school and for use by preschool children.
      Also includes English-as-a-foreign-language dictionaries,
      special-purpose dictionaries and wordbooks. ISBN 0-8352-
      1038-3.
         DICTIONARIES

452. _____. Encyclopedia Buying Guide: A Consumer Guide
      to General Encyclopedias in Print. Third edition. New York:
      R. R. Bowker, 1981. 530p.
         Issued every three years. Series originally titled
      General Encyclopedias in Print. Now grouped in user cate-
      gories. Section V covers multivolume young adult encyclo-
      pedias; Section VI covers multivolume children's encyclopedias;
      Section VII covers small-volume young adult and children's
      encyclopedias. Title-subject index. ISBN 0-8352-1353-6;
      ISBN 0-8352-1409-5 paper.
         ENCYCLOPEDIAS

453. KLEMIN, Diana. The Art of Art for Children's Books: A
      Contemporary Survey. Greenwich, CT: Murton Press, 1982.
      Paper. Illus. 128p. First published, New York: Clarkson
      N. Potter, 1966.
         Is concerned with "the concepts that lie behind the il-
      lustrated book for children." Analysis of 57 artists. Gen-
      eral index. ISBN 0-9608042-0-X.
         ILLUSTRATORS

454. _____. The Illustrated Book: Its Art and Craft. Green-
      wich, CT: Murton Press, 1983. Paper. 167p. First pub-
      lished, New York: Clarkson N. Potter, 1970.
         ISBN 0-9608042-1-8.
         ILLUSTRATION

455. KLIATT YOUNG ADULT Paperback Book Guide.
         Published eight times a year by Kliatt Paperback Book

Guide. Each issue contains critical, descriptive reviews of current YA paperbacks.
PAPERBOUND; YOUNG ADULTS

456. KLOET, Christine A. After "Alice". A Hundred Years of Children's Reading in Britain. Phoenix: Oryx Press, 1977. Paper. 64p. Published by the Library Association, London. Selective, critical, annotated bibliography of books for children. ISBN 0-85365-740-8.
BRITAIN

457. KOHN, Rita [compiler]. Mythology for Young People: A Reference Guide. New York: Garland Publishing, Inc., 1985. 240p.
Bibliography of titles for preschool to young adult under national and topical groupings. Author-illustrator index. Extensive section on skylore by Carl J. Wenning. ISBN 0-8240-8714-3.
MYTHS

457a. _____; Mary Fortney; Catherine Hanley Lutholtz, and Dennis Kelly. Discovering Citizenship Through Family Heritage: A K-3 Resource.... Forthcoming.
Specially prepared for the dual bicentennials of the U.S. Constitution and the Northwest Ordinance of 1787, the thrust is for books emphasizing family and cultural heritage. ISBN [forthcoming].
CITIZENSHIP; FAMILY; CONTEMPORARY ISSUES

458. KREADY, Laura F. A Study of Fairy Tales. Boston: Houghton Mifflin Co., 1916. 313p.
An overview, describing principles of selection, storytelling, history, and sources. Includes synopses of tales suited for dramatization. Index.
FAIRY TALES

459. KREIDER, Barbara. Index to Children's Plays in Collections. Second edition. Metuchen, NJ: Scarecrow Press, 1976. 138p. First edition ©1972, 138p.
Second edition covers 1965 to 1974 and includes one-act plays, skits, monologues, and dialogs, for a total of 950 plays from 42 collections.
First edition contains 500 one-act plays and skits in the English language from 25 collections published between 1965 and 1969.
Both provide a cast analysis and a combined author, title and subject index and a collections index. See TREFNY, Beverly Robin, for third edition. ISBN 0-8108-0494-6 [1972]; ISBN 0-8108-0992-3 [1976].
DRAMATIC LITERATURE

460. KUJOTH, Jean Spealman. Best Selling Children's Books.
      Metuchen, NJ: Scarecrow Press, 1973. 305p.
          A survey to determine which books have influenced
      the most people during the impressionable years of childhood.
      Approximately 1,000 best sellers are discussed. ISBN 0-
      8108-0571-5.
      BEST-SELLING BOOKS

461. KUNITZ, Stanley Jasspon, and Howard Haycraft [editors].
      The Junior Book of Authors. Second edition revised. New
      York: H. W. Wilson, 1951. Illus. 309p. First edition pub-
      lished 1934, with 268 sketches.
          Second edition repeated 160 authors from first edition
      and added 129 new names.
          List of death dates begins with the sixth printing,
      ©1970. ISBN 0-8242-0028-4.
      AUTHORS

462. KUSNETZ, Len. Your Child Can Be a Super Reader: A
      Fun and Easy Approach to Reading Improvement. Illustrated
      by Shelley Kusnetz. Roslyn Heights, NY: Learning House
      Publishers, 1980; 1982. Paper. 143p.
          Includes lists of good books for young readers in three
      basic categories: First books, fiction and non-fiction; and
      discusses magazines. ISBN 0-9602730-0-X.
      ACTIVE READERS, DEVELOPING

463. LA BEAU, Dennis [editor]. Children's Authors and Illus-
      trators: An Index to Biographical Dictionaries. First edi-
      tion. Detroit: Gale Research Co., 1976. 172p. Gale Bio-
      graphical Index Series No. 2.
          Cites 17,686 biographical sketches in 26 biographical
      dictionaries and other reference sources emphasizing twentieth-
      century writers and illustrators.
          [See also SARKISSIAN, Adele] ISBN 0-8103-1078-3.
      AUTHORS; ILLUSTRATORS; BIOGRAPHICAL DICTION-
      ARIES

464. LAI NAM CHEN. Images of Southeast Asia in Children's Fic-
      tion. Singapore: Singapore University Press, 1981. Paper.
      Illus. 114p.
          Study based on critical reading of some 150 titles which
      are described in the annotated bibliography [beware of er-
      rors]. ISBN 9971-69-042-X.
      ASIA

465. LAMME, Linda Leonard. Learning to Love Literature: Pre-
      school through Grade 3. Urbana, IL: National Council of
      Teachers of English, 1981. 98p.

Includes bibliographies. ISBN 0-8141-2787-8.
ACTIVE READERS, DEVELOPING

466. _____, with Vivian Cox; Jane Matanzo; and Miken Olson. Raising Readers: A Guide to Sharing Literature with Young Children. New York: Walker and Co., 1980. 200p.
Compiled in conjunction with the National Council of Teachers of English by its Committee on Literature in the Elementary Language Arts.
Includes selected books and magazines. Multiple indexes. ISBN 0-8027-0654-1.
ACTIVE READERS, DEVELOPING

467. LANDAU, Elliott D. [editor]. Teaching Children's Literature in Colleges and Universities. Urbana, IL: National Council of Teachers of English, 1968. 62p.
ISBN 0-8141-3843-5.
CHILDREN'S LITERATURE, STUDY & TEACHING

468. LANES, Selma G. The Art of Maurice Sendak. New York: Harry N. Abrams, Inc., 1980. Illus. 278p.
Retrospective and overview of Sendak's life and work. Chronology of books. Index. ISBN 0-8109-1600-2.
ILLUSTRATORS

469. _____. Down the Rabbit Hole: Adventures and Misadventures in the Realm of Children's Literature. New York: Atheneum, ©1971, ©1976. Illus. 239p.
Provocative viewpoints. ISBN 0-689-70533-6 [1976]; LC 73-135575 [1971].
CHILDREN'S LITERATURE, HISTORY & CRITICISM

470. LARRICK, Nancy. "Children's Reading" [phonodisc]. [defunct]: National Book Committee, 131949, 1964. One side, 10 inches, 33 1/3 rpm.
Contents: Mother Goose paves the way; On reading aloud; Questions lead to reading; Building a good vocabulary; Start with interests.
ACTIVE READERS, DEVELOPING

471. _____. Children's Reading Begins at Home: How Parents Can Help Their Young Children. Winston-Salem, NC: Starstream Products, 1980. Paper. 53p.
ACTIVE READERS, DEVELOPING

472. _____. A Parent's Guide to Children's Reading. Revised fifth edition. Completely Revised with Illustrations from Favorite Children's Books. Philadelphia: Westminster Press, 1983. Illus. 284p. New York: Bantam Books, 1982. 271p.
First edition, Garden City, NY: Doubleday, 1958; Revised edition, 1964; Third edition, 1969; Fourth edtion, 1975.

Bibliography arranged by subject together with ideas
for at-home reading pleasure. ISBN 0-664-32705-2; ISBN 0-
553-22705-X [Bantam].
ACTIVE READERS, DEVELOPING

473. _____. A Teacher's Guide to Children's Books. Colum-
bus, OH: Charles E. Merrill Books, 1960. Illus. 316p.
Essays on bringing children and their books together
in the elementary grades. Includes bibliographies; index.
ISBN 0-675-09984-6.
ACTIVE READERS, DEVELOPING

474. LASS-WOODFIN, Mary Jo [editor]. Books on American Indians and Eskimos: A Selection Guide for Children and
Young Adults. Chicago: American Library Association,
1978. 254p.
807 titles published between 1950 and 1970 listed by
grade level with a summary of contents and rated on specified
criteria. Subject index. ISBN 0-8389-0241-3.
AMERICAN INDIAN; ESKIMO

475. LATIMER, Bettye I. [editor]. Starting Out Right: Choosing
Books About Black People for Young Children. Washington,
D.C.: Day Care Council of America, Inc., n.d. 96p.
ISBN 0-936746-07-6.
BLACKS

476. LAUGHLIN, Mildred. Reading for Young People: The Great
Plains: North Dakota, South Dakota, Nebraska, Kansas.
Chicago: American Library Association, 1979. Paper. 159p.
Part of "Reading for Young People" series.
368 titles, in every genre, for readers from primary
grades to tenth grade, that focus on the history and character
of the region. Author, title, subject index. Directory of
regional publishers. ISBN 0-8389-0265-0.
U.S., REGIONAL LITERATURE

477. _____. Reading for Young People: The Rocky Mountains.
Chicago: American Library Association, 1980. Paper. 192p.
Part of series.
417 titles on states of Colorado, Montana, Nevada, Utah,
and Wyoming. Author, title, subject index. Directory of
regional publishers. ISBN 0-8389-0296-0.
U.S., REGIONAL LITERATURE

478. LAWRENCE, Carol; Jennabeth Hutcherson; and James L.
Thomas [editors]. Storytelling for Teachers and School Library Media Specialists. Minneapolis: T. S. Denison, 1981.
56p.
Includes bibliography with techniques. Title on cover
reads: "Storytelling for Teachers and Media Specialists."
STORYTELLING

479. LEESON, Robert. Edited by the Children's Rights Workshop.
      Children's Books and Class Society: Past and Present.
      London: Writers & Readers Publishing Cooperative, 1977.
      Paper. 65p. Papers on Children's Literature No. 3.
      Discusses class-biased view of the world as "messages"
      in literature for children. ISBN 0-904613-37-2.
      CLASS BIAS

480. LEHMANN, Terry, and Joi Nobisso. How to Fill an Empty
      Lap: A Bibliography of Picture Books. Water Mill, NY:
      Little Feat, 1980. Illus. Paper. 32p.
      ISBN 0-940112-00-0.
      PICTURE BOOKS

481. LEIF, Irving P. Children's Literature: A Historical and
      Contemporary Bibliography. Troy, NY: Whitston Publish-
      ers, 1977. 338p.
      Trends and history of children's literature today, in
      general and in 31 countries; bibliographic aids for identifying
      early children's books; general biographies and critiques of
      authors and illustrators. Index. ISBN 0-685-88021-4 [ISBN
      0-87875-090-0, 1977 imprint].
      CHILDREN'S LITERATURE, HISTORY AND CRITICISM;
      AUTHORS; ILLUSTRATORS

482. L'ENGLE, Madeleine, and Avery Brooke. Trailing Clouds of
      Glory: Spiritual Values in Children's Books. Philadelphia:
      Westminster Press, 1985. 256p.
      Discussion of "love, commitment, courage, goodness,
      reverence, rejuvenation, punishment, the sense of wonder,
      and faith as they appear in books and in life." Excerpts
      from books cited. ISBN 0-664-32721-4.
      SPIRITUAL VALUES

483. LENZ, Millicent, and Ramona Mahood [editors]. Young Adult
      Literature: Background and Criticism. Chicago: American
      Library Association, 1981 [1980]. 516p.
      A collection of articles and essays. ISBN 0-8389-0302-9.
      YOUNG ADULT

484. LEONARD, Charlotte. Tied Together: Topics and Thoughts
      for Introducing Children's Books. Metuchen, NJ: Scarecrow
      Press, 1980. 261p.
      Ideas for introducing fiction. Approximately 60 titles
      are cited under six broad categories: Outdoors, animals,
      holidays and seasons, family, leisure, and miscellaneous.
      Index to titles, authors, illustrators. ISBN 0-8108-1293-2.
      FICTION

485. LEONARD, Phyllis B. Choose, Use, Enjoy, Share: Library
      Media Skills for the Gifted Child. Paula Kay Montgomery,

editor.   Littleton, CO: Libraries Unlimited, 1985.   153p.
Develops concepts of library and literary skills for
gifted students in the elementary grades.   Bibliographies.
Index.   ISBN 0-87287-4176.
GIFTED

486. _____. For Younger Readers: Braille and Talking Books.
Compiled by National Library Service for the Blind and
Physically Handicapped.   Washington, DC: Library of Congress, biennial.   Paper.   First published 1964 by the American Foundation for the Blind.
Lists Braille, disc and cassette books which have been
announced in Braille Book Review and Talking Book Topics,
by grade and subject areas.   Includes a Spanish-language
section.   Author and title indexes.   ISSN 0093-2825.
TALKING BOOKS; BRAILLE BOOKS

487. LiBRETTO, Ellen V. [compiler and editor]. High/Low Handbook: Books, Materials and Services for the Teenage Problem Reader. Second edition.   New York: R. R. Bowker,
1985.   286p.   First edition ©1981, 210p.
A volume in the Serving Special Populations series.
Full data and plot synopsis of 175 recommended fiction and
nonfiction high/low titles-in-print, with reading levels 1-4,
as a core collection.   Also includes a list as a supplement to
the core collection, and bibliographies and sources of current
reviews.   Title and subject indexes.   ISBN 0-8352-1340-4.
HIGH/LOW

488. _____. New Directions for Young Adult Services. New
York: R. R. Bowker, 1983.   250p.
Of special interest is the section on developing collec-
tions for non-English speaking young adults.   ISBN 0-8352-
1684-5.
NON-ENGLISH SPEAKING; YOUNG ADULT

489. LICKTEIG, Mary J. An Introduction to Children's Literature.
Columbus, OH: Charles E. Merrill Publishing Co., 1975.
Illus.   448p.
Covers full range and lists titles by reading level.
Index.   ISBN 0-675-08716-3.
CHILDREN'S LITERATURE, TEXTBOOKS ON

490. LIMA, Carolyn W. A to Zoo: Subject Access to Children's
Picture Books. Second edition.   New York: R. R. Bowker,
1985.   656p.   First edition ©1982, 464p.
Over 5,000 titles, cataloged under 543 subjects, for
preschool to grade two.   Indexes.   ISBN 0-8352-1400-1.
PICTURE BOOKS

491. LINDER, Leslie. The Art of Beatrix Potter. Revised edition.

An Appreciation by Anne Carroll Moore. Notes to each Section by Enid and Leslie Linder. New York & London: Frederick Warne & Co., 1972. Illus. 406p. First published 1955.
Covers the span of Potter's career. ISBN 0-7232-1457-3.
ILLUSTRATORS

492. _____. The History of the Tale of Peter Rabbit. Anne Emerson, editor. London: Frederick Warne & Co., 1977. Illus.
ISBN 0-7232-1988-5.
PICTURE BOOKS

492a. _____. A History of the Writings of Beatrix Potter; Including Unpublished Work. London: Frederick Warne & Co., 1981. Illus. 446p.
Comprehensive coverage. ISBN 0-7232-1334-8.
AUTHORS; ILLUSTRATORS

493. LINDSKOOG, John, and Kathryn Lindskoog. How to Grow a Young Reader: A Parent's Guide to Kids and Books. Elgin, IL: David Cook, 1978. Paper.
ISBN 0-89191-115-4.
ACTIVE READERS, DEVELOPING

494. A LITTLE PRETTY POCKET-BOOK: John Newbery. Introduced by M. F. Thwaite. New York: Harcourt, Brace & World, 1967. Illus. 184p. First published London: Oxford University Press, 1966.
Bibliography. Index.
FACSIMILE EDITION; CHILDREN'S LITERATURE, HISTORY & CRITICISM; PUBLISHING

495. LIVINGOOD, W. W. [compiler]. Americana as Taught to the Tune of the Hickory Stick. Introduction by Mary Ellen Chase. New York: Women's National Book Association, 1954. 72p [plus 22 pages of advertisements].
Covers readers, spellers, arithmetics, geographies, and United States histories.
U.S., CHILDREN'S TEXTBOOKS

496. LOCHHEAD, Marion. Renaissance of Wonder: The Fantasy Worlds of C. S. Lewis, J. R. R. Tolkien, George MacDonald, E. Nesbit, and Others. San Francisco: Harper & Row, 1980. First published, Edinburgh: Canongate, 1977 under the title The Renaissance of Wonder in Children's Literature.
A study of fantasy writing, primarily British. Bibliographical references; index. ISBN 0-06-250520-3.
FANTASY

497. LONDSDALE, Bernard J., and Helen K. Mackintosh. Children Experience Literature. New York: Random House, 1973. Illus. 540p.
     Full scope textbook. General index. ISBN 0-394-30368-7.
     CHILDREN'S LITERATURE, TEXTBOOKS ON

498. LUCAS, Linda, and Marilyn H. Karrenbrock. The Disabled Child in the Library: Moving into the Mainstream. Littleton, CO: Libraries Unlimited, 1983. 288p.
     Basic information on resources and materials and methods of planning for serving the disabled child. ISBN 0-87287-355-2.
     DISABILITIES

499. LUECKE, Fritz J. [compiler]. Children's Books: Views and Values. Middletown, CT: Xerox Education Publications, 1973. 86p.
     Addresses, essays, and lectures by authors and critics. Includes bibliographic references.
     CHILDREN'S LITERATURE, HISTORY & CRITICISM

500. LUKENS, Rebecca J. A Critical Handbook of Children's Literature. Second edition. Glenview, IL: Scott, Foresman, 1982. Paper. 264p. First edition ©1976.
     Discusses critical standards regarding genre, character, plot, setting, theme, point of view, style, tone, poetry, and nonfiction. Bibliographies. Index. ISBN 0-673-15504-1 paper.
     CHILDREN'S LITERATURE, TEXTBOOKS ON

501. LYNN, Ruth Nadelman. Fantasy for Children: An Annotated Checklist. Second edition. New York: R. R. Bowker, 1983. 444p. First edition ©1979, 350p.
     Comprehensive guide to over 2,000 recommended titles for children in grades 3 to 8. Includes sequels. Arrangement is by type of fantasy with cross-references. Titles available in the United Kingdom and the United States. Indexes. ISBN 0-8352-1732-9 [1983]; ISBN 0-8352-1232-7 [1979].
     FANTASY

502. LYSTAD, Mary. At Home in America: As Seen Through Its Books for Children. Cambridge, MA: Schenkman, 1983. 154p.
     Originally appeared in Children Today, March-April, 1979. ISBN 0-87073-378-8; ISBN 0-87073-379-6 [paper].
     U.S., SOCIAL LIFE

503. _____. From Dr. Mather to Dr. Seuss: Two Hundred Years of American Books for Children. Cambridge, MA: Schenman, 1980. 320p.

Traces development of American social values and behavior on the assumption that books for children reflect the
attitudes and concerns of a people. ISBN 0-87073-210-2
paper.
U.S., SOCIAL LIFE

504. McANDREW, William J., and Peter J. Elliott. Teaching Canada: A Bibliography. Second revised edition. University
of Maine at Orono: NEAPQ (New England-Atlantic Provinces-
Quebec Center), 1974. 102p. First edition ©1971.
Resource bibliography covering fiction, poetry, prose,
drama, and criticism. Includes serials.
CANADA

505. McCULLOCH, Lou W. Children's Books of the Nineteenth
Century. Lombard, IL: Wallace-Homestead Book Co., 1978.
Illus. 152p.
Includes bibliographies and index. ISBN 0-685-50770-X.
CHILDREN'S LITERATURE, HISTORY & CRITICISM

506. McDONOUGH, Irma [editor]. Canadian Books for Children.
Toronto: University of Toronto Press, 1976. Paper. 112p.
Separate listings for French and English language
books. ISBN 0-8020-4547-2.
CANADA

507. _____. Canadian Books for Young People. Toronto: University of Toronto Press, 1980. Illus. Paper. 205p. First
published 1976. Revision ©1978. A revision and expansion
of Canadian Books for Children.
Selected books in print and magazines on a range of
subjects and by grade levels in French and English. ISBN
0-8020-4594-4.
CANADA

508. _____. Profiles: Authors and Illustrators, Children's
Literature in Canada. Ottawa: Canadian Library Association,
1975. Paper. 159p.
44 sketches originally in In Review. ISBN 0-88802-
109-7.
CANADA

509. _____. Profiles 2: Authors and Illustrators, Children's
Literature in Canada. Ottawa: Canadian Library Association,
1982. Paper. 170p.
45 informal biographical sketches originally in In Review.
ISBN 0-88802-163-1.
CANADA

510.   McGOVERN, Edythe M.   They're Never Too Young for Books:
       Literature for Pre-Schoolers.   Los Angeles, CA: Mar Vista,
       1980.   Paper.   294p.
           ISBN 0-9604064-0-9.
           PRESCHOOL

511.   McGUFFEY.   Old Favorites from the McGuffey Readers.
       Edited by Harvey C. Minnich.   Detroit: Singing Tree
       Press, 1969.   Illus.   482p.   First published, New York:
       American Book Company, from 1836-1936.
           Contains material from each of the six readers.   ISBN
       0-8103-3854-8.
           FACSIMILE EDITIONS

512.   McLEAN, Ruari [editor].   The Noah's Ark A.B.C. and 8
       Other Victorian Alphabet Books in Color.   New York:
       Dover, 1976.
           FACSIMILE EDITIONS; ALPHABET BOOKS

513.   McMULLEN, Kate Hall.   How to Choose Good Books for Kids.
       Reading, MA: Addison Wesley Publishing Co., 1984.   Paper.
       Illus.   80p.   Part of "Kids' Care Series."
           Describes important components of good books for
       young readers, gives hints for motivating beginning readers,
       and lists special titles for the problem reader.   Index.
       ISBN 0-201-10809-7.
           SELECTION GUIDE

514.   MacCANN, Donnarae, and Olga Richard.   The Child's First
       Books; A Critical Study of Pictures and Texts.   New York:
       H. W. Wilson Co., 1973.   Illus.   135p.
           Includes historical perspective, stereotypes in illustra-
       tion, graphic elements, outstanding contemporary illustrators,
       book design, literary elements, outstanding contemporary il-
       lustrators, book design, literary elements, outstanding nar-
       rative writers, and specialized texts in discussion of titles.
       Index.   ISBN 0-8242-0501-4.
           PICTURE BOOKS; ILLUSTRATION

515.   _____, and Gloria Woodard [editors].   The Black American
       in Books for Children; Readings in Racism.   Second edition.
       Metuchen, NJ: Scarecrow Press, 1985.   310p.   First edition
       1972.
           Addresses, essays and lectures on Black perspective:
       the basic criterion; Racism in Newbery Prize Books; Modern
       and early examples; Racism and publishing.   Index.   ISBN
       0-8108-0526-X [1972]; ISBN 0-8108-1826-4 [1985].
           BLACKS

516. _____. Cultural Conformity in Books for Children: Further Readings in Racism. Metuchen, NJ: Scarecrow Press, 1977. 215p.
     ISBN 0-8108-1064-6.
     BLACKS

517. MacDONALD, Margaret Read. The Storyteller's Sourcebook: A Subject, Title and Motif Index to Folklore Collections for Children. Detroit: Neal-Schuman Pub., Inc. in association with Gale Research Co., 1982. 818p.
     Indexes 556 folktale collections and 389 picture books. Includes an ethnic and geographic index, along with indexes of motif and titles. ISBN 0-8103-0471-6.
     STORYTELLING; FOLKLORE

518. MacLEOD, Anne Scott [editor]. Children's Literature: Selected Essays and Bibliographies. College Park: College of Library and Information Services, University of Maryland, 1977. Paper. 153p. Student Contribution Series, No. 9. ISBN 0-911808-13-2.
     CHILDREN'S LITERATURE, HISTORY & CRITICISM

519. _____. A Moral Tale: Children's Fiction: American Culture, 1820-1860. Hamden, CT: Archon Books, 1975. 196p.
     ISBN 0-208-01552-3.
     FICTION

520. MacPHERSON, Maud Russel [compiler]. Children's Poetry Index. Boston: F. W. Faxon Co., 1938. 453p.
     Index to 50 collections of poetry in 61 volumes, published between 1907 and 1935. Over 12,000 poems are entered under author, title, and subject.
     POETRY

521. MAGUIRE, Jack. Creative Storytelling: Choosing, Inventing and Sharing Tales for Children. Illus. by Dale Gottlieb. New York: McGraw-Hill, 1985. 189p.
     Especially targeted for parents, emphasis is on lists of stories and collections. No index. ISBN 0-07-039512-8 paper; ISBN 0-07-039513-6.
     STORYTELLING

MAHONY, Bertha E. see also MILLER, Bertha Mahony

522. MAHONY, Bertha E.; Louise Payson Latimer; and Beulah Folmsbee [compilers]. Illustrators of Children's Books, 1744-1945. Boston: Horn Book, 1947. Illus. 527p. One of series. Superseded Contemporary Illustrators of Children's Books, ©1930.
     Brief biographies with listings of works. Multiple indexes. ISBN 0-87675-015-3.
     ILLUSTRATORS

523. MAHONEY, Ellen, and Leah Wilcox. Ready, Set, Read: Best
      Books to Prepare Preschoolers. Metuchen, NJ: Scarecrow
      Press, 1985. 363p.
            Recommended titles. Author and title indexes. ISBN
      0-8108-1684-9.
            PRESCHOOL

524. MALLET, Carl-Heinz. Fairy Tales and Children: The Psy-
      chology of Children Revealed Through Four of Grimm's Fairy
      Tales. Translated by Joachim Neugroschel. New York:
      Schocken Books, Inc., 1984. 256p.
            Contextual analysis of "Little Red Riding Hood," "Han-
      sel and Gretel," "The Goose Girl," and "The Boy Who Set
      Out to Learn Fear." ISBN 0-8052-3897-2.
            FAIRY TALES

525. MANTHORNE, Jane [compiler]. Children's Classics: With
      Lists of Recommended Editions. Boston: Horn Book, 1982.
      Paper. [See also JORDAN, Alice M.]
            ISBN 0-87615-139-X.
            CLASSICS

526. MARSHAK, Bonnie [compiler]. Antiquarian Books for Chil-
      dren: A Catalogue of Catalogues. Revised edition. Green-
      vale, NY: Long Island University, 1983. Paper. 21p.
      First published 1981.
            SPECIAL COLLECTIONS

527. MARSHALL, Margaret Richardson. An Introduction to the
      World of Children's Books. Brookfield, VT: Gower Publish-
      ing Co., 1982. 189p. "A Grafton Book"
            Includes bibliographies. Index. ISBN 0-566-03437-9.
            PUBLISHING; CHILDREN'S LITERATURE, HISTORY &
      CRITICISM

528. MATTHIAS, Margaret, and Diane Thiessen. Children's
      Mathematics Books: A Critical Bibliography. Chicago:
      American Library Association, 1979. Paper. 68p.
            200 tradebooks on math for preschool to grade six, in
      general categories: counting, geometry, measurement, num-
      ber concepts, time. Author, title index. ISBN 0-8389-0285-5.
            MATHEMATICS

529. MEACHAM, Mary. Information Sources in Children's Litera-
      ture: A Practical Reference Guide for Children's Librarians,
      Elementary School Teachers, and Students of Children's Lit-
      erature. Westport, CT: Greenwood Press, 1978. Illus.
      256p. Contributions in Librarianship and Information Science,
      #24.
            Comprehensive bibliography of bibliographies. Criteria
      for evaluating a children's book and building the basic

collection. ISBN 0-313-20045-9.
BIBLIOGRAPHY OF BIBLIOGRAPHIES

530. _____. Reading for Young People: The Northwest.
Chicago: American Library Association, 1981. Paper. 152p.
277 titles on Alaska, Idaho, Oregon, Washington.
Directory of Regional Publishers and Local Book Sources.
Author, title, subject index. ISBN 0-8389-0318-5.
U.S., REGIONAL LITERATURE

531. MEADE, Richard, and Robert Small [editors]. Literature for
Adolescents: Selection and Use. Columbus, OH: Merrill
Publishing Co., 1973. 304p.
Includes bibliographies. ISBN 0-675-09035-0.
YOUNG ADULTS

532. MEALY, Virginia T. From Reader to Writer: Creative Writing in the Middle Grades Using Picture Books. Metuchen,
NJ: Scarecrow Press, 1986. 179p.
Activities presented by months (September-May) and
grade level (4th-6th). Author, title, subject index. ISBN
0-8108-1882-5.
CREATIVE WRITING; MIDDLE GRADES; PICTURE BOOKS

533. MEEK, Margaret; Aidan Warlow; and Griselda Barton [editors].
The Cool Web: The Pattern of Children's Reading. New
York: Atheneum, 1978. 427p.
50 essays, linked by critical commentaries, that show
the critical nature of stories in a child's development. Bibliography. Index. ISBN 0-689-10834-6.
CHILDREN'S LITERATURE, HISTORY & CRITICISM

534. MEIGS, Cornelia Lynde; Anne Eaton; Elizabeth Nesbitt; and
Ruth Hill Viguers. A Critical History of Children's Literature.
Revised edition. Decorations by Vera Bock. New York:
Macmillan, 1969. Illus. 708p. First edition ©1953.
A survey of children's books in English published in
the U.S.A. and Great Britain up to 1967. ISBN 0-02-
583900-4.
CHILDREN'S LITERATURE, HISTORY & CRITICISM

535. MERTINS, Barbara [editor]. Reading for Young People:
Kentucky, Tennessee, West Virginia. Chicago: American
Library Association, 1985. Paper. 157p. Part of series.
300 books on the region selected by librarians. ISBN
0-8389-0426-2.
U.S., REGIONAL LITERATURE

536. METZNER, Seymour. American History in Juvenile Books:
A Chronological Guide. New York: H. W. Wilson, 1966.
329p.

Over 2,000 fiction and nonfiction titles listed by grade levels in time periods from the Age of Discovery (800-1550) to Contemporary America (1920-1960s). Also includes anthologies, collective biographies, general histories, and multiple indexes. LC 66-12299.
AMERICAN HISTORY

537.   . World History in Juvenile Books: A Geographical and Chronological Guide. New York: H. W. Wilson, 1973. 356p.
Companion to American History in Juvenile Books. Approximately 2,700 titles relating to political and social aspects of world history for elementary and junior high school age readers. Multiple indexes. ISBN 0-8242-0441-7.
WORLD HISTORY

538. MEYER, Susan E. A Treasury of the Great Children's Book Illustrators. New York: Harry N. Abrams, 1983. Illus. 272p.
Thirteen artists, including Randolph Caldecott, Walter Crane, Kate Greenaway, Beatrix Potter, Arthur Rackham, John Tenniel, and N. C. Wyeth. ISBN 0-8109-0782-8.
ILLUSTRATORS

539. MILLER, Bertha Mahoney, and Elinor Whitney Field [editors]. Caldecott Medal Books: 1938-1957. Boston: Horn Book, 1957. Illus. 329p. Part of the series.
ISBN 0-87675-001-3.
AWARDS

540.   . Newbery Medal Books: 1922-1955. Boston: Horn Book, 1955. Illus. 458p. Part of the series.
ISBN 0-87675-000-5.
AWARDS

541. MILLS, Gretchen. Discussing Death: A Guide to Death Education. Homewood, IL: ETC Publications, 1976. 140p.
Titles recommended for various concepts at each age level.
DEATH

542. MILLS, Joyce White [editor]. The Black World in Literature for Children: A Bibliography of Print and Nonprint Materials. Atlanta, GA: Atlanta University [School of Library Service], Vol. I, 1975, 42p.; Vol. II, 1976, 45p.; Vol. III, 1977, 56p.
For children ages 3 to 8, titles rated and briefly described.
BLACKS

543. MONSON, Dianne L., and DayAnn McClenathan [editors]. Developing Active Readers: Ideas for Parents, Teachers,

Librarians. Newark, DE: International Reading Association,
1979. Paper. 104p.
   Part I covers ideas for book selection and introduction
of the child to the library. Part II covers ways to help children respond to literature and become book people. ISBN
0-87207-727-6.
      ACTIVE READERS, DEVELOPING

544. MONSON, Dianne L., and Betty J. Peltola. Research in
Children's Literature: An Annotated Bibliography. Newark,
DE: International Reading Association, 1976. Paper. 98p.
   332 entries that include dissertations, ERIC documents,
journal articles and related studies. Index especially designed to locate studies regarding characteristics of the subjects, instruments used, and general content. ISBN 0-87207-
328-9.
      CHILDREN'S LITERATURE, RESEARCH IN

545. MONTEBELLO, Mary. Children's Literature in the Curriculum.
Dubuque, IA: W. C. Brown, 1972. 152p.
   Emphasis is on developing readers. Bibliographies.
ISBN 0-697-06204-X.
      CHILDREN'S LITERATURE, STUDY & TEACHING

546. MOODY, Mildred T., and Hilda K. Limper. Bibliotherapy:
Methods and Materials. Chicago: American Library Associa-
tion, 1971. Illus. with photographs. 161p.
   Compiled in conjunction with the Association of Hospital
and Institution Libraries. Part I covers reading as therapy;
Part II provides books for the troubled child and adolescent.
Title and author index. ISBN 0-8389-3107-3.
      BIBLIOTHERAPY

547. MOORE, Anne Carroll. My Roads to Childhood: Views and
Reviews of Children's Books. Third printing. Introduction
by Frances Clarke Sayers. Includes: Roads to Childhood
[1920]; New Roads to Childhood [1923]; Crossroads to Childhood [1926]. Boston: Horn Book, 1970. Illus. Paper.
399p. First published, New York: Doubleday, Doran and
Co., 1939. Horn Book printings 1961 and 1964.
      ISBN 0-87675-052-8.
      CHILDREN'S LITERATURE, HISTORY & CRITICISM

548. MOORE, Vardine. The Pleasure of Poetry With and By Children: A Handbook. Metuchen, NJ: Scarecrow Press, 1981.
143p.
   Emphasis is on creative uses of poetry. Bibliography.
Index. ISBN 0-8108-1399-8.
      POETRY

549. _____. Pre-school Story Hour. Second edition. Metuchen,

NJ: Scarecrow Press, 1972.   174p.   First edition ©1966.
Techniques and lists of books and recordings.   ISBN
0-8108-0474-3.
STORYTELLING

550. MORANSEE, Jess R. [editor].   Children's Prize Books: An
International Listing of 193 Children's Literature Prizes.
Second Edition Revised and Enlarged.   Introduction by Walter
Scherf.   Hamden, CT: Shoestring Press, 1983.   620p.   New
York: K. G. Sauer, 1983.   First edition, Munchen: Verlag
Dokumentation Saur KG, 1969.   Second edition, Munchen:
K. G. Saur Verlag, 1982, with title Catalogue of the Inter-
national Youth Library.
          Text is in English and German.   ISBN 0-598-03250-1.
PRIZES

551. MORRIS-VANN, Artie M.   Once Upon a Time ... A Guide to
the Use of Bibliotherapy.   Southfield, MI: Aid-U Publishing
Co., 1979.   Paper.   100p.
          ISBN 0-940370-00-X.
BIBLIOTHERAPY

552. MORTIMORE, Arthur Dennis.   Children's Literary Characters
Index, 1981:   The First Supplement to Index to Characters
in Children's Literature.   Winterbourne, Bristol, England:
D. M. Mortimore, 1981.   80p.   Part of a series.   [See below
for fuller description]   ISBN 0-9505665-1-9.
FICTION; CHARACTERS IN CHILDREN'S LITERATURE

553. _____ .   Index to Characters in Children's Literature.
Bristol, England: D. M. Mortimore, 1977.   192p.
          Selective; based on nearly 4,000 books, published in
Britain and internationally, that were available in British libraries in 1975 and 1976.   "The index lists any characters
which were considered likely to be memorable or asked for."
This includes lesser and main characters, animals, magic
creatures, mythological or historical characters and inanimate
objects.   Lists books in series.   Multiple indexes.   ISBN
0-9505665-0-0.
FICTION; CHARACTERS IN CHILDREN'S LITERATURE

554. MOSS, Elaine [compiler].   Picture Books for Young People 9
to 13.   Revised edition.   Nancy Chambers, editor.   Stroud,
Glos., England: Thimble Press, 1985.   Illus.   Paper.   47p.
A Signal Bookguide.   First edition ©1981.
          84 picture books suitable for reading by older children,
described in critical annotations.   ISBN 0-903355-07-8.
PICTURE BOOKS FOR OLDER READERS

555. _____ , and Barbara Sherrard-Smith.   Children's Books of
the Year.   Stroud, Glos, England: Thimble Press, annual.
Illus.   A Julia Macrae Book.

Selection of the "most interesting and significant" books of the year for exhibition at the National Book League in England. Index.
ANNUAL; BEST BOOKS; BRITAIN

556. MUIR, Percival Horace [compiler]. Children's Books of Yesterday. New Edition Revised and Enlarged. Detroit: Singing Tree Press, 1970.
First published, London: National Book League, 1946. ISBN 0-8103-3550-6 [Gale].
CHILDREN'S LITERATURE, HISTORY & CRITICISM; BRITAIN

557. _____. English Children's Books. Third edition. London: Batsford Ltd., 1980. Illus. 256p. First published 1954. Second edition 1969 (New York: Praeger, 1969, 256p.)
Selective, from the 1600s to the 1970s. ISBN 0-7134-2246-7.
CHILDREN'S LITERATURE, HISTORY & CRITICISM; BRITAIN

558. _____. Victorian Illustrated Books. New York: Praeger, 1971. Illus. 287p.
Includes bibliographic references. ISBN 0-275-0735-5.
CHILDREN'S LITERATURE, HISTORY & CRITICISM; BRITAIN

559. MULTI-ETHNIC MEDIA: Selected Bibliographies in Print. David Cohen, coordinator for Task Force on Ethnic Materials Information Exchange, Social Responsibilities Round Table, ALA Chicago: American Library Association, 1975. Paper. 33p.
ISBN 0-8389-3170-7.
MULTIETHNIC

560. MUTISO, Gideon-Cyrus M. Messages, an Annotated Bibliography of African Literature for Schools. Upper Montclair, NJ: Montclair State College Press, 1970.
AFRICA

NATIONAL ASSOCIATION of Independent Schools. Books for Secondary School Libraries, sixth edition see Bowker, R. R.

561. NATIONAL ASSOCIATION of State Educational Media Professionals. Aids to Media Selection for Students and Teachers. McFarland, WI: NASTEMP Division of Publications, 1985. Paper.
List of bibliographies and journals that review print,

media, and software materials for elementary and secondary
schools.
 MEDIA

562. NATIONAL CATALOG of Storytelling Resources. Jonesborough, TN: National Storytelling Resource Center, annual.
 ANNUAL; STORYTELLING

563. NATIONAL CONFERENCE of Christians and Jews (NCCJ).
The Human Family ... Understanding Other People. New
York: National Conference of Christians and Jews, annual.
Paper. Originally titled "Books for Brotherhood: An Anno-
tated Bibliography."
     Selected list of titles published between August and
July of the previous year, which "portray relationships
among people of different origins, races and religions and
depict their varied backgrounds." Suggested age levels.
 ANNUAL; MULTIETHNIC

564. NATIONAL COUNCIL of Teachers of English. Books for You:
A Booklist for Senior High Students. New Edition. Robert
C. Small, Jr., Chair, Committee on the Senior High Booklist
of NCTE. Urbana, IL: National Council of Teachers of English, 1982. Paper. 323p. Revised edition [1976] edited by
Kenneth Donelson [ISBN 0-8141-0362-6].
     Selective listing of 1,400 titles from total of 3,500 based
on the criteria of being enjoyable to read by senior high students. ISBN 0-8141-0359-6.
 SENIOR HIGH SCHOOL

565. _____. Guide to Play Selection: A Selective Bibliography
for Production and Study of Modern Plays. Third edition.
Urbana, IL: National Council of Teachers of English, 1975.
292p.
     First edition by Milton Myers Smith, ©1934; Second edi-
tion ©1958; Third edition by the Liaison Committee. ISBN
0-8352-0862-1; ISBN 0-8141-1946-8 [paper].
 DRAMATIC LITERATURE

566. _____. High Interest--Easy Reading: For Junior and
Senior High School Students. Fourth revised edition. Hugh
Agee, with the Committee to Revise High-Easy Reading. Ur-
bana, IL: National Council of Teachers of English, 1984.
Paper. 98p. First published 1967. Revised every five years.
Second edition 1972; third edition 1979.
     Approximately 400 selected titles to attract unmotivated
readers, grades 7 to 12. Indexes. ISBN 0-8141-2095-4.
 HIGH INTEREST/EASY READING

567. _____. Literature--News That Stays News: Fresh Approaches to the Classics. Candy Carter, chair, and the

Committee on Classroom Practices. Urbana, IL: National Council of Teachers of English, 1985. 120p.
 Bibliographies included with the discussion. ISBN 0-8141-3012-7.
 CLASSICS

568. _____. Poets in the Schools: A Handbook. Michael True, chair, with the Committee on Poets in the Schools. Urbana, IL: National Council of Teachers of English, 1976. Paper. 13p.
 Guidelines and bibliography.
 POETRY

569. _____. Your Reading: A Booklist for Junior High and Middle School Students. Revised edition. Jane Christensen with the Committee on the Junior High and Middle School Booklist. Urbana, IL: National Council of Teachers of English, 1984. Paper. 764 p. First published 1946. This revised edition continues the 1975 edition, Jerry L. Walker, editorial chair.
 For students in grades 7 to 9, wide interest fiction and nonfiction titles, under 45 topics. Annotated listing of over 3,000 fiction and nonfiction books. ISBN 0-8141-5938-9. [See also LAMME, Linda Leonard; TWAY, Eileen; WHITE, Mary Lou.]
 JUNIOR HIGH

570. NATIONAL COUNCIL for the Social Studies/Children's Book Council Joint Committee. Notable Children's Trade Books in the Field of Social Studies. New York: Children's Book Council, annual. Paper. Appeared first in Social Education.
 Covers American and world history and culture, biography, autobiography, folktales, legends, religion, contemporary interests and controversies, and understanding oneself and others.
 ANNUAL; SOCIAL STUDIES

571. NATIONAL EDUCATION ASSOCIATION. The Negro American in Paperback: A Selected List of Paperback Books Compiled and Annotated for Secondary School Students. Washington, DC: National Education Association, 1967.
 BLACKS

572. NATIONAL SCIENCE TEACHERS Association Book Review Subcommittee of the Joint National Science Teachers-Children's Book Council Joint Committee. Outstanding Science Trade Books for Children. New York: Children's Book Council, annual. Paper. First published annually in Science and Children.
 SCIENCE; ANNUAL

573. NEUBURG, Victor E. The Penny Histories: A Study of
      Chapbooks for Young Readers over Two Centuries: Illus-
      trated with Facsimiles of Seven Chapbooks. New York:
      Harcourt, Brace and World, 1969. Illus. 227p. First pub-
      lished, London: Oxford University Press, 1968.
            Discusses chapbooks in England and America. Bibliog-
      raphy. Index.
            FACSIMILE EDITIONS

      NEW YORK PUBLIC LIBRARY. The Black Experience in
      Children's Books see ROLLOCK, Barbara

574. _____. Books for the Teen Age. New York: New York
      Public Library, annual. Illus. Paper. Published February
      of each year since 1929.
            Titles chosen because of special interest and appeal to
      teenage readers. ISBN 0-87104-659-8 [1983]; ISBN 0-87104-
      663-6 [1984].
            TEENAGE; ANNUAL

575. _____. Children's Books ...: One Hundred Titles for
      Reading and Sharing. New York: New York Public Library,
      annual. Paper.
            Annotated list of the best selected by committee of the
      Office of Children's Services.
            BEST BOOKS; ANNUAL

576. _____. Children's Books Suggested as Holiday Gifts. New
      York: New York Public Library, annual. Paper.
            Books of the year in subject areas.
            BEST BOOKS; ANNUAL; GIFT BOOKS

577. _____. On Being Black 1985: A Selected List of Books,
      Films, Filmstrips, Recordings for Young People. New York:
      New York Public Library, 1985. Paper. 19p.
            BLACKS; YOUNG ADULT

      NEWBERY, John see A Little Pretty Pocket Book

578. NEWMAN, Joan E. Girls Are People, Too! A Bibliography
      of Nontraditional Female Roles in Children's Books. Metuchen,
      NJ: Scarecrow Press, 1982. 203p.
            Selective list of 540 fiction and nonfiction titles, pub-
      lished 1971 to 1981, that reject neither feminism nor female-
      ness. Titles are rated. Gives a chronology of notable women.
      General index. ISBN 0-8108-1500-1.
            NONSEXIST

579. NEWS AND NOTES for Children's Theatres. Rowayton, CT:
      New Plays Inc., monthly newsletter.
            Features newly published plays for children, as well as

those from the catalog. Features discuss children's books
specially suited for creative dramatics and includes signed
articles of relevance to librarians, teachers, and play directors.
DRAMATIC LITERATURE

580. NEWTON, Mary Griffin. Books for Deaf Children: A Graded,
Annotated Bibliography. Washington, D.C.: Alexander
Graham Bell Association for the Deaf, 1962. Illus. 173p.
Listing is for nursery and kindergarten through grade
nine.
DEAF

581. NICHOLS, Margaret S., and Margaret N. O'Neill. Multicultural Bibliography for Preschool Through Second Grade: In
the Areas of Black, Spanish-Speaking, Asian American and
Native American Cultures. Stanford, CA: Multicultural Resources, 1972. Paper. 40p.
Includes picture books and story books.
MULTICULTURAL

582. _____. Multicultural Resources for Children. Stanford,
CA: Multicultural Resources, 1977. 205p.
Folktales, myths, legends, picture books, early reading books, poetry, plays, collections, art and music for
preschool through elementary grades in Black, Spanish-
speaking, Asian American, Native American, and Pacific Island cultures. These materials are part of the collection
located at California State University in Hayward. Lists
distributors of children's materials in Spanish and English/
Spanish. Index.
MULTICULTURAL

583. NILSEN, Alleen Pace, and Kenneth L. Donelson. Literature
for Today's Young Adults. Second edition. Glenview, IL:
Scott, Foresman, 1985. Illus. 661p. [See DONELSON,
Kenneth L. for first edition.]
Overview of YA literature. Adds sections on Holocaust
heroes, religious themes, books on humor, poetry, and stage
and screen drama. ISBN 0-673-15933-7.
YOUNG ADULT

584. NOONAN, Eileen F. [compiler]. A Basic Book Collection for
High Schools. First to seventh editions. Chicago: American
Library Association, 1924-1963.
Titles and compilers vary, with Noonan compiler for the
seventh edition.
The list was designed "to serve as an authoritative buy-
ing guide for high school and public libraries," and served
as the model for subsequent lists. Indexes. LC 63-22445.
BASIC COLLECTION; SECONDARY SCHOOL

585.   . Books for Catholic Elementary Schools. Haverford,
PA: Catholic Library Association, 1983. Paper. 16p.
     Selective list of 100 titles for K-8 published 1981-1982
in areas of religion, fine arts, language arts, social studies,
science and mathematics. Directory of publishers. ISBN 0-
87507-024-8.
     CATHOLIC

586.   . Books for Religious Education in Catholic Secondary
Schools. Haverford, PA: Catholic Library Association,
1983. Paper. 14p.
     Selective list of 70 books for a core collection in high
school libraries in areas of reference, Bible study, biography,
catechism, Catholicism, Christology, Church history, death
and dying, marriage, morality, poetry, prayer, religions of
the world, sacraments, and saints. Directory of publishers.
     CATHOLIC

587. NORTHWEST REGIONAL Educational Laboratory, Center for
Sex Equity. Bibliography of Non-Sexist Supplementary Books
(K-12). Phoenix, AZ: Oryx Press, 1983. Paper. 144p.
     Critical discussion on gender, ethnicity, and nationality
of each major character in titles examined. Multiple indexes.
ISBN 0-89774-101-3.
     NONSEXIST

588.   . Guide to Non-Sexist Teaching Activities (K-12).
Phoenix, AZ: Oryx Press, 1984. Paper. 99p.
     Bibliographies of print and nonprint sources, listing of
sex-equity organizations and nonsexist resources. ISBN 0-
89774-100-5.
     NONSEXIST

589. NORTON, Donna E. Through the Eyes of a Child: An Introduction to Children's Literature. Columbus, OH: Charles
E. Merrill Publishing Co., 1983. Illus. 664p.
     Emphasis on evaluation, selection and sharing of chil-
dren's literature. Annual update covers research, issues,
and newly published titles for children. Annotated bibliographies; subject and author/illustrator/title indexes. ISBN
0-675-09832-7.
     CHILDREN'S LITERATURE, TEXTBOOKS ON

590. NORTON, Eloise S. Folk Literature of the British Isles:
Readings for Librarians, Teachers, and Those Who Work with
Children and Young Adults. Metuchen, NJ: Scarecrow
Press, 1978. 272p.
     ISBN 0-8108-1177-4.
     BRITAIN; FOLK LITERATURE

591. NUCLEAR INFORMATION and Resource Service. Growing Up

in a Nuclear World: Annotated Bibliography for Elementary
Grades. Washington, DC: Nuclear Information and Resource
Service, 1982.
　　Lists books, journals, audiovisual materials, curriculum
guides on nuclear weapons and nuclear energy.
　　NUCLEAR ISSUES

592. _____. Nuclear Dangers: Annotated Bibliography for
High Schools. Washington, DC: Nuclear Information and
Resource Service, 1982.
　　NUCLEAR ISSUES

593. OLEXER, Marycile E. Poetry Anthologies for Children and
Young People. Chicago: American Library Association, 1985.
285p.
　　Guide to 300 anthologies and collections of poetry; also
comments on the poets and poems and provides an excerpt
from each book included. ISBN 0-8389-0430-0.
　　POETRY

594. ONTARIO LIBRARY ASSOCIATION. New Paperbacks for
Young Adults. West Toronto, Ontario: Ontario Library As-
sociation, 1979. Paper. 127p.
　　ISBN 0-88969-022-7.
　　CANADA; PAPERBOUND

595. THE OPENHEARTED AUDIENCE: Ten Authors Talk About
Writing for Children. Edited and with an Introduction by
Virginia Haviland. Washington, DC: Library of Congress,
1980. Illus. 198p.
　　Based on The Library of Congress program of lectures,
this volume includes addresses by P. L. Travers, Maurice
Sendak, Joan Aiken, Erik Haugaard, Ivan Southall, Ursula
LeGuin, Virginia Hamilton, John Rowe Townsend, Eleanor
Cameron, and Jill Paton Walsh. Bibliography of their works.
ISBN 0-8444-0288-5.
　　AUTHORS

596. OPIE, Iona, and Peter Opie. Three Centuries of Nursery
Rhymes and Poetry for Children: An Exhibition Held at the
National Book League, May 1973. London: Oxford University
Press, 1973. Paper. 70p.
　　Includes 829 entries, including "illustrious illustrators,"
celebrated characters, alphabet books, histories and inter-
pretations, nursery rhymes in advertising, nursery rhyme
novelties, and poetry for children. ISBN 0-19-211554-5.
　　RHYMES; POETRY

597. OSTERWELL, Wendy [editor]. Alternative Press Publishers
of Children's Books: A Directory. Second edition. Madison,

WI: The Friends of the Cooperative Children's Book Center,
Inc., 1985. Paper. 88p. First edition, 1982.
A fully annotated directory of 150 alternative presses
for children's books in the U.S. and Canada. Includes list
of distributors with the presses each carries. Includes geo-
graphical and bilingual publisher indexes and a subject index.
ISBN 0-931641-00-4.
BILINGUAL; NONSEXIST; PUBLISHERS

598.   OTT, Helen Keating. Helping Children Through Books: A
Selected Booklist. Second edition, revised. Bryn Mawr, PA:
Church and Synagogue Library Association, 1979. Paper.
35p. First edition ©1974.
Designed to help children through minor problems.
Some well-known titles are not included to allow room for
lesser known books. This revised edition updates title to
September 1, 1978. ISBN 0-915324-06-7.
BIBLIOTHERAPY

599.   OWEN, Betty M. A Smorgasbord of Books: Titles Junior
High Readers Relish. Englewood Cliffs, NJ: Scholastic
Book Service, 1974. 96p.
ISBN 0-590-09586-2.
JUNIOR HIGH

PALMER, Eileen C. see TREFNY, Beverly

600.   PALMER, Julia Reed. Read for Your Life: Two Successful
Efforts to Help People Read and an Annotated List of the
Books That Made Them Want To. Metuchen, NJ: Scarecrow
Press, 1974. 510p.
Description of "Library Techniques in Disadvantaged
Areas" and specific activities, with an annotated list of books
recommended as being "most likely to interest people who
have had little or no experience with books." Indexes.
ISBN 0-8108-0654-1.
ACTIVE READERS, DEVELOPING

601.   PALOS HEIGHTS PUBLIC LIBRARY. Bibliography of Children's Literature on Video. Palos Heights, IL: Palos Heights
Public Library, 1984. Paper. 29p.
Listing is by title of the videocassette, with date of
production, length, animation or live, appropriate grade level,
and a content and critical description. This pioneer list was
created as part of a funded project throught he Suburban
Library System, Burr Ridge, Illinois.
VIDEO FORMAT FOR CHILDREN'S LITERATURE

602.   PARLATO, Salvatore J. Films Ex Libris: Literature in 16mm

and Video. Jefferson, NC: McFarland, 1980. Illus. 283p.
Technical, descriptive data for over 1,400 class-length
films based on literature. Index. ISBN 0-89950-006-4.
FILMS, LITERATURE IN; VIDEO

603. PATERSON, Katherine. Gates of Excellence: On Reading
and Writing Books for Children. New York: Elsevier/
Nelson Books, 1981. 127p.
Essays, addresses, lectures on being a novelist for
young readers. ISBN 0-525-66750-4.
AUTHORS

604. PAULIN, Mary Ann. Creative Uses of Children's Literature.
Foreword by Marilyn Miller. Hamden, CT: Library Profes-
sional Publications, 1982. 730p.
Comprehensive discussion of reading guidance tech-
niques with citations of titles. Indexes. ISBN 0-208-01861-1;
ISBN 0-208-01862-X (paper).
ACTIVE READERS, DEVELOPING

605. _____, and Susan T. Berlin [compilers]. Outstanding
Books for the College Bound. Chicago: American Library
Association, 1984. Paper. 112p.
ISBN 0-8389-3302-5.
YOUNG ADULTS

606. PEARL, Patricia [compiler]. Religious Books for Children:
An Annotated Bibliography. Bryn Mawr, PA: Church and
Synagogue Library Association, 1983. Paper. 36p.
Over 400 titles under the categories of: Bible, Old
Testament, New Testament/Jesus Christ, Christian Theology,
Judaism, Buddhism, Hinduism, American Indian religions,
and Religious Holidays. Author and title indexes. ISBN
0-915324-21-0.
RELIGION

607. PELLOWSKI, Anne. Made to Measure: Children's Books in
Developing Countries. New York: Unipub, 1980. Illus.
129p. Paris: UNESCO, 1980. Books About Books: No. 2.
ISBN 92-3-101783-7.
DEVELOPING COUNTRIES, BOOKS IN

608. _____. The Story Vine: A Source Book of Unusual and
Easy-to-Tell Stories from Around the World. Illustrated by
Lynn Sweat. New York: Macmillan, 1984. 116p.
Anthology and guide for telling stories with finger
plays, string, and sand. Extensive bibliographies. ISBN
0-02-044690-X [paper]; ISBN 0-02-770590-0.
STORYTELLING

609. _____. The World of Children's Literature. New York:
R. R. Bowker, 1968. 538p.

Overview of the development of children's literature.
Index.
CHILDREN'S LITERATURE, HISTORY & CRITICISM

610. _____. The World of Storytelling. New York: R. R.
Bowker, 1977. Illus. 296p.
Overview on "worldwide developments in the art of
storytelling." Bibliography of books, periodical, recordings,
films and videotapes. Index. ISBN 0-8352-1024-3.
STORYTELLING

611. PENNYPACKER, Arabelle. Reading for Young People: The
Middle Atlantic. Chicago: American Library Association,
1980. Paper. 164p. Part of series.
362 titles for the states of Delaware, Maryland, New
Jersey, New York and Pennsylvania. Directory of regional
publishers. Author, title, subject index. ISBN 0-8389-
0295-2.
U.S., REGIONAL LITERATURE

612. PEPPIN, Brigid, and Lucy Micklethwait. Book Illustrators of
the Twentieth Century. New York: Arco Publishing, Inc.,
1984. Illus. 336p.
350 entries for a comprehensive overview of British
book illustrators. Data includes a discussion of the artist's
subjects and style, a reference bibliography on the artist,
and a listing of published works and biographical information.
ILLUSTRATORS; BRITAIN

613. PETERSON, Carolyn Sue, and Ann D. Fenton. Index to
Children's Songs: A Title, First Line and Subject Index.
New York: H. W. Wilson, 1979. 318p.
Indexes 5,000 songs and variations in 298 children's
books published between 1909 and 1977. ISBN 0-8242-0638-X.
SONGS

614. _____. Reference Books for Children. Metuchen, NJ:
Scarecrow Press, 1981. 273p. Supersedes Reference Books
for Elementary and Junior High School Libraries.
Selective listing of approximately 900 entries under general references, humanities, recreation, science, social science. Author, title, subject indexes. ISBN 0-8108-1441-2.
REFERENCE BOOKS

615. PETERSON, Carolyn Sue, and Brenny Hall. Story Programs:
A Source Book of Materials. Metuchen, NJ: Scarecrow
Press, 1980. Illus. Paper. 300p.
Handbook in categories of ages 2 to 3, 3 to 5, 6 to 8.
Index. ISBN 0-8108-1317-3.
STORY PROGRAMS

616. PETERSON, Linda Kauffman, and Marilyn Leathers Solt.
      Newbery and Caldecott Medal and Honor Books: An Anno-
      tated Bibliography. Foreword by Daniel Melcher. Boston:
      G. K. Hall and Co., 1982. 427p.
          Summarizes each award book and adds critical commen-
      tary. ISBN 0-8161-8448-8.
      AWARDS

617. PETTUS, Eloise S., and Daniel D. Pettus. Master Index to
      Summaries of Children's Books. Vol. I: A-Z; Vol. II:
      Title and Subject Indexes. Metuchen, NJ: Scarecrow
      Press, 1985. Vol. I, 1036p.; Vol. II, 352p.
          Directs students and teachers of children's literature
      and librarians to sources of summaries of books, published
      1974 to 1980, preschool to grade six. Comprehensive in
      scope. ISBN 0-8108-1795-0.
      SUMMARIES

618. PFLIEGER, Pat. A Reference Guide to Modern Fantasy for
      Children. Westport, CT: Greenwood Press, 1984. 768p.
          From 1863, with the publication of The Water Babies
      by Charles Kingsley, to 1982, with the publication of The
      Borrowers Avenged by Mary Norton, this guide covers 36
      major nineteenth- and twentieth-century British and U.S.
      authors. ISBN 0-313-22886-8.
      FANTASY

619. [PHILADELPHIA], THE FREE LIBRARY OF. Welcome Gifts.
      Philadelphia: Free Library, annual. Paper.
          Annually describes recently published books for year-
      round gift giving. Includes titles for the special child, pa-
      perbacks, and magazines.
      ANNUAL; GIFT BOOKS

620. PILGRIM, Geneva Hanna, and Mariana K. McAllister. Books,
      Young People, and Reading Guidance. Second edition. New
      York: Harper & Row, 1968. First edition ©1960.
          Thrust is to help young people learn to choose books.
      Classified reading lists and sources for the selection and
      evaluation of books along with bibliography. Index. LC
      68-10141.
      ACTIVE READERS, DEVELOPING

621. PILLON, Nancy B. Reaching Young People Through Media.
      Littleton, CO: Libraries Unlimited, 1983. 300p.
          Collection of original articles by YA specialists on
      periodicals, paperbacks, selection of materials, and reading
      interests. ISBN 0-87287-369-2.
      YOUNG ADULT

622. PITZ, Henry Clarence. Illustrating Children's Books:

History, Technique, Production. New York: Watson-
Guphill Publications, 1963. Illus. 207p.
Outlines the development of children's picture books.
Bibliography; index. LC 63-18772.
ILLUSTRATION

623. PLAY INDEX. New York: H. W. Wilson Co., series begins
with 1949-1952, edited by Herbert West and Dorothy Margaret Peake, ©1953, 239p. [ISBN 0-686-66657-7]; 1953-1960,
edited by Estelle A. Fidell and Dorothy Margaret Peake,
©1963, 404p.; indexes 4,592 plays in 1,735 volumes [ISBN
0-686-66658-5]; 1961-1967, edited by Estelle A. Fidelle,
©1968, 464p.; indexes 4,793 plays [ISBN 0-686-66659-3];
1968-1972, edited by Estelle A. Fidell, ©1973, 403p.; indexes
3,848 plays [ISBN 0-686-66660-7]; 1973-1977, edited by
Estelle A. Fidell, ©1978, 457p.; indexes 3,878 plays [ISBN
0-686-66661-5]; 1978-1982, edited by Estelle A. Fidell,
©1983, 480p.; [ISBN 0-317-01196-0].
Each follows the format of playwright, title, subject
index; cast analysis; list of collections indexed; directory of
publishers and distributors.
DRAMATIC LITERATURE

624. POLETTE, Nancy. E Is for Everybody: A Manual for Bringing Fine Picture Books into the Hands and Hearts of Children
--Volume II. Metuchen, NJ: Scarecrow Press, 1982. Illus.
194p. First volume ©1976.
Update reviews the best 126 picture books published
between 1975 and 1982, "appropriate for use in the elementary
grades through junior high school." ISBN 0-8108-1579-6
[Vol. II]; ISBN 0-8108-0966-4 [Vol. I].
PICTURE BOOKS FOR OLDER READERS

625. _____. Picture Books for Gifted Programs. Metuchen,
NJ: Scarecrow Press, 1981. 228p.
Summaries of suggested titles, preschool through ele-
mentary school. ISBN 0-8108-1461-7.
GIFTED; PICTURE BOOKS

626. _____, and Marjorie Hamlin. Celebrating with Books.
Line drawings by Patricia Gilman. Metuchen, NJ: Scarecrow
Press, 1977. Illus. 184p.
Lists books for the usual holidays, special days, and
celebrations. ISBN 0-8108-1032-8.
HOLIDAYS

627. _____. Exploring Books with Gifted Children. Littleton,
CO: Libraries Unlimited, Inc., 1980. 214p.
Based on the wider view of giftedness. Extensive dis-
cussion of selected titles. ISBN 0-872870216-5.
GIFTED

628. _____. Reading Guidance in a Media Age. Metuchen, NJ:
      Scarecrow Press, 1975. Illus. 275p.
      ISBN 0-8108-0873-0.
      ACTIVE READERS, DEVELOPING

629. POLKINGHAM, Anne T., and Catherine Toohey. Creative
      Encounters: Activities to Expand Children's Responses to
      Literature. Illus. by Lynn Welker. Littleton, CO: Libraries
      Unlimited, 1983. Paper. 138p.
          Extends children's literature beyond the story hour
      and the curriculum for grades K to six. Bibliography; in-
      dex. ISBN 0-87287-371-4.
      ACTIVE READERS, DEVELOPING

630. POLLACK, Pamela D. The Best of the Best. New York:
      R. R. Bowker, 1980. Paper. 10p.
          Annotated, retrospective selection of children's books
      from twelve years of School Library Journal's annual choices
      of the "Best Books of the Year." Reprint from SLJ's 25th
      anniversary issue, December 1979.
      BEST BOOKS

631. POPENOE, Cris. Books for Inner Development: The Yes!
      Guide. Washington, D.C.: Yes! Bookshop [distributed by
      Random House]. 1976. Illus. Paper. 383p.
          Lists titles for children (pp. 93-96), along with books
      for adults. ISBN 0-394-73294-4.
      BIBLIOTHERAPY

632- POSNER, Marcia [compiler]. Selected Jewish Children's Books.
  3. New York: JWB Jewish Book Council, 1983. Paper.
      JEWISH

634. PREISS, Byron [editor]. The Art of Leo and Diane Dillon.
      New York: Ballantine Books, 1981. Illus. Unpp. ISBN 0-
      345-28449-6 [paperbound], ISBN 0345-29386-X [clothbound];
      ISBN 0-345-30380-6 [limited edition].
      ILLUSTRATORS

635. PURVES, Alan, and Diane L. Monson. Experiencing Children's
      Literature. Glenview, IL: Scott, Foresman, 1984. Paper.
      216p.
      ISBN 0-63-15348-7.
      CHILDREN'S LITERATURE, HISTORY & CRITICISM

636. PUTNAM, Donalda [compiler]. Sixty Plus: Seniors in Con-
      temporary Fiction. Ottawa: Canadian Library Association,
      1985. Paper.
          Approximately 80 titles, accessible for young adults as
      well as for adults.
      SENIOR ADULTS; CONTEMPORARY FICTION; CANADA

637. QUALE, Eric. The Collector's Book of Children's Books.
      Photographs by Gabriel Monro. New York: Clarkson N.
      Potter, Inc., 1971. 144p.
          A retrospective description of the evolution of "books
      for children's amusement," from the time of the first Eliza-
      beth to 1970. LC 70-154296.
          CHILDREN'S LITERATURE, HISTORY & CRITICISM

638. QUICKE, John. Disability in Modern Children's Fiction.
      Cambridge, MA: Brookline Books, 1984. 176p.
          British and U.S. titles discussed under themes of
      characters with disabilities. ISBN 0-914797-09-3.
          FICTION; DISABILITIES

639. QUIMBY, Harriet B., and Margaret Mary Kimmel. Building
      a Children's Literature Collection: A Suggested Basic Refer-
      ence Collection for Academic Libraries and A Suggested Basic
      Collection of Children's Books. Third edition. Middletown,
      CT: Choice, 1983. Paper. 48p. Choice Bibliographical
      Essay Series, No. 7. First published 1975.
          For this edition, over half the 1,500 titles listed are
      new from previous editions. Covers all genres of children's
      books and all subjects in the study of children's literature.
      ISBN 0-914492-06-3.
          ACADEMIC LIBRARY, BASIC COLLECTION

640. RAHN, Suzanne. Children's Literature: An Annotated Bib-
      liography of the History and Criticism. New York: Garland
      Publishing, 1981. 451p. Garland Reference Library of the
      Humanities.
          Index. ISBN 0-8240-9357-7.
          CHILDREN'S LITERATURE, HISTORY & CRITICISM

641. RAMSEY, Eloise [compiler]. Folklore for Children and Young
      People: A Critical and Descriptive Bibliography for Use in
      the Elementary and Intermediate School. Millwood, NY:
      Kraus Reprint of Philadelphia: The American Folklore Society,
      1952. 110p.
          Scope is international. Part one lists books, part two
      gives selected sources for teachers. Index. ISBN 0-527-
      01127-4.
          FOLKLORE

642. RAPHAEL, Frederick, and Kenneth McLeish [editors]. The
      List of Books. New York: Harmony Books, 1981. 160p.
          Pages 31 to 35 list a choice of readable and read chil-
      dren's classics and "good contemporary books, potentially of
      classic status, too." ISBN 0-517-540177; ISBN 0-517-541521
      [paper].
          BEST BOOKS; CLASSICS

READING RAINBOW   see   discussion in Appendix A, p. 145.

643. READING IS FUNDAMENTAL, INC. Reading Is Fun! Tips
      for Parents of Children Age Birth to 8 Years. Washington,
      DC: Reading Is Fundamental, 1985. Paper.
      ACTIVE READERS, DEVELOPING

644. REASONER, Charles F. Bringing Children and Books To-
      gether: A Teacher's Guide to Early Childhood Literature.
      New York: Dell, 1979. 126p.
      ISBN 0-440-40895-4.
      ACTIVE READERS, DEVELOPING

645. REEDMAN, Russell. Holiday House: The First Fifty Years.
      New York: Holiday House, 1985. 152p.
      Includes chronological list of titles published by Holiday
      House, along with a history of the firm. Bibliography. In-
      dex. ISBN 0-8234-0562-2.
      PUBLISHERS/PUBLISHING

646. REES, David. The Marble in the Water: Essays on Contem-
      porary Writers of Fiction for Children and Young Adults.
      Boston: Horn Book, 1980. 224p.
      Discussion of similarities and differences in fiction for
      young readers in England and the United States. The work
      of 18 authors is covered. ISBN 0-87675-281-4 [paper]; ISBN
      0-87675-280-6.
      FICTION; AUTHORS

647. _____. Painted Desert, Green Shade: Essays on Contem-
      porary Writers of Fiction for Children and Young Adults.
      Boston: Horn Book, 1984. Paper. 197p.
      Examines the work of thirteen authors, six from Brit-
      ain, seven from the United States. ISBN 0-87675-286-5
      [paper].
      FICTION; AUTHORS

648. REID, Virginia M. [editor]. Children's Literature Old and
      New. Champaign, IL: National Council of Teachers of Eng-
      lish, 1964. Paper. 66p. First printed in the May 1963 is-
      sue of Elementary English.
      Includes bibliographies.
      CHILDREN'S LITERATURE, HISTORY & CRITICISM

649. _____. Reading Ladders for Human Understanding. Fifth
      edition. Washington, DC: American Council on Education,
      1972. 346p. First published 1947.
      The four reading ladders: "Creating a positive self-
      image"; "Appreciating different cultures"; "Living with oth-
      ers"; and "Coping with change" are placed within four age
      levels: primary, intermediate, junior, and senior. ISBN

0-8268-1373-9 [paper]; ISBN 0-8268-1375-5.
BIBLIOTHERAPY; MULTICULTURAL

650. RENFRO, Nancy. Puppetry and the Art of Story Creation.
Austin, TX: Nancy Renfro Studios, 1979. Illus. Paper.
165p.
Gives approaches for using folk and fairy tales for
puppet plays. Bibliography of books, pamphlets, and plays.
ISBN 0-931044-02-2.
STORYTELLING

651. RICHARDSON, J. A. Books for the Retarded Reader. Sixth
edition. Mystic, CT: Lawrence Verry, Inc., 1977. Paper.
[See also, HART, J. A.]
ISBN 0-85563-152-X.
RETARDED READERS

652. RICHARDSON, Selma K. [compiler]. Magazines for Children:
A Guide for Parents, Teachers and Librarians. Chicago:
American Library Association, 1983. Paper. 147p.
Discusses approximately 100 magazines for children up
to fourteen years. ISBN 0-8389-0392-4.
MAGAZINES

653. _____. Magazines for Young Adults: Selections for School
and Public Libraries. Chicago: American Library Association,
1984. Paper. 360p.
ISBN 0-8389-0407-6.
MAGAZINES; YOUNG ADULT

654. _____. Periodicals for School Media Programs. Revised
edition. Chicago: American Library Association, 1978.
Paper. 397p.
First published with title "Periodicals for School Li-
braries"; Marion H. Scott, editor.
A buying list of recommended periodicals for K-12.
ISBN 0-8389-0243-X.
PERIODICALS

655. _____. Research About Nineteenth Century Children and
Books: Portrait Studies. Urbana: University of Illinois,
1980. Illus. Monograph No. 17.
ISBN 0-87845-055-6.
CHILDREN'S LITERATURE, HISTORY & CRITICISM

656. ROBERTS, Patricia. Alphabet: A Handbook of ABC Books
and Activities for the Elementary Classroom. Metuchen, NJ:
Scarecrow Press, 1984. 220p.
200 ABC books organized by topics (animals, puzzles,
letter transformations, sign language, transportation) and

80 activities books for primary and middle grades.   ISBN
0-8108-1686-5.
ALPHABET BOOKS

657. ROBINSON, Evelyn Rose [editor].   Readings About Children's
Literature.   New York: Random House, 1973.   431p.   First
published, New York: D. McKay Co., 1966.
    Approximately 60 articles reprinted from journals and
other sources.   Includes bibliographies.
    CHILDREN'S LITERATURE, HISTORY & CRITICISM

658. ROGINSKI, Jim.   Behind the Covers: Interviews with Authors and Illustrators of Books for Children and Young
Adults.   Littleton, CO: Libraries Unlimited, 1985.   263p.
    ISBN 0-87287-506-7.
    AUTHORS; ILLUSTRATORS

659. _____.   Newbery and Caldecott Medalists and Honor Book
Winners: Bibliographies and Resource Material Through
1977.   Littleton, CO: Libraries Unlimited, 1983.   339p.
    Comprehensive bibliography on the 265 authors and
illustrators.   ISBN 0-87287-296-3.
    AWARDS

660. ROLLINS, Charlemae Hill [editor].   The Magic World of
Books.   Illustrated by Lucy Ozone.   Chicago: Science Research Associates, 1954.   40p.   Junior Life Adjustment Booklet.
    BIBLIOTHERAPY; CHILDREN'S LITERATURE, HISTORY
    & CRITICISM

661. _____.   We Build Together: A Reader's Guide to Negro
Life and Literature for Elementary and High School Use.
Third edition.   Urbana, IL: National Council of Teachers
of English, 1967.   71p.   First edition ©1941; revised edition
©1948.
    Covers multiple genres; lists are by grade level.   In-
dexes.
    BLACKS

662. ROLLOCK, Barbara [editor].   The Black Experience in Children's Books.   New York: New York Public Library, 1984.
Paper.   122p.   First published 1957 with title: "Books About
Negro Life for Children," edited by Augusta Baker.   Revisions 1974, 1979.
    Booklist contains selected titles portraying Black life
for children from preschool to age 12.   Covers multiple subjects and all genres.   ISBN 0-87104-637-7.
    BLACKS

663. ROMAN, Susan.   Sequences: An Annotated Guide to

Children's Fiction in Series. Chicago: American Library
Association, 1985.   134p.
    150 different series in sequels and sequences of in-
terest to readers, grades 3 to junior high.   Approximately
125 authors, with titles listed in proper reading order.   Indexes by main character, book title, and series title.   ISBN
0-8389-0428.
    FICTION; SERIES, SEQUELS

664. ROOT, Shelton L., Jr. [editor].   Adventuring with Books.
      Second edition.   New York: Citation Press, 1973.   Paper.
      395p.   First published 1966, edited by Patricia Cianciolo
      (who also edited 1977 edition).
          2,400 titles for pre-K to grade 8 in a span of subjects.
      Compiled with a committee of the National Council of Teachers
      of English.   See also WHITE, Mary Lou for 1981 edition.
      ISBN 0-590-09702-4.
          SELECTION AIDS/GUIDES

665. ROSENBACH, Abraham Simon Wolf.   Early American Children's
      Books in the Free Library at Philadelphia.   New York: Dover
      Publications, 1971.   Paper.   Illus.   Originally published by
      Southworth in 1933.
          ISBN 0-527-77002-7.
          SPECIAL COLLECTIONS

666. ROSENBERG, Judith K., and Kenyon C. Rosenberg.   Young
      People's Literature in Series: An Annotated Bibliographical
      Guide.   Littleton, CO: Libraries Unlimited, 1972.   176p.
          Selective titles published 1955-1972 for readers in grades
      3 to 9, evaluated in terms of plot content, depth and believ-
      ability of characterization, writing style, and book format.
      Series are arranged by author.   Series title index.   ISBN
      0-87287-060-X.
          FICTION; SERIES

667. _____.   Young People's Literature in Series: Fiction, Non-
      Fiction and Publishers' Series, 1973-1975.   Littleton, CO:
      Libraries Unlimited, 1977.   234p.   Supplements above title
      and the volume on Publishers' and nonfiction series.
          2,877 titles includes fiction and nonfiction published
      after 1972 or inadvertently omitted from the earlier editions.
      ISBN 0-87287-140-1.
          FICTION; SERIES

668. ROSENFELT, Deborah Silverton [editor].   Strong Women:
      An Annotated Bibliography of Literature for the High School
      Classroom.   Old Westbury, NY: The Feminist Press, 1976.
      Paper.   58p.
          Inexpensive supplementary readings by and about wom-
      en; selective listing of anthologies, autobiography/biography,

drama, novels, short stories, poetry. Indexes. ISBN 0-912670-40-1.
WOMEN

669. ROSER, Nancy, and Margaret Frith [editors]. Children's
Choices: Teaching with Books Children Like. Newark, DE:
International Reading Association, 1983. Paper. 119p.
ISBN 0-87207-735-7.
BEST BOOKS

670. ROSS, Ramon Royal. Storyteller. Second edition. Columbus, OH: Merrill Publishing Co., 1980. Paper. Illus.
226p. First edition ©1972.
Contains a new chapter on migratory and urban belief
tales. Covers all phases of storytelling. Bibliography. Index. ISBN 0-675-08169-6.
STORYTELLING

671. RUDMAN, Masha Kabakow. Children's Literature: An Issues
Approach. Second edition. New York: Longman, 1984.
476p. Distributed by ALA Publishing Services. First edition
published Lexington, MA: D. C. Heath and Company, 1976,
433p.
Lists books in nine categories: Siblings, divorce,
death and old age, war, sex, the Black, Native American,
the Female. Discusses techniques for evaluation, selection,
and use. Author/Illustrator, title and subject indexes.
ISBN 0-582-28398-1 [Longman]; ISBN 0-669-93203-5 [paper];
ISBN 0-669-00322-0 [cloth] [ALA].
CONTEMPORARY ISSUES; SIBLINGS; DIVORCE; DEATH;
SENIOR ADULTS; WAR; SEX EDUCATION; BLACKS;
AMERICAN INDIANS; WOMEN

672. RUSSELL, William F. Classics to Read Aloud to Your Children. New York: Crown Publishers, 1984. 311p.
Lists titles and provides excerpts for children on three
listening levels: age 5 and up, age 8 and up, age 11 and
up. ISBN 0-517-55404-6.
CLASSICS

673. SADKER, Myra Pollack, and David Miller Sadker. Now Upon
a Time: A Contemporary View of Children's Literature.
New York: Harper-Row, 1977. Illus. 475p.
Discussion and booklists on life's cycle, the American
mosaic, and ecology. Subject and title indexes. ISBN 0-
06-045693-0.
CONTEMPORARY ISSUES

674. SALE, Roger. Fairy Tales and After: From Snow White to

E. B. White. Cambridge: Harvard University Press, 1978.
Illus. 286p.
   Essays covering topics and authors. ISBN 0-674-
29157-3; ISBN 0-674-29165-4 [paper].
   CHILDREN'S LITERATURE, HISTORY & CRITICISM

675. SALWAY, Lance [editor]. Humorous Books for Children.
Stroud, Glos., England: The Thimble Press, 1980. Illus.
Paper. 56p.
   ISBN 0-903355-05-1.
   HUMOR

676. _____ [editor]. A Peculiar Gift: Nineteenth Century
Writings on Books for Children. London: Kestrel Books,
1976. Illus. 500p.
   ISBN 0-7226-5140-6.
   CHILDREN'S LITERATURE, HISTORY & CRITICISM

677. SAPON-SHEVIN, M., and G. M. Kruse [compilers]. A Selected List of Children's Books of Information About Exceptional Children. Revised edition. Chicago: American Library Association, 1980. Paper. 3p.
   EXCEPTIONAL CHILDREN

678. SARKISSIAN, Adele [editor]. Children's Authors and Illustrators: An Index to Biographical Dictionaries. Third revised edition. Detroit: Gale Research Co., 1981. 667p.
Gale Biographical Index Series No. 2.
   This edition retains all materials included in the previous editions. Accesses biographical information on approximately 20,000 persons found in more than 275 reference
books. Includes pseudonyms and pen names. ISBN 0-8103-
1084-4.
   AUTHORS; ILLUSTRATORS; BIOGRAPHICAL DICTION-
ARIES

678a. _____. High Interest Books for Teens: A Guide to Book
Reviews and Bibliographic Sources. Detroit: Gale Research
Co., 1981. 300p.
   ISBN 0-8103-0599-2.
   HIGH INTEREST; TEENAGE

679. _____. Something About the Author: Autobiography
Series. Volume 1. Detroit, MI: Gale Research, 1985. 300p.
   ISBN 0-8103-4450-5.
   AUTHORS

680. _____. Writers for Young Adults: Biographies Master Index. Detroit: Gale Research Co., 1979. 199p. Gale Biographical Index Series No. 6.
   Covers 9,000 names listed in 260 biographies about

novelists, poets, playwrights, nonfiction writers, songwriters and lyricists, and television and screenwriters. ISBN 0-8103-1083-X.
AUTHORS; ILLUSTRATORS; BIOGRAPHICAL DICTION-ARIES

681. SARLES, Christie V. The Witch in the Woods and 449 Other Terrific Books for Libraries to Own and Kids to Read. Concord, NH: New Hampshire State Library, 1985. Paper. 96p.
Titles are classified by age group. New Hampshire authors and illustrators are specially designated. Index.
AUTHORS; BEST BOOKS; ILLUSTRATORS; U.S., REGIONAL LITERATURE

682. SAWYER, Ruth. The Way of the Storyteller. New York: Penguin Books, 1982. Paper. 356p. First published, New York: Viking Press, 1942; first Penguin edition, 1976.
Reading and story lists along with techniques for story telling. Index. ISBN 0-1400-4436-1.
STORYTELLING

683. SAYERS, Frances Clarke. Summoned by Books: Essays and Speeches. Compiled by Marjeanne Jensen Blinn. Foreword by Lawrence Clark Powell. New York: Viking Press, 1965. 173p.
Now classic commentary by a renowned figure in the field of literature for children. LC 65-13361.
CHILDREN'S LITERATURE, HISTORY & CRITICISM

684. SCALES, Pat. Communicate Through Literature: Introducing Parents to the Books Their Teens Are Reading and Enjoying. New York: Pacer Books, 1984. Paper. 47p.
Includes bibliographies with a program using books to foster discussions between parents and teens.
YOUNG ADULTS; TEENAGE

685. SCHERF, Walter [editor]. The Best of the Best: Picture, Children's and Youth Books from 10 Countries or Languages. Second enlarged edition. International Jugendbibliothek, Munich. New York: R. R. Bowker, 1976. Illus. 344p.
Published by Verlag Dokumentation, distributed by Bowker.
Selected list of over 1,800 of the best books for children, ages 3 to 15. ISBN 0-7940-3253-5.
BEST BOOKS

686. SCHILLER, Justin G., Ltd. Children's Books from Four Centuries Including Original Drawings, Manuscripts, and Related Juvenilia. New York: Justin G. Schiller, 1973. Illus. Paper. Unpp.
Catalog No. 29, which offers for sale "scarce and

uncommon children's books." Listed by author. Includes
index of subjects.
SPECIAL COLLECTIONS

687.   SCHIMMEL, Nancy.   Just Enough to Make a Story: A Source-
       book for Storytelling. Revised edition. Berkeley: Sisters'
       Choice Press, 1982. Paper. 54p. First edition ©1978.
           Annotated list of folktales with active heroines. Espe-
       cially applicable to junior high school audiences. ISBN 0-
       932164-00-5.
           STORYTELLING; ACTIVE HEROINES; HEROES &
       HEROINES

688.   SCHINDEL, Morton.   Voices from the Wilderness: The Art
       of Recording Children's Stories [Cassette]. Weston, CT:
       Weston Woods, 1979. One cassette, two sides.
           Using examples from Weston Woods recordings of chil-
       dren's books, Schindel explains the role of the performer
       and the director in capturing the flavor of good literature.
       RECORDING CHILDREN'S LITERATURE

689.   SCHLOBIN, Roger C.   The Literature of Fantasy: An Anno-
       tated Bibliography of Modern Fantasy Fiction. New York:
       Garland Publishing, 1979. Garland Reference Library of the
       Humanities No. 176.
           For high school age readers and adults. ISBN 0-
       8240-9757-2.
           FANTASY

690.   SCHMIDT, Janine, and Barbara Anderson [compilers]. Aus-
       tralian Picture Books. Lindfield, Australia: During-dai
       College of Advanced Education, 1984. 128p. Paper.
           128 titles described. Lists winners of Australian pic-
       ture book awards. ISBN 0-9091-7744-9.
           AUSTRALIA

691.   SCHMIDT, Nancy J.   Children's Books on Africa and Their
       Authors: An Annotated Bibliography. New York and Lon-
       don: African Publishing Co., 1975; 1979 supplement. 291p.
           A list of 837 books from the 1880s to 1973, published
       worldwide but available in the United States. Critical analy-
       sis of African content and competency of authors to write
       about Africa.
           Multiple indexes [geographic, author/illustrator, series,
       subject, title, tribal]. ISBN 0-8419-0166-X; ISBN 0-8149-
       0433-2 [1979 supplement].
           AFRICA

692.   _____. Children's Fiction About Africa in English. Buf-
       falo, NY: Conch Magazine, Ltd., 1981. 260p.

Includes African, European, and U.S. fiction about Africa. ISBN 0-914970-63-1.
AFRICA

693. _____. Children's Literature and Audio-Visual Materials in Africa. Buffao, NY: Conch Magazine, Ltd., 1977. 110p.
Over 100 titles are reviewed or listed. ISBN 0-914970-37-2.
AFRICA

694. SCHMIDT, Velma E., and Earldene McNeill. Cultural Awareness: A Resource Bibliography. Washington, DC: The National Association for the Education of Young Children, 1978. Illus. 121p.
Fiction and nonfiction titles on Asian-, Black-, Native-, and Spanish-speaking Americans. Also includes resources for adults and a system to analyze children's books for racism and sexism. ISBN 0-912674-60-1.
MULTIETHNIC

695. SCHON, Isabel. A Bicultural Heritage: Themes for the Exploration of Mexico and Mexican-American Culture in Books for Children and Adolescents. Metuchen, NJ: Scarecrow Press, 1978. 164p.
Selective list for K-12 classified within five themes: customs, life styles, heroes, folklore, and key historical developments. Author, title indexes. ISBN 0-8108-1128-6.
MEXICAN AMERICAN/MEXICO

696. _____. Books in Spanish for Children and Young Adults: An Annotated Guide/Libros Infantiles y Juveniles en Español: Una Guía Anotada. Metuchen, NJ: Scarecrow Press, 1978. 165p.
A selection guide for books published after 1973 and in print as of 1978. Imprints are from all Spanish-speaking nations. Author, title, subject indexes. ISBN 0-8108-1176-6.
SPANISH, BOOKS IN

697. _____. Books in Spanish for Children and Young Adults: An Annotated Guide, Series II/Libros Infantiles y Juveniles en Español: Una Guía Anotada, Serie No. II. Metuchen, NJ: Scarecrow Press, 1983. 172p.
Critical guide for books in Spanish published after 1978. List of "reliable" book dealers abroad and in the United States. Indexes. ISBN 0-8108-1620-2.
SPANISH, books in

698. _____. Books in Spanish for Children and Young Adults: An Annotated Guide, Series III/Libros Infantiles y Juveniles en Español: Una Guía Anotada, Serie No. III. Metuchen, NJ: Scarecrow Press, 1985. 220p.

Most books listed have been published since 1982 and
in print as of 1984. Titles represent a broad scope of Hispanic cultures. Includes bilingual and nonfiction and Spanish translations of popular fiction and nonfiction. List of
dealers. Author and title indexes. ISBN 0-8108-1807-8
(Serie No. III); ISBN 0-8108-1620-2 (©1983); ISBN 0-8108-
1176 (©1978).
SPANISH, BOOKS IN; BILINGUAL

699.   . A Hispanic Heritage: A Guide to Juvenile Books
About Hispanic People and Cultures. Metuchen, NJ: Scare-
crow Press, 1980. 178p.
Selective guide for K-12 for titles set in South and
Central America and about the Hispanic heritage in the
United States. ISBN 0-8108-1290-8.
HISPANIC HERITAGE

700.   . A Hispanic Heritage, Series II: A Guide to Juve-
nile Books About Hispanic People and Cultures. Metuchen,
NJ: Scarecrow Press, 1985. 164p.
Updates for in-print titles from the 1980 volume. ISBN
0-8108-1727-6.
HISPANIC HERITAGE

701. SCHOOL LIBRARY ASSOCIATION, Primary Schools Sub-
committee. Berna Clark, editor. Books for Primary Children:
An Annotated List. Third edition. London: School Library
Association, 1969. 113p. First edition published as: Primary
School Library Books, ©1960.
Covers fiction and nonfiction. Includes multiple indexes.
The endpapers contain advertisements of titles. ISBN 0-
900641-00-2.
BRITAIN; PRIMARY

702. SCHWARCZ, Joseph H. Ways of the Illustrator: Visual Communication in Children's Literature. Chicago: American Library Association, 1982. Illus. 202p.
Study on how illustration couples with text to enhance
meaning. ISBN 0-8389-0356-8.
ILLUSTRATION

703. SCOTT, Dorothea Hayward. Chinese Popular Literature and
the Child. Chicago: American Library Association, 1980.
181p.
ISBN 0-8389-0289-8.
CHINA

704. SEBESTA, Sam Leaton, and William J. Iverson. Literature
for Thursday's Child. Chicago: Science Research Associates, Inc., 1975. Illus. 565p.
Part I deals with choosing literature, Part II is a

survey of literature, and Part III deals with the literary experience. Booklists. Index. ISBN 0-574-18615-8.
CHILDREN'S LITERATURE, TEXTBOOKS ON

705. SELECTION: Children's Books and Activities for Families to
Share. Published four times a year. Subscriptions to:
P.O. Box 5068, Stanford, CT 94305.
BOOK REVIEWS

706. SHAKESPEARE for the Young Reader. Compiled by the Vol-
unteer Docents of the Folger Shakespeare Library. Washington, DC: Folger Shakespeare Library, 1985. Illus. Paper.
55p.
   150 titles on Shakespeare's life, theatre, works edited
for children, England in the Renaissance, biography, and
historical fiction on Shakespeare and his time.
SHAKESPEARE

707. SHANNON, George W. B. [compiler]. Folk Literature and
Children: An Annotated Bibliography of Secondary Materials.
Westport, CT: Greenwood Press, 1981. 124p.
   Critical materials in three categories: Literature, Edu-
cation and Psychology. Author, title, subject indexes. ISBN
0-313-22808-6.
FOLK LITERATURE

708. SHAPIRO, Lillian [editor]. Fiction for Youth: A Recommended Guide to Books. New York: Neal-Schuman Publishers, Inc., 1981. 252p.
   Selective listing of books published in the twentieth
century and in print as of 1979. Criteria based on readabil-
ity. Title, subject indexes. ISBN 0-918212-34-0.
FICTION; SELECTION GUIDE

709. SHAW, John Mackay. Childhood in Poetry: A Catalogue,
With Biographical and Critical Annotations, Of the Books of
English and American Poets Comprising the Shaw Childhood
in Poetry Collection, Library of the Florida State University,
With Lists of the Poems That Relate to Childhood, Notes and
Index. Detroit: Gale Research Co. Main Catalogue, in five
volumes, published 1968. First Supplement published 1972;
Second Supplement published 1976. Indexes.
      ISBN 0-8103-0477-5.
POETRY; SPECIAL COLLECTIONS

710. SHEDLOCK, Marie L. The Art of the Story-Teller. Third
edition revised. Foreword by Anne Carroll Moore. With a
new Bibliography by Eulalie Steinmetz. New York: Dover
Publications, 1951. Paper. 291p. First published by D.
Appleton & Co., 1915.
      A standard source. ISBN 0-486-20635-1.
STORYTELLING

711. SHERRARD-SMITH, Barbara. Children's Books of the Year.
New York: Franklin Watts, annual. Illus. [around 150p.]
For the year 1979, ©1980, with Elaine Moss.
ISBN 0-531-04178-6 [©1980]; ISBN 0-531-04067-4
[©1981]; ISBN 0-531-04428-9 [©1982]; ISBN 0-531-04678-8
[©1983].
BEST BOOKS

712. SIEGEL, Mary-Ellen. Her Way: A Guide to Biographies of
Women for Young People. Second edition. Chicago:
American Library Association, 1984. 430p. First Edition
under the name of Mary-Ellen Kulkin.
ISBN 0-8389-0396-7.
BIOGRAPHY; WOMEN

713. SILVERMAN, Judith. Index to Collective Biographies for
Young Children. Third edition. New York: R. R. Bowker,
1979. 405p. Formerly Index to Young Readers' Collective
Biographies, ©1975.
Lists 7,245 people in 942 collective biographies. Exten-
sive subject index with cross-references. ISBN 0-8352-1132-0.
BIOGRAPHY

714. SIMMONS, Beatrice [editor]. Paperback Books for Children.
New York: Citation Press, 1972. 130p.
Approximately 700 titles in five divisions: Picture
books, fiction, nonfiction, traditional tales, poetry/rhymes.
Adult guide for selection and use of books for children.
Author and title indexes. ISBN 0-590-09542-0.
PAPERBACK

715. SIMS, Rudine. Shadow and Substance: Afro-American Ex-
perience in Contemporary Children's Fiction. Urbana, IL:
National Council of Teachers of English, 1982. Paper. 111p.
Discussion and booklists. ISBN 0-8141-4376-8 [Dis-
tributed by ALA with the ISBN 0-8389-3278-9].
BLACKS

716. SLOANE, William. Children's Books in England and America
in the Seventeenth Century: A History and a Checklist,
Together with "The Young Christian's Library," the First
Printed Catalogue of Books for Children. New York: King's
Crown Press, Columbia University, 1955. 251p. Index. A
facsimile reproduction of the Bodleian Library copy of the
original issue published in 1710. LC 54-9938.
CHILDREN'S LITERATURE, HISTORY & CRITICISM;
BRITAIN

717. SMITH, Charles A., and Carolyn Lepper Foat. Once Upon a
Mind: Using Children's Books to Nurture Self-Discovery.
Manhattan, KS: Cooperative Extension Service at Kansas

State University, 1983. Illus. Paper. 96p. North Central
Regional Extension Publication No. 169.
    81 selected titles for 3 to 8 year olds, keyed to con-
cepts.
    SELF-DISCOVERY

718. SMITH, Dora Valentine. Fifty Years of Children's Books,
     1910-1960: Trends, Background, Influences. Champaign,
     IL: National Council of Teachers of English, 1963. Illus.
     Paper. 149p.
         Overview and listing of significant books. Indexes.
         CHILDREN'S LITERATURE, HISTORY & CRITICISM

719. SMITH, Elva S. Elva S. Smith's The History of Children's
     Literature: A Syllabus with Selected Bibliographies. Re-
     vised and enlarged edition by Margaret Hodges and Susan
     Steinfirst. Chicago: American Library Association, 1980.
     237p. First published in 1937.
         Covers children's literature from the sixth century to
     the present for England and the U.S. in a full range of
     topics and genres. Author-title index. ISBN 0-8389-0286-3.
         CHILDREN'S LITERATURE, TEXTBOOKS ON; BRITAIN

720. SMITH, Irene. A History of the Newbery and Caldecott
     Medals. New York: Viking Press, 1957; second printing
     1959. 140p.
         Background on the establishment of the awards, how
     winners were selected, and critical commentary on the win-
     ners. Index.
         AWARDS

721. SMITH, James A., and Dorothy M. Park. Word Music and
     Word Magic: Children's Literature Methods. Boston: Allyn
     and Bacon, 1977.
         ISBN 0-205-05587-7.
         CHILDREN'S LITERATURE, TEXTBOOKS ON

722. SMITH, Janet Adam. Children's Illustrated Books. London:
     Collins, 1948. Illus. 50p. Part of "Britain in Pictures"
     series.
         Covers seventh, eighteenth, and nineteenth centuries.
         BRITAIN; PICTURE BOOKS

723. SMITH, Lillian Helene. The Unreluctant Years: A Critical
     Approach to Children's Literature. Chicago: American Li-
     brary Association, 1953. 153p.
         A classic in the study of selection and use of literature
     with children. LC 52-13520.
         SELECTION GUIDE

724. SNOW, Kathleen M.; Esther Gorosh; and Margaret Harper.

Subject Index for Children and Young People to Canadian
Poetry in English. Ottawa: Canadian Library Association,
1983. Paper. 192p.
      For ages 6 to 14. ISBN 0-88802-176-3.
      CANADA; POETRY

725. SOUTHALL, Ivan. A Journey of Discovery: On Writing for
      Children. New York: Macmillan Publishing Co., 1975.
      101p. First published 1968.
      Six essays, addresses, and lectures that point to the
      development of a philosophy. ISBN 0-02-786150-3.
      AUTHOR

726. SPACHE, George Daniel. Good Reading for the Disadvantaged
      Reader; Multi-ethnic Resources. Revised edition. Cham-
      paign, IL: Garrard Publishing, 1975. Paper. 311p. First
      published 1970.
      Emphasis is on helping a minority child develop a posi-
      tive self-concept. ISBN 0-8116-6012-5.
      MULTIETHNIC; DISADVANTAGED READERS

727. _____. Good Reading for Poor Readers. Ninth revised
      edition. Champaign, IL: Garrard Publishing, 1974. Paper.
      303p.. First published 1958.
      Includes trade books, adapted and simplified materials,
      magazines and newspapers, series books along with textbooks,
      workbooks, and games and book clubs. Multiple indexes.
      ISBN 0-8116-6013-3.
      HIGH INTEREST/LOW VOCABULARY

728. SPAIN, Frances Lander [editor]. The Content of the Basket
      and Other Papers on Children's Books and Reading. New
      York: New York Public Library, 1960. Illus. Paper. 83p.
      Lectures given from 1954 to 1960 by Taro Yashima,
      Annis Duff, William Pene du Bois, Elizabeth Gray Vining,
      Elizabeth Enright, Ruth Sawyer, Amelia Munson, Harry Behn,
      and Elisabeth Nesbitt. LC 60-53296.
      AUTHORS

729. SPIRT, Diana. Introducing More Books: A Guide to the
      Middle Grades. New York: R. R. Bowker, 1978. 240p.
      Continues series which includes Juniorplots and Introducing
      Books [see KOHLBERG; ELKIND].
      Plot summaries of 72 books with listing of approximately
      500 titles appropriate for the 8 to 15 age range. ISBN 0-
      8352-0988-1.
      BOOKTALKING

730. STANFORD, Barbara Dodds, and Karima Amin. Black Litera-
      ture for High School Students. Urbana, IL: National Coun-
      cil of Teachers of English, 1978. Paper 273p.

Paper text edition from Teachers College Press, Columbia University. ISBN 0-8141-0330-8.
BLACK; SECONDARY SCHOOLS

731. STENSLAND, Anna Lee. Literature By and About the American Indian: An Annotated Bibliography for Junior and Senior High School Students. Second edition. Urbana, IL: National Council of Teachers of English, 1979. 383p. First published 1973.
    Includes myth, legend, oratory, poetry, fiction, drama, biography, autobiography, history, anthropology, archaeology, modern life and problems, music, arts, and crafts. ISBN 0-8141-2984-6 [paper].
    AMERICAN INDIAN

732. STEWIG, John Warren. Children and Literature. Chicago: Rand McNally College Publishing Co., 1980. 562p.
    Instructional strategies and literary analysis. ISBN 0-395-30748-1.
    CHILDREN'S LITERATURE, TEXTBOOKS ON

733. STINTON, Judith [editor]. Racism and Sexism in Children's Books. New York: Writers and Readers, 1981. Illus. 148p. Papers on Children's Literature series.
    ISBN 0-906495-19-9; ISBN 0-906495-18-0 [paper].
    RACISM; SEXISM

734. STOTT, Jon C. Children's Literature from A to Z: A Guide for Parents and Teachers. New York: McGraw-Hill, 1984. Illus. Paper. 318p.
    Essays on authors, illustrators, literature by genre and themes. A selective approach. Bibliography. Index. ISBN 0-07-061791-0.
    SELECTION GUIDE

735. STREET, Douglas [editor]. Children's Novels and the Movies. New York: Ungar, 1983. Illus. Paper. 304p. Part of Ungar Film Library series.
    23 essays on children's books and their film adaptation. Not inclusive for all books made into movies. Appendices include a selective filmography, a bibliography and film rental sources for children's novels made into movies. ISBN 0-8044-2840-9; ISBN 0-8044-6883-4 [paper].
    FICTION; MOVIES ADAPTED FROM NOVELS

736. SUTHERLAND, Zena [editor]. The Best in Children's Books: The University of Chicago Guide to Children's Literature 1973-1978. Chicago: University of Chicago Press, 1980. 547p. Ongoing series.
    Selective reviews already published in the Bulletin of the Center for Children's Books. Indexes by title, curricular

use, reading level, subject and type of literature. ISBN 0-
226-78059-7.
BEST BOOKS

737. _____. History in Children's Books: An Annotated Bib-
liography for Schools and Libraries. Brooklawn, NJ: Mc-
Kinley Publishing Co., 1967. 248p. McKinley Bibliographies
Vol. V.
Chronological treatment by geographical sections and
historic periods. Author and title index.
HISTORY

738. _____; Dianne L. Monson; and May Hill Arbuthnot. Chil-
dren and Books. Sixth edition. Glenview, IL: Scott,
Foresman and Co., 1981. Illus. 678p. [See also ARBUTH-
NOT, May Hill.]
Practical guide to book evaluation and selection. Com-
prehensive bibliographies by topic. A standard text since
1947. ISBN 0-673-15377-0.
CHILDREN'S LITERATURE, TEXTBOOKS ON

739. SUTTON-SMITH, Brian, in collaboration with David M. Ab-
rams, et al. The Folkstories of Children. Philadelphia:
University of Pennsylvania Press, 1981. 311p. Publications
of the American Folklore Society: New Series; volume 3.
Emphasis is on children as authors in the oral tradition.
ISBN 0-8122-7781-3; ISBN 0-8122-1108-1 [paper].
FOLKSTORIES

740. SWINGER, Alice K. Children's Books: A Legacy for the
Young. Bloomington, IN: Phi Delta Kappa Educational
Foundation, 1981. Paper. 45p. Diamond Jubilee Series.
ISBN 0-87367-164-3.
CHILDREN'S LITERATURE, HISTORY & CRITICISM

741. TANDY, Lynette [compiler]. Books for Kids About Moving:
A Survival Guide for Parents. Los Angeles: The Bekins
Co. Paper.
Free to public libraries from the Public Relations De-
partment of the Bekins Company, 1335 S. Figueroa Street,
Los Angeles, CA 90015.
MOVING

742. TANYZER, Harold, and Jean Karl [compilers and editors].
Reading, Children's Books, and Our Pluralistic Society.
Prepared by a Joint Committee of the International Reading
Association and the Children's Book Council. Newark, DE:
International Reading Association, 1972. Paper. 89p.
Prospectives in Reading No. 16.
Papers and bibliography growing out of the

Prospectives in Reading Conference. LC 77-190455.
MULTIETHNIC; MULTICULTURAL

743. TARBERT, Gary C. [editor]. Children's Book Review Index.
Detroit: Gale Research Co., annual. Children's Book Review
Index Series.
Vol. 9: 1983 reviews indexed; ©1984 ISBN 0-8103-0634-4
Vol. 8: 1982 reviews indexed; ©1983 ISBN 0-8103-0633-6
Vol. 7: 1981 reviews indexed; ©1982 ISBN 0-8103-0632-8
Vol. 6: 1980 reviews indexed; ©1981 ISBN 0-8103-0631-X
Vol. 5: 1979 reviews indexed; ©1980 ISBN 0-8103-0630-1
Vol. 4: 1978 reviews indexed; ©1979 ISBN 0-8103-0629-8
Vol. 3: 1977 reviews indexed; ©1978 ISBN 0-8103-0628-X
Vol. 2: 1976 reviews indexed; ©1977 ISBN 0-8103-0627-1
Vol. 1: 1975 reviews indexed; ©1976 ISBN 0-8103-0626-3
ANNUAL; BOOK REVIEWS

744. _____. Children's Review Index: A Master Cumulation,
1969-1981. 4 vols. Detroit: Gale Research Co., 1982. 2059p.
ISBN 0-8103-2045-2.
BOOK REVIEWS

745. TARG, William [editor]. Bibliophile in the Nursery: A Book-
man's Treasury of Collector's Lore on Old and Rare Children's
Books. Metuchen, NJ: Scarecrow Publishing Co., 1969.
First published, Cleveland: World Publishing Co., 1957.
Illus. 503p.
RARE BOOKS

746. TAYLOR, Donna [editor]. The Great Lakes Region in Chil-
dren's Books: A Selected Annotated Bibliography. Brighton,
MI: Green Oak Press, 1980. 481p.
Hard and softcover books, magazines, and pamphlets
on Illinois, Indiana, Michigan, Minnesota, Ohio, Ontario,
Wisconsin, and the Great Lakes area in general. Multiple
indexes. ISBN 0-931600-01-4.
U.S., REGIONAL LITERATURE; CANADA

747. TERRY, Ann. Children's Poetry Preferences; A National
Survey of Upper Elementary Grades. Urbana, IL: National
Council of Teachers of English, 1974. 72p.
POETRY

748. THOMAS, Carol H. [editor]. Merlin's Magic: A Reading
Activities Idea Book for Use with Children. Phoenix, AZ:
Oryx Press, 1984. Illus. Paper. 96p. Part of Fun With
Reading Series.
Emphasis is on the planning and organizing of reading
programs in public and school libraries. ISBN 0-89774-091-2.
ACTIVE READERS, DEVELOPING

748a. _____. Sports Splash: A Handbook of Reading Activities
for Use with Children. Phoenix, AZ: Oryx Press, 1983.
Illus. Paper. 110p. Part of Fun With Reading Series.
ISBN 0-89774-000-9.
SPORTS

749. THOMAS, James L. Sharing Books with Young Children.
Phoenix, AZ: Oryx Press, 1981. ISBN 0-912700-99-8.
ACTIVE READERS, DEVELOPING

750. _____. Turning Kids On to Print Using Nonprint. Illus-
trated by Carol H. Thomas; Photos by James L. Thomas.
Littleton, CO: Libraries Unlimited, 1978. Illus. 168p.
Bibliography; index. ISBN 0-87287-184-3.
ACTIVE READERS, DEVELOPING

751. _____, and Ruth M. Loring [editors]. Motivating Children
and Young Adults to Read. Vol. 2. Phoenix, AZ: Oryx
Press, 1983. 208p. Vol. 1, 1979, 189p.
Compilation of recent journal articles on how to motivate
students to read. Bibliography of sources. Index. ISBN
0-912700-34-3 [vol. 1]; ISBN 0-89774-046-7 [vol. 2, paper].
ACTIVE READERS, DEVELOPING

752. THOMISON, Dennis. Reading About Adolescent Literature.
Metuchen, NJ: Scarecrow Press, 1970. 222p.
Addresses, essays, and lectures. Includes bibliograph-
ical references. ISBN 0-8108-0282-1.
ADOLESCENT LITERATURE

753. THWAITE, M. F. From Primer to Pleasure: An Introduction
to the History of Children's Books in England from the In-
vention of Printing to 1900, With an Outline of Some Develop-
ments in Other Countries. Revised edition. Boston: Horn
Book, Inc., 1972. Illus. 340p. First published, London:
Library Association, 1963.
Comprehensive coverage. ISBN 0-87675-275-X.
BRITAIN; CHILDREN'S LITERATURE, HISTORY &
CRITICISM

754. TIEDT, Irish M. [editor]. Drama in Your Classroom: Annotated Bibliography. Urbana, IL: National Council of Teachers of English, 1974.
DRAMATIC LITERATURE

755. _____. Exploring Books with Children. Boston: Hough-
ton Mifflin, 1979. 560p. Includes bibliographies; index.
ACTIVE READERS, DEVELOPING; CHILDREN'S LITER-
ATURE, TEXTBOOKS ON

756. TORONTO PUBLIC LIBRARIES; Boys and Girls Division.
The Osborne Collection of Early Children's Books, 1566-1910:

A Catalogue. Introduction by Edgar Osborne. Judith St. John, editor. Vol. 1: 1566-1910, 561p.; Vol. 2: 1476-1910. Toronto: Toronto Public Libraries, 1958; 1966; 1975.
Approximately 3,000 books from the collection in this catalogue. The intent of the collection is to be "representative of the various streams of writing for children." ISBN 0-919486-25-8 [Vol. 1]; ISBN 0-919486-54-1 [Vol. 2].
CANADA; SPECIAL COLLECTIONS; BRITAIN

757. _____. Osborne Collection: Toronto Public Library Early English Children's Books. Illustrated by Holp Shuppan. Topsfield, MA: Merrimack Publishing Circle, n.d. 35 bks.
ISBN 0-370-30371-7.
CANADA; SPECIAL COLLECTIONS

758. TOWNSEND, John Rowe. A Sense of Story: Essays on Contemporary Writers for Children. Philadelphia: J. B. Lippincott, 1971, 1975. Boston: Horn Book, Inc., 1973. 216p.
Discusses work of 10 English language writers from the U.S., Great Britain, and Australia, with a bibliography for each author. LC 79-155797 [Lippincott]; ISBN 0-87675-276-8 [Horn Book].
AUTHORS

759. _____. A Sounding of Storytellers: Essays on Contemporary Writers for Children. New and Revised. New York: J. B. Lippincott, 1971, 1979. 218p.
Covers 14 authors, with bibliographies for each. ISBN 0-397-31882-0.
AUTHORS

760. _____. Written for Children: An Outline of English-Language Children's Literature. Second revised edition. Philadelphia: J. B. Lippincott, 1983. 384p. First edition ©1965; first revised edition 1975.
Notes and bibliography. Index. ISBN 0-397-31528-7.
CHILDREN'S LITERATURE, HISTORY & CRITICISM

761. TREFNY, Beverly Robin, and Eileen C. Palmer. Index to Children's Plays in Collections. Third edition. Metuchen, NJ: Scarecrow Press, 1986. [See KREIDER, Barbara, for second edition.]
ISBN 0-8108-1893-0.
DRAMATIC LITERATURE

762. TRELEASE, Jim. The Read-Aloud Handbook. Revised edition. Photographs by Joanne Rathe. New York: Penguin Books, 1985. Paper. 240p. First published 1979; annual editions.
300 recommended titles include wordless picture books; short novels; novels; poetry; and anthologies. Author-

illustrator index. ISBN 0-14-046727-0 [1985]; ISBN 0-8446-6172-4 [1984 edition, Peter Smith]; ISBN 0-8423-5251-1 [1983 edition, Tyndale]; ISBN 0-14-046534-0 [1982 edition].
READING ALOUD

763. TUCKER, Nicholas [editor]. Suitable for Children?: Controversies in Children's Literature. Berkeley: University of California Press, 1976. 224p.
Contrasting views on what children like to read, what adults think children should like, and what some of the effects of reading are. ISBN 0-520-03236-5.
CHILDREN'S LITERATURE, HISTORY & CRITICISM

764. TUER, Andrew W. Pages and Pictures from Forgotten Children's Books. Detroit: Singing Tree Press, 1969. 510p. First published, London: The Leadenhall Press, Ltd., 1898-99.
Introduction describes coloring process of the early books. Index. ISBN 0-405-09034-X.
FACSIMILE EDITIONS

765. _____. Stories from Old-Fashioned Children's Books, Brought Together and Introduced to the Reader. Detroit: Singing Tree Press, 1968. Illus. 439p. First published, London: The Leadenhall Press, Ltd., 1899-1900.
Eighteenth-century stories. LC 68-31438.
FACSIMILE EDITIONS

766. TWAY, Eileen [editor]. Reading Ladders for Human Relations. Sixth edition. With National Council of Teachers of English Committee on Reading Ladders for Human Relations. Washington, DC: American Council on Education, 1981. Paper. 398p. Editions One to Three edited by M. M. Heaton; Edition Four edited by M. E. Crosby; Edition Five edited by Virginia M. Reid.
Ladder I, growing into self; II, relating to others; III, interacting in groups; IV, appreciating different cultures; V, coping in a changing world. Author and title indexes. ISBN 0-8268-1414-X.
MULTIETHNIC

767. TYMN, Marshall B.; Kenneth J. Zahorski; and Robert H. Boyer. Fantasy Literature: A Core Collection and Reference Guide. New York: R. R. Bowker, 1979. 273p.
68 titles for children in this "all ages" guide. ISBN 0-8352-1153-3.
FANTASY

768. ULLOM, Judith C. [compiler]. Folklore of the North American Indians: An Annotated Bibliography. Washington, DC: Children's Book Section, Library of Congress, 1969. Illus. 126p.
152 entries in eleven culture areas: Eskimo, Mackenzie,

Plateau, North Pacific, California, Plains, Central Woodland, Northwest Woodland, Iroquois, Southeast, Southwest. Includes children's anthologies. Index. LC 70-601462.
AMERICAN INDIAN; FOLKLORE

769. UNIVERSITY PRESS BOOKS for Secondary School Libraries. Sixteenth edition. Chicago: American Library Association, 1983. Paper. 73p. Updated every three years.
Sixteenth edition describes 242 fiction and nonfiction titles suitable for secondary school students. ISBN 0-8389-6573-3.
SECONDARY SCHOOLS; ANNUAL

770. VANDERGRIFT, Kay E. Child and Story: The Literary Connection. Jane Anne Hannigan, editor. New York: Neal-Schuman Publishers, 1980. Paper. 340p. Diversity and Directions in Children's Literature Series.
Includes bibliography, index. ISBN 0-918212-42-1.
CHILDREN'S LITERATURE, HISTORY & CRITICISM

771. VAN ORDEN, Phyllis J. Collection Program in Elementary and Middle Schools: Concepts, Practices, and Information Sources. Illustrated by William R. Harper. Littleton, CO: Libraries Unlimited, 1982. Illus. 301p. Library Science Text Series.
Includes bibliographies; index. ISBN 0-87287-335-8.
CORE COLLECTION

772. _____. The Collection Program in High Schools: Concepts, Practices and Information Sources. Illus. by William R. Harper. Littleton, CO: Libraries Unlimited, 1985. Illus. 289p. Library Science Text Series.
Lists of associations and agencies, as well as bibliographies and selection tools. Index. ISBN 0-87287-483-4.
CORE COLLECTION

773. VAN TASSEL, D. [editor]. Computers, Computers, Computers: In Fiction and Verse. Nashville, TN: Thomas Nelson, Inc., 1977. 192p.
Range is from humorous to serious. ISBN 0-8407-6542-8.
COMPUTERS

774. VARLEJS, Jana [editor]. Young Adult Literature in the Seventies: A Selection of Readings. Metuchen, NJ: Scarecrow Press, 1978. 462p.
59 articles on reading interest, minorities in YA literature, nonficiton, and titles "to get kids hooked on books." Lists of books. ISBN 0-8108-1134-0.
YOUNG ADULTS

775. VELLEMAN, Ruth A. Serving Physically Disabled People.
New York: R. R. Bowker, 1979. 392p.
     Core collection suggested. Subject index. ISBN 0-
8352-1167-3.
     DISABILITIES

776. VIGEURS, Ruth Hill; Marcia Dalphin; and Bertha Mahony
Miller. Illustrators of Children's Books, 1946-1956. Boston:
Horn Book, 1958. Illus. 299p. Part of the illustrators
series.
     Approximately 500 illustrators discussed. Multiple in-
dexes. LC 57-31264.
     ILLUSTRATORS

777. _____. Margin for Surprise: About Books, Children and
Librarians. Boston: Little Brown, 1964. 175p.
     Essays that continue to inspire. LC 64-21491.
     ACTIVE READERS, DEVELOPING; CHILDREN'S LITERA-
TURE, HISTORY & CRITICISM

778. VRIES, Leonard de [editor]. Flowers of Delight: From the
Osborne Collection of Early Childrens Books.... Designed
by Eric Ayers. New York: Pantheon Books, 1965. Illus.
232p.
     Notes on the original books, authors, illustrators, and
publishers, along with presentation of books. LC 65-23741.
     SPECIAL COLLECTIONS; CANADA

779. _____. Little Wide Awake: An Anthology from Victorian
Children's Books in the Collection of Anne and Fernand G.
Renier. Introduction by M. F. Thwaite. Cleveland: World
Publishing Co., 1967. Illus. 240p.
     Notes on the presentation. LC 67-23362.
     SPECIAL COLLECTIONS; CANADA

780. WAGGONER, Diana. The Hills of Faraway: A Guide to Fantasy. New York: Atheneum, 1978. Illus. 326p.
     530 titles for children. Indexes.
     FANTASY

781. WALKER, Elinor [editor-compiler]. Book Bait: Detailed Notes
on Adult Books Popular with Young People. Third edition.
Chicago: American Library Association, 1979. Paper. 172p.
First published 1957; revised 1968.
     Books of interest to 13 to 16 year olds. Descriptions
complete enough to use as book talks. ISBN 0-8389-0279-0.
     YOUNG ADULTS; FICTION

782. _____. Doors to More Mature Reading: Detailed Notes on

Adult Books for Use with Young People. Second edition.
Chicago: American Library Association, 1981. Paper. 233p.
125 fiction and nonfiction titles described. ISBN 0-
8389-0344-4.
YOUNG ADULTS

783. WALSH, Frances [compiler]. That Eager Zest: First Dis-
coveries in the Magic World of Books. New York: J. B.
Lippincott, 1961. 251p.
Noted writers tell of their childhood reading experi-
ences.
AUTHORS; CHILDREN'S LITERATURE, HISTORY &
CRITICISM

784. WARD, Martha E., and Dorothy A. Marquardt. Authors of
Books for Young People. Supplement to the Second Edition.
Metuchen, NJ: Scarecrow Press, 1979. 302p. First edi-
tion, 1964; supplement to the first edition, 1967; second
edition, 1971.
Selective regarding inclusion. ISBN 0-8108-1159-6
[1979]; ISBN 0-8108-0404-0 [1971].
AUTHORS

785. _____. Illustrators of Books for Young People. Second
edition. Metuchen, NJ: Scarecrow Press, 1975. 233p.
First edition, 1970.
750 biographies, including Caldecott recipients. ISBN
0-8108-0819-6.
ILLUSTRATORS

786. _____. Photography in Books for Young People. Metuchen,
NJ: Scarecrow Press, 1985. 107p. Introduction by Barbara
S. Bates.
Covers 376 titles, illustrated with photographs. In-
cludes data on photographers. Author and title indexes.
ISBN 0-8108-1854-X.
PHOTOGRAPHY; ILLUSTRATION

787. WASS, Hannelore, and Charles A. Corr [editors]. Helping
Children Cope with Death: Guidelines and Resources. Washington, DC: Hemisphere Publishing Corporation, 1982. Illus.
194p.
Title index to books on graded levels. ISBN 0-89116-
247-X.
DEATH

788. WEHMEYER, Lillian Biermann. Images in a Crystal Ball:
World Futures in Novels for Young People. Littleton, CO:
Libraries Unlimited, 1981. 211p.
Discusses 150 novels published since 1964 that are set
in a future time and are written for students in grades 8

or below. ISBN 0-87287-219-X.
    FUTURISM; FICTION

789. WEISS, Jaqueline Shachter. Prizewinning Books for Children:
    Themes and Stereotypes in U.S. Prizewinning Prose Fiction
    for Children. Lexington, MA: D. C. Heath, 1983. 480p.
    Part of Libraries & Librarianship Special Series.
        Over 700 fiction and picture books that have won U.S.
    awards, grouped within grade levels by genres. ISBN 0-
    669-06352-5.
        PRIZEWINNING BOOKS

790. WELLNER, Cathryn J. Witness to War: A Thematic Guide
    to Young Adult Literature on World War II, 1965-1981.
    Metuchen, NJ: Scarecrow Press, 1982. 287p.
        Covers all aspects of World War II for books published
    in or translated into English, French, and German. ISBN
    0-8108-1552-4.
        WORLD WAR II

791. WENZEL, Evelyn L. [compiler]. Time for Discovery: Infor-
    mational Books. Glenview, IL: Scott, Foresman, 1971.
        INFORMATIONAL BOOKS

792. WESTON WOODS. Weston Woods Catalog.
        Sound filmstrips, recordings, and motion pictures re-
    lated to outstanding children's books. Paper. Annual.
        MULTIMEDIA

793. WHALLEY, Joyce Irene. Cobwebs to Catch Flies: Illustrated
    Books for the Nursery and Schoolroom, 1700-1900. Berkeley:
    University of California Press, 1975.
        Critical analysis by topical listing. ISBN 0-520-02931-3.
        ILLUSTRATION

794. WHEELBARGER, Johnny J. Children's Literature Handbook.
    New York: MSS Information Corp., 1974. 94p.
        Includes bibliography. ISBN 0-8422-0442-3.
        CHILDREN'S LITERATURE, HISTORY & CRITICISM

795. WHITE, Gabriel. Edward Ardizzone: Artist and Illustrator.
    New York: Schocken Books, 1980. Illus. 192p.
        Pictorial record of Ardizzone's work. ISBN 0-8052-
    3754-2.
        ILLUSTRATOR

796. WHITE, Mary Lou [editor]. Adventuring with Books: A
    Booklist for Preschool-Grade 6. Urbana, IL: National Coun-
    cil of Teachers of English, 1981. Paper. 500p.
        Approximately 2,500 children's titles selected from
    10,000 books published between 1977 and 1980. All books

listed "are recommended for their literary merit, high poten-
tial interest for children and equitable treatment of minorities." Replaces earlier edition edited by Patricia Cianciolo
[1966, 1977]. ISBN 0-8141-0075-9; ISBN 0-686-86378-X
[text edition for members].
PRESCHOOL; MIDDLE GRADES; SELECTION GUIDE

797. WHITE, Virginia L., and Emerita S. Schulte [editors]. Books
About Children's Books: An Annotated Bibliography. Newark,
DE: International Reading Association, 1979. 48p. IRA
Annotated Bibliography Series.
Includes materials on bibliographies, biographies, criti-
cism, history, indexes, research, teaching methodology,
textbooks. Index. ISBN 0-87207-333-5.
BIBLIOGRAPHY OF BIBLIOGRAPHIES

798. WHITEHEAD, Robert J. Children's Literature: Strategies of
Teaching. New York: Prentice Hall, 1968.
ISBN 0-13-132589-2.
CHILDREN'S LITERATURE, TEXTBOOKS ON

799. _____. A Guide to Selecting Books for Children. Metuch-
en, NJ: Scarecrow Press, Inc., 1984. 323p.
Description and analysis of 13 genre divisions for infants through beginning readers and 19 genre divisions for
readers aged 8 to 11. ISBN 0-8108-1691-1.
SELECTION GUIDE

800. WILKIN, Binnie Tate. Survival Themes in Fiction for Chil-
dren and Young People. Foreword by Jerome Cushman.
Metuchen, NJ: Scarecrow Press, 1978. 262p.
Themes include the individual, pairings and groupings,
and views of the world. Discussion is on impact of society
on the individual and the group. Age levels given. General
Index. ISBN 0-8108-1048-4.
BIBLIOTHERAPY; FICTION

801. WILKINSON, J. P. Canadian Juvenile Fiction and the Library
Market. Ottawa: Canadian Library Association, 1976. Pa-
per. 87p.
ISBN 0-88802-112-7.
CANADA; FICTION

802. WILLIAMS, Helen Elizabeth. The High/Low Consensus. Williamsport, PA: Bro-Dart Publishing Co., 1980. Paper.
259p.
1,100 titles grouped within reading levels from 1 to 10,
with full descriptions. Subject index and title, author index.
ISBN 0-87272-088-8.
HIGH INTEREST/LOW VOCABULARY

803.   _____, with Katherine Mary Gloden. Independent Read-
       ing, K-3. Williamsport, PA: Bro-Dart Publishing Co.,
       1980. Paper. 120p. Supersedes bibliography by Gayle
       Syphen Jacob, ©1975.
           1,274 titles grouped for reading levels by subjects and
       subheads. Author, title index. ISBN 0-87272-089-6.
           INDEPENDENT READING

804. WILMS, Denise Murcko [editor]. Science Books for Children:
       Selections from Booklist, 1976-1983. Chicago: American Li-
       brary Association, 1985. Paper. 192p.
           Annotations of some 500 of the best trade science books
       that have been reviewed in Booklist, 1976-1983. Includes ti-
       tles for all reading levels and interests; arranged by Dewey
       Classification. Author/Title and Subject indexes. ISBN 0-
       8389-3312-2.
           SCIENCE

805. WILSON, A. E. Penny Plain, Two Pence Coloured: A His-
       tory of the Juvenile Drama. Foreword by Charles B. Coch-
       ran. New York: The Macmillan Company, n.d. Illus.
       118p.
           Covers nineteenth-century and early twentieth-century
       plays for young audiences. Lists of publishers, including
       West's Plays 1811-1831. Bibliography of works published
       between 1868 and 1925. Indexes of people and plays.
           DRAMATIC LITERATURE

806. WILSON, Barbara Ker. Writing for Children: An English
       Author and Editor's Point of View. New York: Franklin
       Watts, Inc., 1961 [©1960]. 128p.
           It's one person's approach to authorship and editing.
       Bibliography; list of Carnegie Medal winners; index. LC
       61-11336.
           AUTHORS; PUBLISHING; BRITAIN

807. WILSON, Geraldine L. An Annotated Bibliography of Chil-
       dren's Picture Books: An Introduction to the Literature of
       Head Start's Children. Washington, DC: U.S. Government
       Printing Office (Head Start Bureau), 1979. Paper. 85p.
           Has lists for seven minority groups: African Ameri-
       cans, Chicano/Mexican Americans, Chinese, Franco-
       Americans, Japanese, American Indians, and Puerto Ricans.
       ISBN 0-017-092-00038-3.
           PICTURE BOOKS; MULTIETHNIC

THE H. W. WILSON COMPANY see Children's Catalog;
Junior High School Library Catalog; Senior High School Library Catalog. For Junior Authors and Illustrators Series
see DEMONTREVILLE, Doris; FULLER, Muriel; HOLTZE,
Sally Holmes; and KUNITZ, Stanley J.

808. WILSON, Jane B. [compiler]. Children's Writings: A Bib-
      liography of Works in English. Jefferson, NC, and London:
      McFarland, 1982. 187p.
          "This is an eclectic bibliography, partially annotated,
      of books by or about children and youth who wrote and, in
      most instances, published manuscripts by the age of 21 or
      younger." The 737 entries are listed by author. Appendix
      A is an essay on seven-year-old writers; Appendix B is an
      essay on teenage-girl diarists. ISBN 0-89950-043-9.
          CHILDREN'S WRITINGS

809. _____. The Story Experience. Metuchen, NJ: Scarecrow
      Press, 1979. 177p.
          Includes storytelling techniques; filmography; list of
      radio programs; audio tapes; storytelling sources and re-
      sources, thirteenth century to the present; descriptions of
      storytellers. Includes bibliographies; index. ISBN 0-8108-
      1224-X.
          STORYTELLING; FILMOGRAPHY

      WILTS, John E. see CRIDLAND, Nancy

      WINKEL, Lois see THE ELEMENTARY SCHOOL Library Col-
      lection

810. WINTLE, Justin, and Emma Fisher. The Pied Pipers: Inter-
      views with the Influential Creators of Children's Literature.
      New York: Paddington Press, Ltd., 1975. Illus. 320p.
          Interviews of 23 major figures coming on the children's
      literature scene after World War II. ISBN 0-8467-0038-7.
          BRITAIN; AUTHORS; ILLUSTRATORS

811. WISCONSIN LIBRARY ASSOCIATION. Children's Films.
      Madison: Wisconsin Library Association, n.d. Paper. 20p.
          180 titles of films, with full annotation and citation,
      to tie-in with books.
          FILMOGRAPHY

812. WISE, Bernice Kemler. Teaching Materials for the Learning
      Disabled: A Selected List for Grades 6-12. Chicago: Amer-
      ican Library Association, 1980. Paper. 64p.
          Includes fiction and nonfiction for classroom and per-
      sonal use. Reading and interest levels are noted. Includes
      publishers and address; author/title index. ISBN 0-8389-
      0311-8.
          DISABILITIES

813. WITHROW, Dorothy E.; Helen B. Carey; and Bertha M. Hir-
      zel. Gateways to Readable Books, Fifth Edition: An Anno-
      tated, Graded List of Books in Many Fields for Adolescents
      Who Are Reluctant to Read or Find Reading Difficult. New

York: H. W. Wilson Co., 1975. 299p. First edition, ©1944
by Ruth Strang, Alice Checkovitz, Christine Gilbert, and
Margaret Scoggin. Subsequent editions, ©1952, ©1958, ©1966.
Includes approximately 1,000 titles classified according
to 74 subjects and sub-heads, with brief annotations that
include grade level. Mutliple indexes. ISBN 0-8242-0566-9.
HIGH INTEREST/LOW VOCABULARY

814. WITUCKE, Virginia. Children's Informational Books. New
York: R. R. Bowker Co., 1983. 192p.
Includes titles on a broad range of subjects. ISBN
0-89774-079-3.
INFORMATIONAL BOOKS

815. _____. Literature for Children: Poetry in the Elementary
School. Pose Lamb, consulting editor. Dubuque, IA: Wm.
C. Brown Co., 1970. Paper. 115p.
Covers what poetry is, how to locate poems and poets,
and how to set up a viable poetry program in the elementary
school. Extensive bibliographies; index. ISBN 0-697-06206-6.
POETRY

816. WOLFE, Ann G. About 100 Books ... A Gateway to Better
Intergroup Understanding. Seventh edition. New York:
American Jewish Committee, Institute of Human Relations,
1972. Illus. Paper. 48p. First published 1962.
MULTIETHNIC

817. WOLFF, Kathryn, and Jill Storey [compilers and editors].
AAAS Science Book List Supplement. Washington, DC:
American Association for the Advancement of Science, 1978.
First published 1959.
Listing of approximately 2,850 selected trade and text
books appropriate for junior and senior high school levels.
Extends coverage from third edition to titles published be-
tween 1969 and 1977. ISBN 0-87168-218-4.
SCIENCE

818. WOLFF, Kathryn; Joellen M. Fritsche; Elina N. Gross; and
Gary T. Todd [compilers and editors]. The Best Science
Books for Children: A Selected and Annotated List of Sci-
ence Books for Children Ages Five Through Twelve. Wash-
ington, DC: American Association for the Advancement of
Science, 1983. 276p.
Approximately 1,300 books within detailed subject in-
dexes with age group designations and ordering information.
Publication dates range from mid-1970s to 1982. Title and
author indexes. ISBN 0-87168-307-5.
SCIENCE

819. WOOLMAN, Bertha. The Caldecott Award: The Winners and

the Honor Books.   Minneapolis: T. S. Denison, Paper.
1978; 1981. 96p.
Questions and answers about award winners and honor
books; brief biographies of all winners, listed in alphabetical
order by last name; title index. ISBN 0-513-01718-6.
AWARDS

820. _____. The Newbery Award: These Are Winners: The
Books and Their Authors. Minneapolis: T. S. Denison,
1978. Paper. 78p.
Information on each author, up to 1977, includes references to biographical and critical data. Geared for young
people, the format provides clues about an award book and
its author so that the reader can supply the title and author's
name. LC 78-67193.
AWARDS

821. THE WORLD BOOK ENCYCLOPEDIA. "Literature for Children"
reprint. Zena Sutherland, contributing editor. Chicago:
World Book-Childcraft International, Inc., 1981. Paper.
28p.
Lists of books for all ages and genres. Also available
are reprints on authors and illustrators, characters and
works, genres, personalities, and awards in literature for
children. These reprints are updates for encyclopedia articles.
CHILDREN'S LITERATURE, HISTORY & CRITICISM

822. WYNAR, Christine Gehrt. Guide to reference Books for
School Media Centers. Second edition. Littleton, CO: Libraries Unlimited, 1981. 377p. First edition, ©1973, 473p.;
Supplement, ©1976, 131p.
Subjects treated are those generally included in cur-
ricular and extracurricular topics. Entries are arranged by
author under 54 main subject headings, with paperback editions indicated where available. Also reviews sources, selection aids for print and nonprint titles, including videotapes
and minicomputer programs. The three volumes cover approximately 5,000 books. ISBN 0-87287-256-4 [1981]; ISBN
0-87287-069-3 [1973]; ISBN 0-82787-121-5 [1976].
REFERENCE BOOKS

YESTERDAY'S AUTHORS of Books for Children   see COM-
MIRE, Ann

823. YOLEN, Jane. Touch Magic: Fantasy, Faerie and Folklore
in the Literature of Childhood. New York: Philomel Books,
1981. 128p.
Collection of essays on the importance of fairytale and

fantasy. Bibliography. ISBN 0-399-20830-5.
       FANTASY; FOLKLORE; CHILDREN'S LITERATURE,
       HISTORY & CRITICISM

824. YONKERS PUBLIC LIBRARY Children's Services. A Guide
      to Subjects and Concepts in Picture Book Format. Second
      edition. Dobbs Ferry, NY: Oceana Publications, Inc., 1979.
      163p. First published 1974.
           Extensive bibliography of titles with and without words,
      under 55 main-subject categories with subheadings and cross-
      references. While the titles are limited to those in the Yonk-
      ers Public Library, the list does contain some 2,000 entries.
      ISBN 0-379-20276-X [1979]; ISBN 0-379-00131-4 [1974].
           PICTURE BOOKS

825. YOUNG, Sharon. Mathematics in Children's Books: An An-
      notated Bibliography Preschool Through Grade 3. Palo Alto,
      CA: Creative Publications, 1979. Paper. 96p.
           Titles selected can initiate or supplement mathematics
      instruction. Organization is by topic, with subtopics, alpha-
      betically by author, and including reading level. Topics in-
      clude numbers, arithmetic operations, measurement, time and
      money, geometry and special topics. List of publishers;
      title index. ISBN 0-88488-116-4.
           MATHEMATICS

826. YOUNG RELATIONSHIPS. Compiled by British Columbia
      Teacher-Librarians's Association. Hope, British Columbia:
      BCT-LA, 1984. 150p.
           American and British titles, published since 1978, un-
      der coping, delinquency, family problems, first love, handi-
      caps, peer relationships, suicide. Subject and title indexes.
           INTERRELATIONSHIPS; BOOKTALKING; YOUNG ADULT;
      CONTEMPORARY ISSUES

827. ZIEGLER, Elsie B. Folklore: An Annotated Bibliography
      and Index to Single Editions. Westwood, MA: F. W. Faxon
      Co., 1973 [1975]. 203p.
           A location aid divided into six sections: Annotated
      Title Bibliography, Subject Index, Motif Index, Country In-
      dex, Type of Folklore Index, and Illustrator Index. ISBN
      0-87305-100-9.
           FOLKLORE

828. ZIPES, Jack. The Trials and Tribulations of Little Red Rid-
      ing Hood: Versions of the Tale in Sociocultural Context.
      South Hadley, MA: Bergin and Garvey, 1983. Illus. 298p.
           Contains the texts of 31 versions of the tale, in chrono-
      logical order of publications. Bibliography of "Red Riding

Hood Texts." ISBN 0-89789-023-X.
    FOLKTALES

829. ZISKIND, Sylvia. Telling Stories to Children. New York:
    H. W. Wilson Co., 1976. 157p.
        Bibliography on "how to" titles. Index. ISBN 0-
    8242-0588-X.
        STORYTELLING

APPENDIX A: RESOURCE LOCATIONS

Resource locations for lists, reviews and other publications on literature for young people, that do not appear in the main Resource Guide.*

The Advertising Council Inc.
825 Third Avenue
New York, NY 10022
    Supports and promotes national public service advertising campaigns.

Alexander Graham Bell Association for the Deaf
1537 Thirty-fifth Street, NW
Washington, DC 20007
    Publishes a graded, annotated list, "Books for Deaf Children."

American Association for Gifted Children
15 Gramercy Park
New York, NY 10003
    Publishes list available upon request.

American Association of Retired Persons
P.O. Box 199
Long Beach, CA 90801
    With the National Retired Teachers Association publishes guides available upon request.

The American Books Awards
One Park Avenue
New York, NY 10016
    Publishes a catalog of nominated books.

American Educational Research Association
1230 Seventeenth Street, NW
Washington, DC 20036
    Lists available upon request.

---

*The addresses provided are those known at the time of the completion of the manuscript. They cannot be guaranteed to be accurate at the time this volume is published. If a request is returned, a new address can be verified through standard sources available in most libraries.

American Federation of Labor and Congress of Industrial Organizations
815 Sixteenth Street, NW
Washington, DC 20006
    Guides on career-related titles available upon request.

American Folklore Society
University of Pennsylvania Press
3933 Walnut Street
Philadelphia, PA 19104
    Catalog of materials available.

American Institute of Architects
1735 New York AVenue, NW
Washington, DC 20006
    Catalog of trade books related to architects and architecture.

American Institute of Graphic Arts (AIGA)
1059 Third Avenue
New York, NY 10021
    Publishes illustrated catalog of outstanding children's books
    in relation to exhibits it sponsors.

American Society for Aerospace Education
1750 Pennsylvania Ave, NW, Suite 1303
Washington, DC 20006
    Lists of related trade books available.

Association for Children with Learning Disabilities
4156 Library Road
Pittsburgh, PA 15234
    Guides available.

Auromere
1291 Weber Street
Pomona, CA 91768
    Catalog of children's books from India available.

The Authors Guild, Inc.
234 West 44th Street
New York, NY 10036
    Quarterly bulletin publishes articles related to young people's
    literature; could be a source for data on authors.

Big Brothers/Big Sisters of America
220 Suburban Station Building
Philadelphia, PA 19103
    Related trade titles issued as guides, periodically.

Canadian Book Information Center
70 The Esplanade
Toronto, Ontario, Canada M5E 1A6

Publishes "A Guide to Selecting Canadian Materials" which includes literature for young readers.

Canadian Children's Literature Association
Box 335
Guelph, Ontario, Canada N1H 6K5
Offers a variety of materials on selection and use of literature for young readers.

Center for Children's Books
University of Chicago Graduate School Library
Chicago, IL 60637

Center for Early Adolescence
Suite 223, Carr Mill Mall
Carrboro, NC 27510

Center for Inter-American Relations, UNICEF
381 East 38th Street
New York, NY 10016
Information on children's cultures.

Center for Sex Equity
Publications are available through Oryx Press.

Center for Urban Education
33 West 42nd Street
New York, NY 10036

Child Care Action Campaign
Box 313
New York, NY 10185

The Children's Book Centre
229 College Street, 5th Floor
Toronto, Ontario, Canada M5T 1RA

Children's Book Centre
140 Church Street
London, W 8, England

Children's Defense Fund
122 C Street, NW
Washington, DC 20001

Children's Divorce Center Press
264 Amith Road
Woodbridge, CT 06525

The Children's Literature Association (ChLA)
c/o Ruth MacDonald, Dept. of English, Box 3E

New Mexico State University
Las Cruces, NM 88003
    (In 1985 announced a new award, called the Phoenix Award,
    to be given to the children's author whose work has passed
    the test of time and been deemed of high literary quality.)
    Publishes Children's Literature: An International Journal
    (annual).

Children's Literature Foundation
Box 370
Windham Center, CT 06280

Children's Radio Theatre
Box 53057
Washington, DC 20009

Church and Synagogue Library Association
P.O. Box 1130
Bryn Mawr, PA 19010

Cooperative Children's Book Center
P.O. Box 5288
(Room 411 West, State Capitol)
Madison, WI 53702
    Among other things, publishes Alternative Press Publishers
    of Children's Books: A Directory.

The Council for Exceptional Children
1920 Association Drive
Reston, VA 22091

Cultural Information Service
P.O. Box 786, Madison Square Station
New York, NY 10159
    Publishes viewers' guides on year-round television program-
    ming, including reviews of books.

Family Guidance Center
910 Edmond, Suite 100
St. Joseph, MO 64501

Feminists on Children's Media
162-11 Ninth Ave.
Whitestone, NY 11357

Folklore Society
c/o University College London
Gower Street
London, WC 1E 6BT, England

Illinois State Library
Springfield, IL 62756

One annual issue of <u>Illinois Libraries</u> is on services and materials for young readers.

Information Center on Children's Culture (ICCC)
U.S. Committee for UNICEF
331 E. 38th St.
New York, NY 10016
   Book lists and materials available.

Initial Reading Alphabet Publications, Inc.
20 East 46th Street
New York, NY 10027

Institute of Modern Languages
Silver Spring, MD 20900

International Board on Books for Young People
Elizabethstrasse 15
8000 Munich 40, Federal Republic of Germany
   Publishes papers on the IBBY Congresses.

Modern Language Association of America
Division on Children's Literature
62 Fifth Ave.
New York, NY 10011
   Seminar on Children's Literature at the annual MLA meetings.

Montana Reading Publications
Level 4, Stapleton Bldng.
Billings, MT 59101
   "Provides a series of brochures which list high interest low-reading level books which are indigenous to American Indian culture, background and experiences."

Music Library Association
343 S. Main St., Room 205
Ann Arbor, MI 48108

National Art Education Association
1201 Sixteenth St. NW
Washington, DC 20036

National Association for Education by Radio-Television
1201 Sixteenth St. NW
Washington, DC 20036

National Association for Gifted Children
5100 North Edgewood Dr.
St. Paul, MN 55112

National Association for the Advancement of Colored People (NAACP)
186 Remsen St.
Brooklyn, NY 11201

National Association for the Preservation and Perpetuation of Story-
     telling
Box 112
Jonesborough, TN 37659
     Publishes National Storytelling Journal and The Yarnspinner.

National Association of Independent Schools
Four Liberty Square
Boston, MA 02109

National Committee for Citizens in Education
Suite 410, Wilde Lake Village Green
Columbia, MD 21044

The National Committee for the Prevention of Child Abuse
322 S. Michigan, Suite 1250
Chicago, IL 60604

National Congress of Parents and Teachers
700 N. Rush St.
Chicago, IL 60611

National Council for Children and Television
20 Nassau Street
Princeton, NJ 08540

National Council of Teachers of English
1111 Kenyon Rd.
Urbana, IL 61801

National Information Center for Special Education Materials
University of Southern California
University Park
Los Angeles, CA 90007

National Information Center for the Handicapped
Box 1492
Washington, DC 20013

National Information Center on Deafness
Gallaudet College
Kendall Green
Washington, DC 20002

The National Library Service for the Blind and Physically Handi-
     capped
Library of Congress
Washington, DC 20542

National Science Teachers Association
1201 Sixteenth St. NW
Washington, DC 20036

Navaho Curriculum Center
Rough Rock Demonstration School
Chinle, AZ 86503

Navajo Social Studies Project
College of Education
University of New Mexico
Albuquerque, NM 87106

The Negro Bibliographic and Research Center, Inc.
117 R. Street NE
Washington, DC 20002

New Hampshire State Library
20 Park St.
Concord, NH   03301

North Central Regional Educational Materials Project
111 N. Curtiss Hall
Iowa State University
Ames, IA 50011
        Offers publications on selection and use of books.

Pan American Union
17th and C Street NW
Washington, DC 20006

Parents Anonymous
22330 Hawthorne Blvd., Suite 208
Torrence, CA 90505

Planned Parenthood
810 Seventh Ave.
New York, NY 10019

Racism/Sexism Resource Center
1814 Broadway
New York, NY 10023

Reading Is Fundamental, Inc.
600 Maryland Ave. SW, Suite 500
Washington, DC 20560

Social Science Education Consortium, Inc.
855 Broadway
Boulder, CO 80302

Society for the Study of Myth and Tradition
150 Fifth Ave.
New York, NY 10011
  Publishes Parabola, with information on literature for young
  readers.

Society for Visual Education, Inc.
1345 W. Diversey Pkwy.
Chicago, IL 60614

Society of Children's Book Writers (SCBW)
P.O. Box 296, Mar Vista Station
Los Angeles, CA 90066
  Information source on writers, illustrators, editors, publish-
  ers, editors.

Syracuse University
The Reading and Language Arts Center
508 University Place
Syracuse, NY 13210
  Publishes a graded bibliogrpahy for children with reading
  difficulties.

Theatre Library Association
111 Amsterdam Ave.
New York, NY 10023
  Publishes a quarterly, Broadside, with information on dramatic literature for young people.

United Nations Association of the United States of America, Inc.
300 East 42nd Street
New York, NY 10017

U.S. Board on Books for Young People
P.O. Box 355
Enon, OH 45323
  Supports the International Board on Books for Young People,
  which provides "reading materials of merit to young people
  worldwide."

U.S. Office of Education
400 Maryland Ave. SW
Washington, DC 20202

Westchester Library System
8 Westchester Plaza
CWEP
Elmsford, NY 10523

GENERAL RESOURCES STATEWIDE

Cooperative Extension Services

Departments of Education in state governments and state universities

Library Associations

National Endowment for the Humanities, through state Committees for the Humanities

SPECIAL PROGRAMS OF UNIQUE VALUE TO LITERATURE FOR YOUNG PEOPLE

"Jump Over the Moon: Sharing Literature with Young Children"
A Telecommunications series coproduced by the South Carolina ETV Network and the University of South Carolina.
Contact:
University of South Carolina
915 Gregg Street
Columbia, SC 29208

"Not for Children Only": Let's Talk About It, Reading and Discussion Programs in America's Libraries
A series developed to introduce and reacquaint adults with the literature of their childhood that continues to have relevance to children now and in the future. Contact:
American Library Association
50 East Huron Street
Chicago, IL 60611

"Reading Rainbows"
A national program that linked summer reading with a television series on public television.

SOURCES FOR CHILDREN'S BOOKS ADAPTED INTO FILMSTRIPS, MOTION PICTURES, RECORDINGS

Catalog

Educational Filmlocator of the Consortium of University Filmcenters and R. R. Bowker Company
New York: R. R. Bowker Company
Listing of titles held by member libraries of CUFC. Classifications includes titles appropriate for children at levels from K-grade 12, with subject listings that include folklore, stories, and children's literature, among others.

Firms Producing Audiovisual Materials for Use with Literature Programs

Coronet Instructional Films
65 East South Water Street
Chicago, IL 60601

Encyclopaedia Britannica Educational Corp.
425 North Michigan Ave.
Chicago, IL 60611

Miller Brody Productions, Inc.
342 Madison Avenue
New York, NY 10017

Weston Woods Studios, Inc.
Weston, CT 06880

Firms Producing Phonograph Recordings of Literature for Young People

Caedmon Records
D.C. Heath and Company
2700 North Richardt Ave.
Indianapolis, IN 46219

CMS Record, Inc
14 Warren St.
New York, NY 10007

Folkways/Scholastic
906 Sylvan Avenue
Englewood Cliffs, NJ 07632

Spoken Arts, Inc.
310 North Avenue
New Rochelle, NY 10801

Guides/Lists

Action for Children's Television
46 Austin Street,
Newtonville, MA 02160
> One of their publications, Exploring the Arts: Films and Video Programs for Young Viewers, by Paula Rohrlick (1982), evaluates a number of titles dealing with fairy tales and myths for the two to fifteen age range.

Dell Publishing Co., Inc.
Education Sales Dept.
245 East 47th Street
New York, NY 10017

An available pamphlet, <u>Media Resource Guide to Dell Paper-
backs</u>, lists films and recordings based on Dell paperbacks
for all grades. This pamphlet includes a directory of media
distributors to the education market. Also given is a list of
Dell authors who are the subjects of interviews and profiles.

APPENDIX B: REVIEW SOURCES

Appraisal: Children's Science Books. Children's Science Book Review Committee. Harvard Graduate School of Education.
Published 3 times a year; ratings by a librarian and subject specialist who do not confer. Covers pure and applied sciences.

Audio-Visual Instructor. Association of Educational Communication and Technology (1126 16th St., NW, Washington, DC 20036).
Published 10 times a year.

Babbling Bookworm: Monthly Newsletter. Babbling Bookworm (935 Private Rd., Winnetka, IL 60093).
Reviews current children's books.

BAYA Reviews. BAYA (410 Magnolia Ave., Modesta, CA 95354).
Bimonthly reviews includes 50 to 75 titles that represent popular preferences of young adults.

Bookbird. International Board on Books for Young People (IBBY) and International Institute for Children's Literature. (U.S. Associate Editor, Barbara Elleman, c/o Booklist, ALA, 50 E. Huron St., Chicago, IL 60611).
Quarterly journal dealing with aspects of international children's literature. Includes an eight-page Spanish-language summary in each issue.

The Booklist. American Library Association.
Biweekly guide to current print and nonprint materials.

The Book Report. Linworth Publishing (2950 N. High St., P.O. Box 14466, Columbus, OH 43214).
A magazine for junior and senior high school librarians.

Bulletin: Interracial Books for Children. Council on Interracial Books for Children (1841 Broadway, New York, NY 10023).
Reviews and recommends materials.

Bulletin of the Center for Children's Books. Graduate Library School, University of Chicago Press (5801 Ellis Ave., Chicago, IL 60637).
Monthly review of children's books and lists for professional and parental reading/guidance.

The Calendar. Children's Book Council, Inc.
   Highlights titles and personalities and events in the publishing industry.

Canadian Children's Literature: A Journal of Criticism and Review.
Canadian Children's Literature Association and Canadian Children's
Press (Box 335, Guelph, Ontario N1H 6K5, Canada).
   Quarterly of criticism and review of books for Canadian chil-
   dren.

Canadian Library Journal.
   Bimonthly, with reviews and articles.

Catholic Library World. Catholic Library Association (461 W. Lancaster Ave., Haverford, PA 19041).
   Reviews and features.

Childhood Education. Association for Childhood Education Interna-
tionale.
   Bimonthly journal with about 25 reviews of books. Every
   three years, reviews are compiled into Bibliography of Books
   for Children.

Children's Book News. Children's Book Centre (140 Church St.,
London W8, England).
   Monthly review of new books.

Children's Book Reviews. OHIONET (1500 West Lane Ave., Columbus, Ohio 43221).
   "Reviews the whole extent of children's literature" with review cards and review lists along with annotated ratings list.

Children's Book Review Index. Gale Research Co.
   Three issues per year with annual cumulation covering K-5
   books.

Children's Book Review Service. Edited by Ann L. Kalkhoff (220
Berkeley Place, #10, Brooklyn, NY 11217).
   Published monthly, with two special supplements in the Fall
   and Spring. Realistic fiction, fantasy and nonfiction are
   reviewed with an emphasis on "interests of contemporary
   children."

Children's Literature Abstracts. C. H. Ray, editor (45 Stephenson
Tower, Station St., Birmingham, England).
   Published quarterly.

Children's Literature: Annual of the Modern Language Association.
Division on Children's Literature and the Children's Literature Association.

Children's Literature in Education. APS Publications, Inc. (150
Fifth Ave., New York, NY 10011).
    Published quarterly.

ChLA Quarterly. Children's Literature Association.

Choice. American Library Association (100 Riverview Center, Middletown, CT 06457).
    Published ten times a year. Includes professional materials
    for librarians, teachers, researchers.

CM: Canadian Materials for Schools and Libraries.
    Evaluates books, magazines, films, etc. for early childhood
    to post-secondary level.

Elementary English. National Council of Teachers of English.
    Eleven issues a year with articles and book reviews.

Emergency Librarian. Dyad Services (P.O. Box 4696, Station D,
London, Ontario N5W 5L7, Canada).

English Journal. National Council of Teachers of English.
    Published monthly with emphasis on books for young adults.

Fanfare. Horn Book.
    Selections from Horn Book Reviews.

Grade Teacher. Macmillan Professional Magazines, Inc. (One
Fourth Place, Greenwich, CT 06830).
    Reviews books.

Growing Point. Margery Fisher, editor (Ashton Manor, Northamp-
ton, England).
    Review of children's books.

The High/Low Report. Riverhouse Publications (20 Waterside Plaza,
New York, NY 10010).
    Monthly newsletter.

Horn Book Crier. Horn Book.
    Published bimonthly with latest events in children's publish-
    ing field.

The Horn Book Magazine. Horn Book. Published six times a year.
    Reviews, criticism, features.

In Review: Canadian Books for Children. Provincial Library Service, Ministry of Culture and Recreation (Queens Park, Toronto,
Ontario M7A 2R9, Canada).
    Published quarterly, it also includes sketches of authors and
    illustrators.

Instructor. Instructor Publications, Inc. (P.O. Box 6099, Duluth, MN 55806).
Monthly, includes reviews of trade and textbooks under subject headings.

Interracial Books for Children. Council on Interracial Books for Children (29 W. 15th St., New York, NY 10011).
Published eight times a year; includes articles, commentary, and book reviews.

Journal of Education. Boston University School of Education. (765 Commonwealth Ave., Boston, MA 02215).
Quarterly; contains commentary and reviews of views.

Journal of Reading. International Reading Association.

Judaica Book News. (303 West 10th St., New York, NY 10014).

Kidstuff: A Treasury of Early Childhood Enrichment Materials. GuideLines Press (1307 S. Killian Dr., Lake Park, FL 33403).
Published monthly; includes suggestions for books.

Kirkus Reviews Service. (200 Park Ave., South, New York, NY 10003).
Published biweekly as a prepublication announcement.

Kliatt: Young Adult Paperback Book Guide. (425 Watertown St., Newton, MA 02158).
Published eight times a year; about 300 paperbacks are reviewed per issue. Covers original, reprints, and reissues in all genres.

Language Arts Magazine. National Council of Teachers of English.
Published eight times a year. 25 to 40 books with an elementary focus are reviewed in each issue.

Lector. California Spanish Language Data Base (P.O. Box 4273, Berkeley, CA 94704).
Bimonthly review journal of Spanish-language and bilingual materials.

Library Journal. R. R. Bowker Co. (Dept. C, Box 1807, Ann Arbor, MI 48106).
Published bi-weekly, it reviews and recommends titles.

The Lion and the Unicorn: A Critical Journal of Children's Literature. Brooklyn College, Department of English (Brooklyn, NY 11210).
Concentrates on theme-centered criticism on a semi-annual publication schedule.

McNaughton Young Adult Reviews. McNaughton Book Service
(P.O. Drawer 926, Williamsport, PA 17705).
    Reviews 30 to 35 YA titles for the rental plan.

Magazine of Books. Chicago Tribune.
    Weekly, on Sunday.

Mass Media Newsletter. Mass Media Newsletter Association (2116
North Charles St., Baltimore, MD 21218).

Media and Methods. North American Publishing Co. (401 N. Broad
St., Philadelphia, PA 19108).
    Monthly reviews of children's and YA books.

Media Digest. National Education Film Center (4321 Skyesville Rd.,
Finksburg, MD 21048).

Media Index. (343 Manville Rd., Pleasantville, NY 10570).

Media Review. University of Chicago Laboratory Schools (1362 E.
59th Street, Chicago, IL 60637).
    Monthly; evaluates about 40 films, filmstrips, filmloops, and
    slides for children, including titles adapted from books for
    children.

MS: the new magazine for women. MS Magazine Corp. (370 Lexington Ave., New York, NY 10017).
    Up-to-date titles for young readers regarding sexism.

The National Storytelling Journal. (NAPPS, P.O. Box 112, Jonesborough, TN 37659).

New York Times Book Review.
    Weekly on Sunday. Fall and Spring special sections on chil-
    dren's books.

News from ALAN. Assembly on Literature for Adolescents of NCTE.
    Bimonthly newsletter reviews approximately 20 titles per issue.

Openers: America's Library Newspaper. American Library Association.
    Seasonal and standard approaches to descriptive lists and
    features on books and authors/illustrators for young readers
    and adults.

Parents' Choice: A Review of Children's Media--Books, Television,
Movies, Music, Story Records, Toys and Games. Parents' Choice
Foundation (Box 185, Waban, MA 02168).
    Quarterly.

Perspectives. Cooperative Services for Children's Literature
(Snyder Building, University of Toledo, Toledo, OH 43606).

Published three times a year, free to teachers in Ohio. Reviews books for elementary school children and suggestions for incorporating literature into the curriculum.

Phaedrus: A Journal of Children's Literature Research. Phaedrus, Inc. (14 Beacon St., Boston, MA 02108).
Annual.

Publishers Weekly. R. R. Bowker.
Weekly and special announcement issues for Fall, Spring and Summer.

Ranger Rick's Naturescope. National Wildlife Federation (1412 16th St. NW, Washington, DC 20036).
A bimonthly newsletter available during the school year; includes booklists.

School Libraries in Canada. Canadian School Library Association.

School Library Journal. R. R. Bowker.
Monthly reviews and recommendations along with articles and commentary. Special issues for "Best Books" and roundups of outstanding books.

Science and Children. National Science Teachers Association. (1742 Connecticut Ave., NW, Washington, DC 20009).
March issue features outstanding science trade books of the previous year.

Science Books: A Quarterly Review. American Association for the Advancement of Science.
Trade, text and reference books in pure and applied sciences for elementary and secondary school students.

Science Fiction and Fantasy Book Review. Science Fiction Research Association (1226 Woodhill Dr., Kent, OH 44240).
Ten issues a year with critical reviews of value to young readers as well as adults.

Social Education. National Council for Social Education (2030 M. St., NW, Suite 400, Washington, DC 20036).
April issue features notable children's trade books in the eight fields of social studies.

Teacher. Macmillan Professional Magazines, Inc. (22 W. Putnam Ave., Greenwich, CT 06830).
Eleven issues; includes reviews of old and new books for children and ways to use them.

Top of the News. Association for Library Service to Children and Young Adult Services Division.

Quarterly; contains articles and book reviews of material for adults working with children.

The WEB: Wonderfully Exciting Books. Center for Language, Literature, and Reading. The Ohio State University.

"Why Children's Books?" A Newsletter for Parents. Horn Book.
Recommends titles and suggests use of books and selection techniques.

Wilson Library Bulletin. H. W. Wilson.
Monthly reviews and articles.

Young Adult Alternative Newsletter. Carol Starr, editor (37167 Mission Boulevard, Fremont, CA 94536).

A. B. Bookman's Weekly
P.O. Box AB
Clifton, NJ 07015

Abingdon Press
201 Eighth Ave. South
Nashville, TN 37202

Harry N. Abrams, Inc.
110 East 59th Street
New York, NY 10022

Academy Chicago Limited
425 N. Michigan Ave.
Chicago, IL 60611

Addison-Wesley Publishing
Co.
One Jacob Way
Reading, MA 01867

Africana Publishing Co.
(A Division of Holmes &
Meier, Inc.)
30 Irving Place
New York, NY 10003

Agathon Press, Inc.
150 Fifth Ave.
New York, NY 10011

Aid-U Publishing Co.
17220 W. Eight Mile Rd.,
Bldg. B, Suite 24
Southfield, MI 48075

The Allen Press
1041 New Hampshire St.
Lawrence, KS 666055

Allyn and Bacon, Inc.
150 Tremont St.
Boston, MA 02111

Alphabet Press
60 N. Main St.
Natick, MA 01760

American Association for the
Advancement of Science
1101 Vermont Ave., NW, 10th
Floor
Washington, DC 20005

American Bibliographic Center,
Clio Press
Riviera Campus, 2040 A.P.S.
Box 4397
Santa Barbara, CA 93103

American Council on Education
One Dupont Circle
Washington, DC 20036

American Folklife Center
Library of Congress
Washington, DC 20540

American Friends Service
International-Intercultural Programs
010 East 10th St.
New York, NY 10017

American Friends Service Committee
160 North 15th St.
Philadelphia, PA 19102

American Guidance Service, Inc.
4201 Woodland St.
Publishers' Building
Circle Pines, MN 55014

American Industrial Arts Association

1914 Association Drive
Reston, VA 22091

American Jewish Committee
165 East 56th Street
New York, NY 10022

American Library Association
50 East Huron St.
Chicago, IL 60611

American Library Publishing
Co.
275 Central Park, West
New York, NY 10024

American Theatre Association
now called National Edu-
cational Theatre Association

Anchorage Press, Inc.
(formerly The Children's
Theatre Press)
P.O. Box 8067
New Orleans, LA 70182

Anti-Defamation League of
B'nai B'rith
1640 Rhode Island Ave., NW
Washington, DC 20036

APS Publications, Inc.
150 Fifth Ave.
New York, NY 10011

Arbeitskreis für Jugend-
literatur e.V.,
Elizabethstrasse 15,
8000 Munich 40,
Federal Republic of Germany

Arco Publishing Inc.
215 Park Ave. South
New York, NY 10003

Arden Library
Mill and Main Streets
Darby, PA 19023

Association for Childhood
Education International

3615 Wisconsin Ave., NW
Washington, DC 20016

Association of American Indian
Affairs [AAIA]
95 Madison Ave.
New York, NY 10016

Association of American Publishers, Dept. BF
220 E. 23rd Street
New York, NY 10010

Association of American Univer-
sity Presses
One Park Ave.
New York, NY 10016

Atheneum Publishers
597 Fifth Ave.
New York, NY 10017

Atlanta University
School of Library Service
Atlanta, GA 30314

Austin Bilingual Language Edi-
tions
P.O. Box 3864
Austin, TX 78764

Australian Council for Educational Research
Hawthorn, Vic., Australia

Avon Books
(A Division of Hearst Corp)
Education Department
959 Eighth Ave.
New York, NY 10019

Bank Street College of Education
610 West 112th Street
New York, NY 10025

Bantam Books, Inc.
666 Fifth Ave.
New York, NY 10103

Batsford Ltd.

4 Fitzhardinge St.
London, W1H OAH, England

Bay Area Young Adult Li-
brarians
116 Karen Way
Mountain View, CA 94040

Beautiful Day Books
5008 Berwyn Rd.
College Park, MD 20740

The Bekins Co.
1335 S. Figueroa St.
Los Angeles, CA 90015

Bergin and Garvey Publishers, Inc.
670 Amherst Road
South Hadley, MA 01075

Berkley Medalion Books
Berkley Publishing Corporation
200 Madison Ave.
New York, NY 10016

Biblio Press
P.O. Box 22
Fresh Meadows, NY 11365

Blue Engine Express
173 E. Iroquois
Pontiac, MI 48053

The Bodley Head Ltd.
9 Bow Street
London, WC2E 7AL, Eng-
land

Boston Public Library
P.O. Box 286
Boston, MA 02117

Boston University School
of Education
765 Commonwealth Ave.
Boston, MA 02215

R. R. Bowker Co.
1180 Avenue of the Americas
New York, NY 10036

Bradbury Press
(An affiliate of Macmillan, Inc.)
866 Third Ave.
New York, NY 10022

Braille Institute of America
741 N. Vermont Ave.
Los Angeles, CA 90029

Bramhall House Book see Clarkson N. Potter, Inc.

British Columbia Teacher-
Librarians Association
Box 985
Hope, British Columbia, Canada
VOX 110

Bro-Dart Foundation
1609 Memorial Ave.
Williamsport, PA 17701

Brookline Books
29 Ware St.
Cambridge, MA 02138

Wm. C. Brown Company Pub-
lishers
2460 Kerper Blvd.
Dubuque, IA 52001

Bureau of Indian Affairs, Lan-
guage Arts Branch
Indian Education Resource
Center
P.O. Box 1788
Albuquerque, NM 87103

John Gordon Burke Pub., Inc.
P.O. Box 1492
Evanston, IL 60204

California Library Association
717 K Street, Suite 300
Sacramento, CA 95814

Cambridge Jackson Ltd.
80 Wrentham St.
Birmingham B5 6QT, England

Cambridge University Press

(Press Syndicate of the University of Cambridge)
32 East 57th Street
New York, NY 10022

Canadian Library Association
151 Sparks St.
Ottawa, ON K1P 5E3, Canada

[Press of] Case Western Reserve University
Cleveland, OH 44106

Catholic Library Association
461 West Lancaster Ave.
Haverford, PA 19041

The Catholic University of America Press
620 Michigan Ave. NE
Washington, DC 20064

Center for International Cooperation
National College of Education
2840 Sheridan Road
Evanston, IL 60201

Century House Pubs.
Old Irelandville
Watkins Glen, NY 14891

Chelsea House Pubs.
133 Christopher St.
New York, NY 10014

The Child Study Assn. of America/Wel-Met, Inc.
853 Broadway
New York, NY 10003

Children's Book Council, Inc.
67 Irving Place
New York, NY 10003

Children's Literature Association Publications
210 Education Building,
Purdue University
West Lafayette, IN 47907

Children's Magazine Guide
7 N. Pinckney St.
Madison, WI 53703

Children's Theatre Association
(Affiliate of American Theatre Association)
now called Youth Theatre Directors

Choice
100 Riverview Center
Middleton, CT 06457

Citation Press
(Division of Scholastic Book Service)
50 West 44th Street
New York, NY 10036

Citizens Committee for Children
P.O. Box 6133, Station J
Ottawa, Ontario K2A 1T2,
Canada

Charles W. Clark Co., Inc.
Farmingdale, NY

Clarkson N. Potter, Inc.
(The Crown Publishing Group)
One Park Ave.
New York, NY 10016

Cleveland Public Library
Publications Office, Information Dept.
325 Superior St.
Cleveland, OH 44114

Collier
(Imprint of Macmillan)

Collins
14 St. James' Place
London, England

Collins, William, Inc.
2080 W. 117th St.
Cleveland, OH 44111

Columbia University Press

562 W. 113th St.
New York, NY 10025

The Combined Book Exhibit,
Inc.
Scarborough Park, Albany
Post Road
Briarcliff Manor, NY 10510

Conch Magazine
102 Normal Ave.
Buffalo, NY 14213

David C. Cook, Publishing
Co.
850 N. Grove Ave.
Elgin, IL 60120

Cooperative Children's Book
Center
P.O. Box 5288
Madison, WI 53705

Council on Interracial Books
for Children, Inc. (CIBC)
1841 Broadway, Room 500
New York, NY 10023

Creative Publications
P.O. Box 10328
Palo Alto, CA 94303

Thomas Y. Crowell Company
201 Park Ave. South
New York, NY 10036

Cuyahoga County Public Library
4510 Memphis Ave.
Cleveland, OH 44144

David and Charles (Holdings)
Ltd.
Brunel House
Newton Abbott, Batsford,
Devon TQ12 4PU, England

Day Care Council of Amer-
ica, Inc.
1602 17th Street NW
Washington, DC 20009

The John Day Company, Inc.
62 West 45th St.
New York, NY 10036

Delacorte Press
(c/o Dell Publishing Co.)
1 Dag Hammarskjold Plaza, 245
E. 47th St.
New York, NY 10017

Dodd, Mead and Co.
79 Madison Ave.
New York, NY 10016

Doubleday & Co., Inc.
501 Franklin Ave.
Garden City, NY 11530

Dover Publications, Inc.
180 Varick St.
New York, NY 10014

The Dramatic Publishing Co.
4150 N. Milwaukee Ave.
Chicago, IL 60641

Dryden Press
(Division of Holt, Rinehart &
Winston)
901 N. Elm
Hinsdale, IL 60521

During-gai College of Advanced
Education
P.O. Box 222
Lindfield, N.S.W. 2070 Aus-
tralia

Ebsco Subscription Service
P.O. Box 1943
Birmingham, AL 35201

Emporia State University
Emporia, KS 66801

Enoch Pratt Free Library
400 Cathedral St.
Baltimore, MD 21201

M. Evans & Co., Inc.
216 E. 49th St.

New York, NY 10017

Faber & Faber, Inc.
99 Main Street
Salem, NH 03079

F. W. Faxon Co., Inc.
15 Southwest Park
Westwood, MA 02090

The Feminist Press
Box 334
Old Westbury, NY 11568

Five Owls Press Ltd.
67 High Road, Wormley
Broxbourne, Herts.,
   England

Flatiron Book Distributors
   Inc.
175 Fifth Ave., Suite 814
New York, NY 10010

Folger Shakespeare Library
201 E. Capitol, SE
Washington, DC 20003

Follett Publishing Co.
65 E. Water St.
Chicago, IL 60601

Four Winds Press
(A Division of Scholastic)
730 Broadway
New York, NY 10003

Franklin, Burt, Pub.
(Distributed by Lenox Hill
   Publishing-Distributing
   Corp.)
235 E. 44th St.
New York, NY 10017

Free Library of Philadelphia
Logan Square
Philadelphia, PA 19103

Gale Research Co.
Book Tower
Detroit, MI 48226

Garland Publishing, Inc.
136 Madison Ave.
New York, NY 10016

Garrard Publishing Co.
P.C. Box A
Champaign, IL 61820

David R. Godine Pub., Inc.
306 Dartmouth St.
Boston, MA 02116

Gower Publishing Co.
Old Post Rd.
Brookfield, VT 05036

Green Oak Press
9339 Spicer Rd.
Brighton, MI 48116

Greenwillow Books
(Div. of William Morrow & Co.,
   Inc.)
105 Madison Ave.
New York, NY 10016

Greenwood Press
88 Post Road, West
P.O. Box 5007
Westport, CT 06881

Grossett & Dunlop, Inc.
51 Madison Ave.
New York, NY 10010

Guidelines Press
1307 S. Killian Dr.
Lake Park, FL 33403

G. K. Hall & Co.
70 Lincoln St.
Boston, MA 02111

Hanes Corporation
P.O. Box 2222
Winston-Salem, NC 27102

Harcourt Brace Jovanovich, Inc.
757 Third Ave.
New York, NY 10017

Harmony Books
(A Division of Crown Pub-
    lishers)
One Park Ave.
New York, NY 10016

Harper & Row, Inc.
10 E. 53rd St.
New York, NY 10022

Harvard Common Press
535 Albany St.
Boston, MA 02118

Harvard University Press
Cambridge, MA 02138

Haworth Press
28 E. 22nd St.
New York, NY 10010

D. C. Heath & Co.
125 Spring St.
Lexington, MA 02173

Heinemann Educational Books,
    Inc.
4 Front St.
Exeter, NH 03833

Heldref Publications
Suite 302, 4000 Albermarle
    St., NW
Washington, DC 20016

Hemisphere Publishing Cor-
    poration
1025 Vermont Ave. NW
Washington, DC 20005

Hodder and Stoughton Ltd.
47 Bedford Square
London, WC1B 30P, England

Holiday House, Inc.
18 E. 53rd St.
New York, NY 10022

Holt, Rinehart and Winston,
    Inc.
383 Madison Ave.
New York, NY 10017

The Horn Book, Inc.
Park Square Bldng.
31 St. James Ave.
Boston, MA 02116

Houghton Mifflin Co.
One Beacon St.
Boston, MA 02108

Indiana University Press
10th & Morton Sts.
Bloomington, IN 47405

Institute of Race Relations
36 Jermyn St.
London SW1 England

Interbook Inc.
545 Eighth Ave.
New York, NY 10018

International Center on Deafness
Gallaudet College
800 Florida Ave, NE
Washington, DC 20002

International Reading Association
800 Barksdale Road, P.O. Box
    8139
Newark, DE 19711

Japan Library Association
1-1-10 Taishido, Setagaya-ku
Tokyo 154, Japan

Japanese American Curriculum
    Project
414 East Third Ave.
San Mateo, CA 94401

Japanese Board on Books for
    Young People
P.O. Box 5024
San Francisco, CA 94101

Joint Council on Economic Edu-
    cation
1212 Ave. of the Americas
New York, NY 10036

Julia MacRae Books
12A Golden Square
London W1R 3AF, England

JWB Jewish Book Council
15 E. 26th St.
New York, NY 10010

Kansas State University
North Central Regional Edu-
    cational Materials Project
Office of Cooperative Exten-
    sion Service
Manhattan, KS 66506

Kennikat Press Corp.
90 S. Boyles Ave.
Port Washington, NY 11050

Kestrel Books
(Penguin Books Ltd., Chil-
    dren's Division)
536 Kings Rd.
London SW10 0UN, England

Alfred A. Knopf, Inc.
(Subsidiary of Random House,
    Inc.)
201 E. 50th St.
New York, NY 10022

Knowledge Industry Publica-
    tions
White Plains, NY 10604

Kraus Reprint
Rte. 100
Millwood, NY 10546

Laurel-Leaf Books
(c/o Dell Publishing Co.,
    Inc.)
1 Dag Hammarskjold Plaza
245 E. 47th St.
New York, NY 10017

Learning House Publishers
38 South St.
Roslyn Heights, NY 11577

Libraries Unlimited Inc.
P.O. Box 263
Littleton, CO 80160

Library Association
7 Ridgemount St.
London WC1E 7AE England

Library of Congress see U.S.
    Government Printing Office

Library Professional Publications
995 Sherman Ave.
Hamden, CT 06514

J. B. Lippincott & Co.
(Harper & Row, Pub., Inc.)
10 E. 53rd St.
New York, NY 10022

Little, Brown & Co.
34 Beacon St.
Boston, MA 02106

Little Feat
Box 150
Water Mill, NY 11976

Lollipop Power, Inc.
P.O. Box 1171
Chapel Hill, NC 27514

Longman, Inc.
1560 Broadway
New York, NY 10036

Lothrop, Lee & Shepard Books
(Div. of Wm. Morrow & Co.,
    Inc.)
105 Madison Ave.
New York, NY 10016

McFarland & Co., Inc. Publishers
Box 611
Jefferson, NC 28640

McGraw-Hill Book Co.
1221 Ave. of the Americas
New York, NY 10020

McKinley Publishing Co.
Brooklawn, NJ 08030

Macmillan Publishing Co., Inc.
Front & Brown Sts.
Delran Township, Riverside,
NJ 08075

Mar Vista
11917 Westminster Pl.
Los Angeles, CA 90066

Meeting Street School
Rhode Island Easter Seal
Society
667 Waterman Ave.
East Providence, RI 02914

Meridian Press
2915 Providence Rd.
Charlotte, NC 28211

Charles E. Merrill Pub. Co.
(Div. of Bell & Howell Co.)
1300 Alum Creek Dr.
Columbus, OH 43216

Merrimack Publishers Circle
458 Boston St.
Topsfield, MA 01983

Modern Curriculum Press, Inc.
13900 Prospect Road
Cleveland, OH 44136

Montana Council for Indian
Education
517 Rimrock Road
Billings, MT 59101

Montgomery Co. Public
Schools
Rockville, MD 20850

The Moretus Press, Inc.
274 Madison Ave.
New York, NY 10016

Wm. Morrow & Co., Inc.
105 Madison Ave.
New York, NY 10016

D. M. Mortimore
72, Friary Grange Park
Winterbourne, Bristol BS17 1NB,
England

Mosaic Press
P.O. Box 1032
Oakville, Ontario L6J 5E9

Multicultural Resources
Box 2945
Stanford, CA 94305

The Murton Press
26 Anderson Rd.
Greenwich, CT 06830

Nancy Renfro Studios
1117 W. 9th St.
Austin, TX 78703

National Association for the Education of Young Children
Publications Dept.
1834 Connecticut Ave. NW
Washington, DC 20009

National Association of State
Educational Media Professionals
Division of Publications
2879 Exchange St.
McFarland, WI 53558

National Book League
7 Albermarle St.
London W1X 4BB England

National Conference of Christians and Jews
71 Fifth Ave., Suite 1100
New York, NY 10008

National Council for the Social
Studies
3501 Newark St., NW
Washington, DC 20016

National Council of Teachers of
English

111 Kenyon Rd.
Urbana, IL 61801

National Education Association
1201 Sixteenth St. NW
Washington, DC 20036

National Library of Canada
395 Wellington St.
Ottawa, K1A ON4 Canada

National Storytelling Resource
   Center
P.O. Box 112
Jonesborough, TN 37659

Neal-Schuman Publishers
23 Cornelia St.
New York, NY 10014

Thomas Nelson, Inc.
P.O. Box 946
407 Seventh Ave. South
Nashville, TN 37203

New Hampshire State Library
Concord, NH 03301

New Plays-Books Incorpor-
   ated
Box 273
Rowayton, CT 06853

New Readers Press
Box 131
Syracuse, NY 13210

New York Public Library
Office of Children's Services
8 East 40th Street
New York, NY 10016

Nuclear Information and Resource Service
1346 Connecticut Ave. NW
Washington, DC 20036

Odyssey Press
(Distributed by Bobbs-
   Merrill Co., Inc.)

4300 W. 62nd St.
P.O. Box 7080
Indianapolis, IN 46206

Ontario Library Association
Suite 402
73 Richmond St. West
Toronto, Ontario M5H 1ZA
   Canada

Oryx Press
2214 N. Central Ave.
Phoenix, AZ 85004

Oxford University Press
200 Madison Ave.
New York, NY 10016

Pacer Books for Young Adults
51 Madison Ave.
New York, NY 10010

Paddington Press Ltd.
(Two Continents Publishing
   Group)
30 East 42nd Street
New York, NY 10017

Palos Heights Public Library
12501 South 71st Ave.
Palos Heights, IL 60463

Pantheon Books
(Division of Random House, Inc.)
201 E. 50th St.
New York, NY 10022

Penguin Books, Inc.
625 Madison Ave.
New York, NY 10022

Pergamon Press
Fairview Park
Elmsford, NY 10523

Phaedrus, Inc.
14 Beacon Street
Boston, MA 02108

Philomel Books

467

(Putnam Publishing Group)
200 Madison Ave. Suite 1405
New York, NY 10016

Plays, Inc.
8 Arlington St.
Boston, MA 02116

Pluto Press
(Dist. by Flatiron Book Distributors inc.)
175 Fifth Ave. Suite 814
New York, NY 10010

Portland Public School
P.O. Box 3107
Portland, OR 97208
atn: Educational Media Dept.

Clarkson N. Potter, Inc.
419 Park Ave. South
New York, NY 10016

Frederick A. Praeger, Inc.
Publishers
111 Fourth Ave.
New York, NY 10003

The Putnam Publishing Group
51 Madison Ave.
New York, NY 10010

Random House, Inc.
400 Hahn Road
Westminster, MD 21157

Routledge & Kegan Paul
Ltd.
9 Park St.
Boston, MA 02108

Rowman & Littlefield, Inc.
(Division of Littlefield,
Adams & Co.)
81 Adams Dr., Box 327
Totowa, NJ 07511

The Ryerson Press
350 Victoria Street
Toronto, Ontario M5B 2K3
1E8 Canada

St. Cloud State University
Center for Economic Education
Joint Council on Economic Education
1212 Avenue of the Americas
New York, NY 10036

St. Martin's Press, Inc.
175 Fifth Ave.
New York, NY 10010

The Scarecrow Press, Inc.
P.O. Box 4167
Metuchen, NJ 08840

Schenkman
3 Mount Auburn Place
Cambridge, MA 02138

Justin G. Schiller, Ltd.
P.O. Box 1667, F.D.R. Station
New York, NY 10022

Schocken Books
67 Park Ave.
New York, NY 10016

Scholastic Book Services
50 West 44th St.
New York, NY 10036

Science Research Associates,
Inc.
(Subsidiary of IBM)
155 N. Wacker Dr.
Chicago, IL 60606

Scott, Foresman and Company
1900 E. Lake Avenue
Glenview, IL 60025

Charles Scribner's Sons
597 Fifth Ave.
New York, NY 10017

The Shoestring Press, Inc.
Hamden, CT 06514

Simon & Schuster Inc.
1230 Ave. of the Americas
New York, NY 10020

Singapore University Press
Kent Ridge, Singapore 0511

Singing Tree Press
1249 Washington Blvd.
Detroit, MI 48226

Sisters' Choice Press
1409 Fifth Street
Berkeley, CA 94710

John Russell Smith
4, Old Compton St., Soho
   Square,
London, England

Southern Illinois University
   Press
P.O. Box 3697
Carbondale, IL 62901

Star Publications
1211 W. 60th Terrace
Kansas City, MO 64113

Stark County District Library
715 Market Ave.
North Canton, OH 44720

Starstream Products
P.O. Box 2222
Winston-Salem, NC 27102

State University College at
   Buffalo
1300 Elmwood Ave.
Buffalo, NY 14222

Stipes Publishing Co.
P.O. Box 526
Champaign, IL 61820

Taplinger Publishing Co.,
   Inc.
132 W. 22nd St.
New York, NY 10011

Temple University Press
Broad & Oxford Sts.
Philadelphia, PA 19122

Telos Press, Ltd.
Box 3111
St. Louis, MO 63130

The Thimble Press
Lockwood, Station Road,
South Woodchester,
Stroud. Glos. GL5 5EQ England

Frederick Ungar Publishing Company
36 Cooper Square
New York, NY 10003

Unipub
(A Xerox Publishing Co.)
205 E. 42nd St.
New York, NY 10017

United States Government Print-
   ing Office
Supt. of Documents
Washington, DC 20402

University of Arizona Press
(Center for Latin American
   Studies)
P.O. Box 3398
Tucson, AZ 85722

University of California Press
2223 Fulton St.
Berkeley, CA 94720

University of Chicago Press
5801 S. Ellis Ave.
Chicago, IL 60637

University of Colorado
Bureau of Educational Research
School of Education
Boulder, CO 80302

University of Georgia
Dept. of Educational Media &
   Librarianship
607 Aderhold Hall
Athens, GA 30602

University of Minnesota Press

2037 Universith Avenue
Southeast
Minneapolis, MN 55414

University of Northern Iowa
Extension Service
Cedar Falls, IA 50613

University of Pennsylvania
Press
3933 Walnut St.
Philadelphia, PA 19104

University of Pittsburgh
Press
127 North Bellefield Ave.
Pittsburgh, PA 15260

University of Texas Press
P.O. Box 7819, University
Station
Austin, TX 78712

University of Toronto Press
5201 Dufferin St.
Downsview, Ontario M3H 5T8
Canada

University Press Books
302 Fifth Ave.
New York, NY 10001

Upstart Press
Box 889
Hagerstown, MD 21741

Lawrence Verry, Inc.
Mystic, CT 06355

Viking Press, Inc.
625 Madison Ave.
New York, NY 10022

Henry Z. Walck, Inc.
19 Union Square West
New York, NY 10003

Walker & Co.
720 Fifth Ave.
New York, NY 10019

Wallace-Homestead
580 Waters Edge Rd.
Lombard, IL 60148

Frederick Warne & Co.
2 Park Ave.
New York, NY 10016

Watson-Guptill Publications
(Division of Simon & Schuster)
1230 Ave. of the Americas
New York, NY 10020

Franklin Watts, Inc.
(Subsidiary of Grolier, Inc.)
387 Park Ave. South
New York, NY 10019

Westchester Library System
8 Westchester Plaza, CWEP
Elmsford, NY 10523

Westminster Press
925 Chestnut St.
Philadelphia, PA 19107

Weston Woods
Weston, CT 06880

Whitston Publishing Co., Inc.
P. O. Box 958
Troy, NY 12181

Whittlesey House
(Part of McGraw-Hill Book and
Educational Services Group)
1221 Avenue of the Americas
New York, NY 10020

H. W. Wilson
950 University Ave.
Bronx, NY 10452

Women's National Book Association, Inc. (WNBA)
160 Fifth Ave.
New York, NY 10010

World Book-Childcraft Interna-
tional, Inc.
(A Subsidiary of the Scott &
Fetzer Co.)
Merchandise Mart Plaza, Box

3565
Chicago, IL 69654

The World Publishing Co.
2231 West 110 St.
Cleveland, OH 44102

Writer, Inc.
8 Arlington St.
Boston, MA 02116

Writers and Readers
(Div. of W. W. Norton Co.)

500 Fifth Ave.
New York, NY 10110

Yale University Press
92A Yale Station
New Haven, CT 06520

Yes! Bookshop
1035 31st St. NW
Washington, DC 20007

Zondervan Publishing House
Grand Rapids, MI 49506

NOTE: Where applicable, journal articles that are relevant to the intent of this book are listed under a subject heading. These journal articles are not listed in the Resource Guide.

the Sands of Time: Biography for Children" by Gertrude
Herman.
School Library Journal, May 1981: "What Do We Do About Bad
    Biographies?" by Jo Carr.
School Library Journal, February 1985: "A Question of Accura-
    cy: Errors in Children's Biographies" by Ann W. Moore.
Top of the News, Fall 1985: "Trends in Juvenile Biography:
    Five Years Later" by Virginia Witucke.
Blacks 72, 101, 144, 233, 254, 267, 313, 475, 515, 516, 542, 571,
    576, 661, 662, 671, 715, 730
Blind, Books for the see Braille Books; Disabilities/Disabled,
    Books for the; Talking Books; Young Adult
Book Clubs
    Top of the News, Winter 1984: "School Book Club Expurgation
        Practices" by Gayle Keresey.
Book Dealers 262; see also Annual; Publishing
Book Fairs 365; see also Annual; Exhibitions of Books
Book Reviews/Book Reviewing 31, 203, 249, 705, 743, 744; see
    also Children's Literature, History & Criticism
    Horn Book, April 1984: "Critical Decisions: Reflection on the
        Changing Role of a Children's Book Reviewer" by Elaine Moss.
    Top of the News, Winter 1979: "The Young Adult Book Review
        Media" by Audrey B. Eaglen.
    "The Reviewing of Children's and Young Adult Books" by
        Rosemary Weber.
Book Shows see Exhibition of Books
Booklists by Libraries--Significant contributions to the develop-
    ment of topical bibliographies are made by libraries of all
    sizes. Exchanges can be arranged where lists are not ad-
    vertised for sale. The Indianapolis-Marion County Public
    Library system is one example of an on-going program of
    attractive publications for local use.
Booktalking 88, 106, 184, 344, 347, 348, 729, 826; see also Fiction
    English Journal, October 1984: "Booktalking Seventeen Hundred
        Students at Once--Why Not?" by Pamela Spencer.
    School Library Journal, August 1984: "Booktalking Them Off
        the Shelves" by Hazel Rochman.
    School Library Journal, January 1986: "'No, But I Read the
        Book!': Booktalks at Miller Ave. School" by William Silver
        and Nancy Westover.
Boys' Books 265
    School Library Journal, August 1983: "Bringing Boys' Books
        Home" by Hazel Rochman.
Braille Books 133, 486
    Booklist, August 1985 and March 1, 1986: "Children's Books
        for the Blind and Physically Handicapped."
Britain/British 99, 143, 205, 220, 240, 251, 304, 312, 361, 391,
    428, 456, 555, 556, 557, 558, 590, 612, 701, 716, 719, 722, 753,
    756, 806, 810; see also Children's Literature, History & Criticism
Brotherhood see Bias-free; Multiethnic
Buying Guides 111; see also Awards; Best; Selection Aids/Guides

Caldecott Medal see Awards
Canada 65, 71, 103, 153, 199, 244, 289, 345, 504, 506, 507, 508,
    509, 594, 636, 724, 746, 756, 757, 778, 779, 801; see also Annual;
    Children's Literature, History & Criticism; French, Books in
    In Review, February 1981: "The Modern Canadian Child's World
    of Books" by Irma McDonough.
    School Library Journal, September 1980: "The Red and The
    White: Canadian Books for Children" by Joan McGrath.
Careers 97, 342
    School Library Journal, February 1980: "Doctor, Teacher,
    Fireman: Career Books by Children" by Sandra J. Ridenour.
    School Library Journal, continuing column: "Working Papers"
    lists titles in various career options.
Catholic 227, 585, 586
Censorship; see also Children's Literature, History & Criticism
    Childhood Education, September/October 1984: "Protecting the
    Children: Huckleberry Finn, E. T. and the Politics of Cen-
    sorship" by Anthony Magistrale.
    Top of the News, Fall 1984: "Censorship, Book Selection, and
    the Marketplace of Ideas" by Tony Fiociello.
    Top of the News, Fall 1984: "Censorship, Book Selection, and
    the Marketplace of Ideas" by Tony Fiociello.
    Top of the News, Winter 1984: "Who Me, Censor?" by Carol
    Hole.
    Top of the News, Spring 1985: "Yeah, Me Censor: A Response
    to Various Critics" by Carol Hole.
    "Being Banned" by Norma Klein.
Central America
    School Library Journal, December 1985: "Books on Central
    America: Sparse and One-sided" by Isabel Schon.
Chants see Folklore; Poetry
Characters in Children's Literature 316, 552, 553; see also Sequels
    & Series, Books in
Chicano 157; see also Hispanic; Latino; Mexican-American; Multi-
    ethnic; Spanish
Children's Literature, History & Criticism 53, 57, 79, 85, 99, 152,
    158, 159, 164, 170, 179, 201, 229, 251, 257, 269, 287, 291, 298,
    303, 304, 307, 311, 312, 324, 327, 350, 358, 366, 374, 379, 382,
    385, 389, 396, 402, 441, 448, 469, 481, 494, 499, 505, 518, 527,
    533, 534, 547, 556, 557, 558, 609, 635, 637, 640, 648, 655, 657,
    660, 674, 676, 683, 716, 718, 740, 753, 760, 763, 770, 777, 783,
    794, 821, 823
    English Journal, January 1981: "Bait: Literature Isn't Supposed
    to Be Realistic" by G. Robert Carlsen and Norma Bagnell.
    School Library Journal, November 1980: "Books by the Numbers:
    The Mass-Market Children's Book" by Pamela D. Pollack.
    School Library Journal, April 1985: "A Celebration of Tradition
    in Children's Literature" by Kay E. Vandergrift and Jane
    Anne Hannigan.
    Top of the News, the May Hill Arbuthnot Honor Lectures: Also
    available in reprints from the American Library Association.

Handicapped, Books for the   see   Disabilities
Handicrafts   see   Crafts
Health   68, 69
Heroes and Heroines   7, 67, 687
    Horn Book, April 1983:   "A Need for Heroes" by Mollie Hunter.
High Interest/Low Vocabulary   21, 323, 487, 566, 678a, 726, 802,
    813
    Booklist, April 1, 1984:   "High Interest/Low Reading Level Book-
        list 1983."
    Booklist, June 15, 1985:   "High Interest/Low Reading Level Book-
        list 1985."
High School   see   Senior High School; Secondary Schools
Hispanic   699, 700; see also Chicano; Latino; Mexican-Americans;
    Multiethnic; Spanish-speaking
    Booklist, December 1, 1985:   "Ethnic Groups in Children's Books:
        Hispanics" compiled by Isabel Schon.
    School Library Journal, January 1981:   "Hispanic Picture Books"
        by L. Michael Espinosa.
Historical Fiction   332, 407, 408, 419
    Language Arts, April 1981:   "Yesterday Comes Alive for Readers
        of Historical Fiction" by Patricia Cianiolo.
    School Library Journal, August 1982:   "Criteria for Historical
        Fiction" by Christopher Collier.
    School Library Journal, November 1985:   "The Overstuffed Sen-
        tence and Other Means for Assessing Historical Fiction for
        Children" by Joan W. Blos.
Historical Nonficiton   420
History   737; see also American History; World History
Holidays   86, 93, 626; see also Religion
Hospital Experience   4; see also Bibliotherapy
How To Books   435
Human Relations   see   Multiethnic
Human Values   235
Humor   675
    Reading Teacher, May 1982:   "What's So Funny? Action Research
        & Bibliography of Humorous Children's Books--1975-1980" by
        John E. Bennett.
Hungarian
    Booklist, June 15, 1985:   "Hungarian Children's Books" compiled
        by Frances Povsic and Kalman Szekely.

Illness   4, 69
Illustrated Books   see   Picture Books
Illustration in Books   211, 308, 454, 514, 622, 702, 786, 793
Illustrators   54, 98, 221, 222, 250, 259, 271, 326, 388, 398, 399,
    400, 428, 444, 445, 453, 463, 468, 481, 491, 492a, 522, 538,
    612, 634, 658, 678, 680, 681, 776, 785, 792, 795, 810
Immigrants   186, 421, 803
Indian   see   American Indian
Informational Books   134, 383, 791, 814

Medal Books   see   Awards
Media   see   Multimedia
Mexican American/Mexico   431, 695;   see also   Chicano; Hispanic
   Heritage: Latino; Spanish, Books in
Middle Grades   347, 532, 796
Moral Development
   Young Children, May 1985:   "'But What About Sharing?' Chil-
     dren's Literature and Moral Development" by Suzanne Krogh
     and Linda Lamme.
Mother Goose   76
Movies Adapted from Children's Fiction   735
Movies, Books on
   Top of the News, Spring 1984:   Journal Articles.   "Movie Books:
     A Bibliography" compiled by the ALSC Liaison with Mass
     Media Committee
Moving   741
Multicultural/Multiethnic   66, 112, 154, 162, 178, 223, 317, 436,
   559, 563, 581, 582, 648, 694, 726, 742, 766, 807, 816
   English Journal, February 1981:   "Ethnic Literature" by Rosalie
     B. Kiah
   The Reading Teacher, January 1984:   ERIC/RCS: Understanding
     Other Cultures Through Literature" by Anne Auten.
   School Library Journal, December 1983:   "Legacies for Youth:
     Ethnic and Cultural Diversity in Books."
Multimedia   362, 561, 792
Mysteries
   School Library Journal, every May and December: "Round-up
     of Mystery and Suspense Books."
   School Library Journal, November 1980:   "Mysteries Too Good to
     Miss" by Robert E. Unsworth.
   School Library Journal, March 1985:   "Why Johnny (and Jane)
     Read Whodunits in Series" by Barbara S. Moran and Susan
     Steinfirst.
Myths   226, 284, 417, 418, 457

Native Americans   see   American Indian
Nature   339
Negro   see   Blacks
Newbery Award Medal   see   Awards
Non-English Speaking   488, 63
Nonfiction   35, 166, 315
   Children's Literature in Education, Autumn 1980:   "The Possibil-
     ities of Nonfiction: A Writer's View" by Milton Meltzer.
Nonsexist   2, 12, 39, 206, 253, 578, 587, 588, 597
   English Journal, April 1983:   "Non-nonsexist Guidelines: A
     Happy Neutrality" by Frank Zepezauer.
Nonstereotyped   131
Nostalgia
   School Library Journal, September 1984:   "Looking Homeward:
     Nostalgia in Children's Literature" by Mary Renck Jalongo
     and Melissa Ann Renck.

Promotional Materials   192
Pseudonyms   425
Publishers/Publishing   127, 130, 192, 276, 299, 300, 358, 494, 527,
    597, 645, 806
    School Library Journal, February 1982: "Small Press Children's
        Books and Where to Find Them" by Susan C. Griffith and
        Michele A. Seipp.
Pulps   265
Puppetry   see   Storytelling

Racism   207, 733
Rare Books   198, 745
Reading Aloud   37, 191, 443, 762
    Language Arts, November/December 1981: "Parents Reading to
        Their Children: What We Know and Need to Know" by William
        Teale.
    The Reading Teacher, October 1984: "Inexpensive, Worthwhile,
        Educational Parents Reading to Children" by John Lauten-
        schlager and Karl Hertz.
Reading Guidance   see   Active Readers, Developing
Reading Preferences
    Top of the News, Fall 1985: "Gender Gap in the Library: Dif-
        ferent Choices for Girls and Boys" by Glenda T. Childress.
Recording Literature   688
Reference Books   63, 120, 433, 614, 822
    School Library Journal, December 1980:   "Recommended Reference
        Sources for School Media Centers."
    "Sports, Math and Reference Books Team Up" by Joanne
        Troutner.
    School Library Journal, May 1984 and May 1985:   "Reference
        Books Roundup" by Linda Blaha, Priscilla Drach and Craigh-
        ton Hippenhammer.
Religion   244, 606;   see also   Catholic; Christian; Jewish Theme,
    Books on; Spiritual Values
    Booklist, February 15, 1985:   "Religious Books for Children"
        compiled by Barbara Elleman.
    Top of the News, Summer 1979:   "Religious Books: Which Are
        the Best?"
Reluctant Readers/Retarded Readers   38, 175, 213, 320, 323, 371,
    651;   see also   Active Readers, Developing; High Interest/Low
    Vocabulary
    English Journal, January 1984:   "Turning Reluctant Readers
        into Lifetime Readers" by Judy Beckman.
    Top of the News, Winter 1980:   "Getting Reluctant Readers to
        Read: A Hi-Lo Booklist" compiled by the Education Committee,
        Young Adult Services Division, ALA.
Reviews   see   Book Reviews
Rhymes   256, 286, 596;   see also   Mother Goose; Poetry
Role-free   see   Nonsexist
Romance

Talking Books   486; see also Braille Books; Disabilities/Disabled,
    Books for the
Teenage, Books for the   161, 305, 574, 678a, 684; see also Junior
    High School; Senior High School; Young Adult
Telecourse on Children's Literature
    Top of the News, Winter 1984: "Jump Over the Moon: The
        Development of a Telecourse in Children's Literature" by
        Pam Barron.
Television and Books   238
Trade Books
    Childhood Education, May/June 1985: "Teaching Content with
        Trade Books: A Strategy" by Betty Holmes and Richard
        Ammon.
Traditional Tales; see also Folklore/Folktales
    Signal, September 1985: "Translator's Notebook: On Approach-
        ing the Traditional Tales" by Anthea Bell.
Translation; see also Traditional Tales
    Children's Literature in Education, Winter 1980: "Translation
        and Internationalism in Children's Literature" by Marianne
        Carus.

UFOs   see   Extraterrestrial
United States, Children's Textbooks in the   495
United States History   see   American History
United States, Regional Literature   59, 270, 335, 369, 380, 393,
    392, 476, 477, 530, 535, 611, 681, 746
United States, Social Life in Children's Books   502, 503

Verse   see   Poetry
Videocassettes, Children's Books on   601, 602
Visually Impaired, Books for the   see   Blind, Books for the; Talk-
    ing Books
Vocational Guidance   see   Career Planning

Western Fiction
    School Library Journal, January 1982: "Cowboys from Way Back
        When: Western Fiction for YA's" by Marcia Melton and Ken
        Donelson.
Women   668, 671, 712
World History   537
World Understanding   see   Multiethnic
World War II   790
    School Library Journal, February 1984: "The Second World War"
        by Milton G. Hathaway.
Writers   see   Authors

Young Adult Literature   10, 11, 26, 43, 44, 89, 101, 103, 104, 106,

156, 218, 224, 268, 278, 348, 455, 483, 488, 531, 577, 583, 605, 621, 653, 684, 774, 781, 782, 826; see also Junior High School; Senior High School; Teenage

Booklist, December 7, 1981: "Teenage Trauma: An Update on Realistic YA Fiction."

Booklist, March 1, 1985: "Self-Helpers 2: More Information and Guidance for Today's YA's" compiled by Stephanie Zvirin (updates the March 1, 1981 list).

Booklist, July 1985: "Contemporary Classics for Young Adults" compiled by YA Books Staff.

Booklist, November 15, 1985: "Books for the Blind and Physically Handicapped Young Adult."

Horn Book, April 1983: "Coming Full Circle: From Lesson Plans to Young Adult Novels" by Richard Peck.

Horn Book, July/August 1985: "Young Adult Books and Politics: The Last Taboo" by Jack Forman.

Horn Book, September/October 1985: "Young Adult Books: Childhood Terror" by Hazel Rochman.

The Library Quarterly, April 1985: "Young Adult Realism: Conventions, Narrators, and Readers" by Catherine Ross.

School Library Journal, January and February 1980: "Short, Important Books for the Older YA's" by Vicki M. Sherouse.

School Library Journal, August 1980: "Adult Novels for Young Teens" by Linda R. Silver.

School Library Journal, September 1980: "In the YA Corner, Clip 'n Read Files: A Bibliography of Articles on Selection and Book Reviews of Young Adult Books" by Thomas W. Downen and Barbara Goodman.

School Library Journal, October 1983: "'Grokking' the YA Cult Novels" by Roger Sutton.

Top of the News, Spring issues, annually: "Best Books for Young Adults."

Top of the News, Fall 1981: "Young Adults Books From an Editor's Perspective" by Nancy Vasilakis.
"View From the Inside: How the Best Books for Young Adults Committee Really Works" by Jane Bodart.

Top of the News, Winter 1983: "Young Adult Publishing: A Blossoming Market" by Kristin Ramsdell.

Top of the News, Winter 1984: "Involving Young Adults in Fiction Selection" by Robert Swisher, Mildred Laughlin, Donnice Cochenour, Linda Cowen, and Evelyn Healey.

Top of the News, Summer 1985: "Romance Versus Reality: A Look at YA Romantic Fiction" by Susan Kundin.

Top of the News, Winter 1985: "A Refreshing Breeze in Young Adult Literature" by Jeffrey S. Copeland